AF478158

Leadership in Democracy

Leadership in Democracy

Also by Paul Brooker

THE FACES OF FRATERNALISM: Nazi Germany, Fascist Italy, and Imperial Japan

TWENTIETH-CENTURY DICTATORSHIPS: The Ideological One-Party States

DEFIANT DICTATORSHIPS: Communist and Middle Eastern Dictatorships in a Democratic Age

NON-DEMOCRATIC REGIMES: Theory, Government and Politics

LEADERSHIP IN DEMOCRACY: From Adaptive Response to Entrepreneurial Initiative

NON-DEMOCRATIC REGIMES: MODERN STATELESS WARFARE

Leadership in Democracy

Second edition

Paul Brooker

First published 2005
Second edition published 2010 by
PALGRAVE MACMILLAN

Palgrave Macmillan in the UK is an imprint of Macmillan Publishers Limited, registered in England, company number 785998, of Houndmills, Basingstoke, Hampshire RG21 6XS.

Palgrave Macmillan in the US is a division of St Martin's Press LLC, 175 Fifth Avenue, New York, NY 10010.

Palgrave Macmillan is the global academic imprint of the above companies and has companies and representatives throughout the world.

Palgrave® and Macmillan® are registered trademarks in the United States, the United Kingdom, Europe and other countries.

ISBN: 978–0–230–24815–1 hardback

This book is printed on paper suitable for recycling and made from fully managed and sustained forest sources. Logging, pulping and manufacturing processes are expected to conform to the environmental regulations of the country of origin.

A catalogue record for this book is available from the British Library.

A catalog record for this book is available from the Library of Congress.

10 9 8 7 6 5 4 3 2 1
19 18 17 16 15 14 13 12 11 10

Printed and bound in Great Britain by
CPI Antony Rowe, Chippenham and Eastbourne

Contents

Preface to the Second Edition

The second edition of a book provides an opportunity for updating, for second or more ambitious thoughts, and for adding new topics or material. The updating has been confined to a few cases of giving someone their due and has not attempted to extend the 1960s–90s assessment of entrepreneurial democracy into the twenty-first century, which seems to be following the tendencies that appeared in the last decades of the previous century. A more important updating has been the use of works that appeared at the same time or later than the first edition, notably North's evolutionary analysis of economic change. Now it has been possible to use his landmark work to support the evolutionary approach adopted in the book's third chapter and in its development of a leadership-evolutionary model of democratic politics.

The most obvious addition is the new chapter on presidential leadership that has been added to Part II. As this chapter is focused on presidential pioneering in foreign policy, it also rectifies Part II's failure to pay much attention to foreign policy. And it provides an opportunity to examine Neustadt's classic leadership model of a presidential democracy and to make some comparisons with Schumpeter's and other leadership models of democracy.

In fact the most important or ambitious addition is the reorientation of the book's overall approach to pay more attention to political leadership in general rather than focusing so much on entrepreneurial-style, pioneering leadership. Thus the first edition's chapter on political entrepreneurship has been removed to provide space for expanding the Introduction and opening two chapters to include a wider perspective on Schumpeter's leadership model. The new perspective highlights the originality and pioneering status of the leadership dimension to his theory of democracy. Even if his leadership model of democracy failed to use any analogies with entrepreneurship, it pioneered the use of economic analogies with the market and the firm, and it provided pioneering accounts of the two main types of political leadership – the market-like deliberative type and the command-like authoritative type. The opening chapters also point out that he was foreshadowing Downs's and Schattschneider's use of these economic analogies in their classic leadership models of democracy, which have had a marked influence upon more recent conceptions of leadership in democracy.

Furthermore, the opening chapters include a new emphasis on adaptive innovation and on the institutional framework or foundation of leadership models. The emphasis on institutions is partly due to the conceptual influence of the analogy with the firm, of the institutional economics of the firm and of the political-economy notion of institutions being 'populated' by individuals with market-like motivations. But it is also due to the role that institutional factors play in leadership models and approaches discussed in these chapters, such as Schattschneider's classic leadership model or the more recent case of Elgie's institutional approach to leadership in liberal democracies. As for the new emphasis on adaptive innovation, this involves using Drucker's business-management theory of innovation to highlight similarities and differences between the political and economic forms of adaptive innovation. And it produces an analysis of innovation-averse leadership that applies to adaptive innovation as well as to pioneering initiatives and responses.

The new emphasis on adaptive innovation is also evident in the Conclusion, which presents some pessimistic second thoughts about the future of innovative leadership. The optimistic scenario has been discarded and the pessimistic scenario for entrepreneurial democracy has been extended to include a pessimistic appraisal of the prospects for even the merely adaptive form of innovative leadership. In particular, there is no confidence in democracies' ability to produce the required adaptive innovations if a crisis requires something better than the New Deal innovations that US democracy produced in response to the Great Depression.

Finally, the inclusion of prophetic leadership in this edition's typology of political leadership confirms that a key point should be added to the first edition's Preface. It suggested that modern politics be viewed as a spectrum or continuum extending from the coercive political criminality of dictatorship to the free political commerce of democracy. But clearly above or beyond the forensic-to-economic range of analysis and analogy lies an additional, religious dimension of analysis and analogy that can be applied to a few dictatorships and occasionally to a democracy. The political religions espoused by Nazi Germany, Fascist Italy and Imperial Japan are the obvious examples of how this religious dimension can be applied to a few dictatorships, as I described some twenty years ago when presenting a Durkheimian interpretation of these regimes. And the prophetic, visionary type of democratic leadership is the obvious example of how the religious dimension can be applied to a few occasions in the history of a democracy. Although such prophetic leadership is rare and becoming rarer, it takes democratic leadership above and beyond the 'practical and sometimes grubby business' of everyday politics.

Another important addition to the first edition's Preface are some new acknowledgements. I owe many thanks to Jon Johansson for encouraging me to broaden the perspective on Schumpeter's leadership model, to Mark Gerrard for reminding me to look at IT cases of entrepreneurship and adaptive innovation, and to the Department of Political Science at the University of Canterbury for helping me finish off a few projects in academic semi-retirement.

Introduction

> But collectives act almost exclusively by accepting leadership –
> this is the dominant mechanism of practically any collective
> action which is more than a reflex.
>
> Schumpeter (1974 [1947])

> And we define: the democratic method is that institutional
> arrangement for arriving at political decisions in which indi-
> viduals acquire the power to decide by means of a competitive
> struggle for the people's vote … free competition for a free vote.
>
> Schumpeter (1974 [1947])

Leadership is one of those important things that scientists find difficult to measure but easy to model, so it is not surprising that political scientists have been constructing models of political leadership for more than half a century. These leadership models of politics have often combined an institutional perspective on leadership with an economic perspective on politics. Their institutional or structural perspective on leadership has viewed a leader as a person performing the direction-setting role of giving a lead to other people; their economic or quasi-economic perspective on politics has involved the use of economic analogies – with the market, the entrepreneur or the firm – and the use of economic concepts of collective action, market competitiveness, entrepreneurial innovation or principal–agent relationships. The combination of these two perspectives has produced very effective leadership models that have helped to explain democracies' electoral and policy-making processes and to explain change in democracies' public policies, political issues or political institutions (in the broad sense of everything from organisations to constitutions and even informal rules of the game).

Such great political scientists as Downs and Schattschneider developed early forms of a leadership model of democracy but it was first pioneered by the economist Joseph Schumpeter in his 1940s classic *Capitalism, Socialism and Democracy*. The theory of democracy which he presented in this work included a leadership model of democracy that used economic analogies with the firm and the market. But, surprisingly, it did not use any analogy with the entrepreneur, despite the fact that Schumpeter's reputation as an economist rests largely upon the theories of entrepreneurship that he presented in *Capitalism, Socialism and Democracy* and in some of his other economic writings.

This book therefore aims to provide the missing piece of Schumpeter's leadership model of democracy by adding an analogy with the entrepreneur – and specifically with the form of entrepreneur described in Schumpeter's famous theory of entrepreneurship. In addition to rectifying this surprising omission, it aims to provide an exposition of his leadership model that will reveal its true stature and potential. They have been obscured by his use of analogies and comparisons with economic institutions and processes, which have had a more dramatic effect upon his audience and also seem to have distracted him from presenting a more systematic description of his leadership model and of the types of leadership that it incorporated.

Schumpeter's theory of democracy aimed to explain how representative democracy can produce orderly and coherent collective action by a large-scale and modern political community – which might number tens of millions, be spread across a continent and contain a diverse range of interests and opinions. As is quoted above, he believed that leadership was the key to overcoming such collective-action problems and, as is described in Chapter 1, his theory included an extensive leadership model of democracy that was presented in the form of a wide-ranging analysis of the 'logic' of British parliamentary democracy. Both this leadership model and his overall theory of democracy were characterised by a quasi-economic perspective that involved an extensive use of economic analogies and comparisons. This quasi-economic perspective is evident even in his definition of democracy, quoted above, as a method for arriving at political decisions in which individuals acquire the power to decide by means of a competitive struggle for the people's vote.

The very notion of individuals acquiring the 'power to decide' through 'the people's vote' contained an implicit or latent analogy with the firm. It begs comparison with how a business corporation's mass of shareholder-owners can use their voting rights to replace the executives who manage the firm on their behalf. Schumpeter actually used this analogy with the firm when he noted that describing a democracy's government as the 'executive' is appropriate so long as it is used in the same sense as the term 'executives' of a business corporation. He was pioneering an analogy that has become something of a cliché and now includes adopting the principal–agent approach employed by institutional economists to analyse relationships within the firm, such as the relationship between shareholders and managers. Not only is the democratic state owned collectively by its citizens as equal shareholders with equal voting rights but also these citizens constitute a 'collective principal' that by some form of majority vote chooses 'agents' to use the state's public offices/powers on the collective principal's behalf. This application of a principal–agent approach has even included comparisons with managers 'shirking' their responsibility to be conscientious agents of the shareholders – and comparisons with economists' analyses of how such shirking is deterred or discovered and remedied.

However, Schumpeter used the analogy with the firm to create the underlying framework for a *leadership*, not managerial, model of democracy. For example, he used the concept of leadership, not management, to highlight the fact that elections involve consent as well choice. His comment that the 'true' function of the electorate's vote is the acceptance of leadership was pointing out, in an exaggerated manner, that elections are not simply about choice. In principal–agent terms, elections involve not only the people choosing agents but also the people consenting to these elected individuals acting as a special type of agent. In terms of Schumpeter's leadership model, the people are accepting these individuals as the formal leaders of the political community and are accepting the authoritative type of leadership that they will provide through their 'power to decide'.

Authoritative political leadership is a military-like type of leadership that sets a direction by giving a command-like lead, which the recipients of the lead obey because they are inspired by this leadership or simply because obedience is obligatory and/or coerced. For example, the most formal authoritative leads are given through legislation, which is not only obligatory but also underwritten by the state's law-enforcement machinery. Clearly by accepting authoritative leadership, a large-scale democratic political community gives itself the opportunity to engage in collective action and bring about change in an orderly manner. However, no large-scale democracy elects only one formal leader; it elects a hundred or more to represent the diversity of the political community and to ensure that the 'power to decide' is not monopolised by one individual leader. It is true that often a President or Prime Minister is formally pre-eminent among the elected leaders and may well act as spokesperson for their collective decision-making and authoritative leadership, for someone needs to provide the 'personal touch', the personalised direction-setting, that is characteristic of leadership and cannot be provided by a faceless committee or assembly. But he or she has to share power with the other elected leaders, and to a greater degree than a firm's chief executive who shares power with a board of directors. Thus Schumpeter's leadership model depicted a parliamentary democracy's Prime Minister as a leader whose power is restricted by sub-leaders, namely the other Cabinet Ministers, with whom the Prime Minister discreetly competes for leadership of the government and/or policy areas.

Indeed *competition* for leadership is the key feature of Schumpeter's leadership model of democracy. While the analogy with the firm provided the model's underlying or skeletal framework, he used the analogy with market competition to 'flesh out' this skeleton and to explain how democracy continually produces changes in issues, policies and institutions. Somewhat paradoxically, his pioneering use of market and business analogies or comparisons has in fact proved to be the most influential aspect of his theory of democracy, and his reputation as a political scientist rests largely upon his market-analogous description of democracy as involving a competitive struggle for the people's vote and, specifically, free competition for a free vote. Yet much of this quasi-economic aspect of his theory was oriented towards leadership and was incorporated into his leadership model of democracy. He depicted the market-like competition for power as being competition between political (party) leaders who lead the people's electoral deliberation and choice. And he was well aware that between elections the competing party leaders and other politicians continue to lead the people's deliberation and choice. Their competition to retain or acquire leadership roles motivates them, like firms competing in a market, to compete in 'selling' leads that may well set a new direction by raising new issues or proposing new policies or institutions.

In contrast to the authoritative type of political leadership, this market-like type does not inspire, obligate or coerce the recipient of the lead to accept it. The lead is being sold to a potential customer who has the choice of whether or not to 'buy' it or indeed to prefer a different, competing lead from another seller. The market-like type of leadership sets a direction not by obedience but by choice and consent; it gives a lead that if accepted, will have been considered on reflection or after debate to be the best option available. It therefore inspires thought rather than action and in fact is best labelled *deliberative* leadership.

Deliberative leadership is characteristic of any situation of collective choice or consultation in decision-making, whether by an electorate, assembly, committee or any combination of two or more people within the same or different institutions. Schumpeter recognised that this market-like leadership occurs within parliamentary democracies' cabinet governments, whose internal competition for leadership of the government and/or particular policy areas will result in these holders of elected public office leading one another's deliberation and choice. But as will be shown in Chapter 4, if this leadership-oriented market analogy is to reach its full potential, it must be taken further by (1) extending it to presidential democracies' congressional legislatures and congressional-presidential relations, and (2) applying it to individuals who are informal political leaders and may not even be known by the public. These informal, even publicly anonymous leaders include (1) policy advocates who give a lead to the electorate, the politicians and the civil service when they are deliberating about the policy advocate's area of expertise and (2) civil servants who lead the deliberation of governments and legislatures in highly technical or relatively routine policy areas.

Furthermore, Chapter 3 shows that the effectiveness of this market-analogous leadership for change is reduced by the equivalent of market 'rigidity'. The competitive aspect of deliberative leadership may be reduced by habits of thought, the resistance of vested interests or other factors that reduce the diversity and strength of competition among the leads that are being sold by and to leaders. In addition, one or more of the competing leads may be enjoying extraneous or 'undeserved' competitive advantages. These are analogous to the advantages created by superior sales and marketing activities or by larger amounts of capital being invested in these activities. Such presentational advantages arise from investing the political capital produced by a leader's formal position and personal prestige, from the political salesmanship that is one of a leader's most important personal qualities and from the political marketing advantages that are exemplified by a President's or Prime Minister's use of prime-time television to give/sell a lead to the people's deliberations about public affairs.

Although market-analogous, deliberative leadership is a characteristic of democratic political systems, the analogy with the firm shows that modern democracies also contain a large amount of authoritative leadership. Just as the non-market mechanism of 'command' plays an important role in the many 'mixed' market/command economies, so too does authoritative leadership in the mixed deliberative/authoritative representative democracies. Elected public officials not only provide a large amount of authoritative leadership to their political community's citizenry but also give directives or orders to their subordinates in the state machinery of civil servants, police and armed forces, as when a US President gives orders to his country's armed forces in his capacity as Commander-in-Chief. However, this authoritative leadership usually involves a formal decision that has been influenced by deliberative leadership's selling of policy proposals, whether in public debate or in private discussions behind closed doors.

Democracies also sometimes experience the relatively rare 'prophetic' type of political leadership. Schumpeter perhaps not surprisingly did not mention this type, even though such luminaries as Weber and Freud had presented well-known analyses of prophetic religious leadership. The political version is similar to the religious in presenting a vision that changes the attitude of its audience, if only by creating a more hopeful or determined attitude. Perhaps the best examples of prophetic political leadership in modern times have been Churchill's 'blood, toil, tears and sweat' and 'finest hour' speeches, Kennedy's 'new generation' inaugural address and Martin Luther King's 'I have a dream' and 'the promised land' speeches. The similarities between political and religious versions of prophetic leadership have never been more obvious than in King's 'the promised land' speech, in which he prophesied the night before he was killed: 'I have seen the promised land. I may not get there with you. But I want you to know tonight that we, as a people, will get to the promised land.'

Prophetic political leadership also has similarities with the authoritative and deliberative types. As it *inspires* a change in attitude, it is similar to those occasions when authoritative leadership inspires obedience – and an enthusiastic obedience – rather than relying on being obligatory and/or coercive. Furthermore, like the lead sold by a deliberative leader, the inspirational vision presented by a prophetic leader has to compete in a market-like manner with alternative visions, even when it is presented by the country's President or Prime Minister. Such preeminent formal leaders usually perform the role of prophetic leader at least once during their career, and in fact they are expected to provide some prophetic leadership when a dramatic crisis or change requires the political community to transcend the mundane concerns of 'business as usual' in the political marketplace.

Schumpeter implied that democracy's ordinary, 'business as usual' cases of leadership for change were similar to the incremental adaptive responses that a market economy makes through its market processes.

The economy will be making adaptive responses to changes in the economic environment and its various other environments, such as the physical, social and international. Similarly, a democratic political community will be making adaptive responses to changes in its various environments and will be making the responses through market-like deliberative leadership for change that precedes the formal decisions and authoritative leadership. Furthermore, a democracy's adaptive responses are similar to those of a market economy in normally being a gradual, incremental form of change that is comparable to biological adaptation.

In contrast, truly innovative changes are typically the result of pioneering initiatives by economic entrepreneurs or entrepreneurial political leaders. Drawing the analogy between innovative political leadership and economic entrepreneurship produces an important leadership model of how and why a democracy changes its policies, issues and institutions. But it also raises the question of why Schumpeter, the great economic theorist of entrepreneurship, did not use the analogy with entrepreneurship in his theory of democracy – why is there no leadership-oriented analogy with entrepreneurs?

Schumpeter had some reason to be wary of using comparisons or analogies with economic entrepreneurship. Democracies do not experience a political leadership as informal and self-contained (in the sense of not having to convince or impress people) as entrepreneurs' leadership of the economy in new directions. Nor have democracies experienced a political or policy equivalent of the recurring creative-destructive economic revolutions instigated by Schumpeterian entrepreneurs. On the other hand, democracies have often experienced more humble political or policy innovations, and the analogy with economic entrepreneurship helps to distinguish the innovative, pioneering kind of political leadership from the standard, adaptive kind that is concerned merely with making adaptive responses to events. Furthermore, although their political evolution lacks the revolutionary dynamism of capitalist economic evolution, democracies' political and policy changes arise from the same evolutionary process: the selection of adaptive responses and the occasional pioneering, entrepreneurial-style initiative.

This book therefore aims to expand Schumpeter's analysis of leadership in democracy by exploring his adaptive-pioneering conception of leadership. Chapter 1 describes his analysis of the competition for leadership that occurs in democracy, not only the electoral competition but also the between-elections competition for leadership that occurs even within the collective, collegial governments of parliamentary democracies. It also compares his leadership model of democracy with those developed by Downs, Schattschneider and more recent theorists of leadership in democracy. Chapter 2 is concerned with the key question of what distinguishes entrepreneurial-style, pioneering leadership from the standard, adaptive form of political leadership provided by competitive careerists. It also examines two forms of leadership that fall between the pioneering initiative and the adaptive response, namely (1) the partly pioneering, creative response and (2) the adaptive innovation, which has become a prominent feature of modern business management – in theory as well as practice. Chapter 3 develops a Schumpeterian evolutionary perspective on politics, which uses the notion of 'selection of variations (in issues, policies and institutions) for preservation' to describe the process of democratic political evolution. Finally, Chapter 4 completes Part I by presenting a Leadership-Evolutionary model of the democratic political system. It adds an evolutionary perspective to Schumpeter's leadership model of parliamentary democracy and also extends it into other areas: presidential democracies' independent, congressional legislatures; modern democracies' highly influential administrative bureaucracies; and the many informal and specialised policy-based sectors of a democratic political system.

The LE model also provides a background and framework to Part II: Assessing Entrepreneurial-Style, Pioneering Leadership, which assesses whether this unusual, pioneering kind of democratic leadership has become more prevalent in recent decades. The assessment covers the 1960s–90s period and is based upon cases highlighted in secondary sources, which have often depicted these cases as some form of political entrepreneurship. Entrepreneurial-style, pioneering leadership in the electoral/party system is covered in Chapter 5, which assesses leaders' marketing of innovative political issues in their electoral competition for the people's vote. In contrast, Chapter 6 assesses top-down, governmental pioneering leadership by holders of executive public office. It follows Schumpeter in focusing on the British case of leadership provided by the Prime Minister of a parliamentary democracy. However, Chapter 7 balances this bias by focusing on US presidential pioneering, using Neustadt's famous model of presidential leadership, and it also shifts the emphasis from domestic to foreign policy. Chapter 8 keeps the focus on the US by assessing the entrepreneurial-style legislative leadership that occurs when a legislator introduces or promotes an innovative bill in Congress. Chapters 9 and 10 cover the informal entrepreneurial-style, pioneering leadership that has been offered by, respectively, some public administrators and some policy advocates. Normally it has been a publicly anonymous form of pioneering leadership but occasionally an administrator or policy advocate has become a public figure, as in the famous cases of FBI boss J. Edgar Hoover and consumer advocate Ralph Nader. Both Chapters 9 and 10 are based upon American cases and studies not only because of the relative abundance of secondary literature but also because these forms of entrepreneurial-style, pioneering leadership are much more prevalent in the United States than in any other democracy. Finally, the Conclusion makes some suggestions about the likely future of innovative leadership in democracy – taking into account the assessments in Part II and also past experience of how democracies adapt to crisis conditions.

Part I
Theory

1
Schumpeter's Leadership Model of Democracy

The quasi-economic aspect of his theory of democracy

The theory of democracy that Schumpeter presented more than sixty years ago in *Capitalism, Socialism and Democracy* is much better known for its quasi-economic features than for its emphasis on leadership.[1] There seems to be a strong economic flavour to his actual definition of democracy: 'that institutional method for arriving at political decisions in which individuals acquire the power to decide by means of a competitive struggle for the people's vote' – through being successful in 'free competition for a free vote'.[2] And his theory stimulated Downs's 1950s classic, *An Economic Theory of Democracy*, which in turn became one of the most influential examples of the rational-choice approach to political science.[3]

Schumpeter's theory is only *quasi*-economic but he used a number of comparisons and analogies with economics, businessmen and business activities. For example, he pointed out that in a democracy everyone is free to compete for the electorate's support 'in the same sense in which everyone is free to start another textile mill'.[4] Similarly, he used a comparison between trade associations and party politicians to illustrate his argument that the shift from independents to party politicians constitutes an attempt to regulate political competition.[5]

His conception of politicians' activities and motivation was presented through analogies with businessmen. He quoted a politician's remark that: 'What businessmen do not understand is that exactly as they are dealing in oil so I am dealing in votes.'[6] And he endorsed such a narrow view of politicians' activities and motivation by drawing an analogy with how economists' schematic models adopted a simplified view of businessmen's motivation by focusing on profit-seeking and excluding any altruistic motives.[7]

> Similarly, the social meaning or function of parliamentary activity is no doubt to turn out legislation and, in part, administrative measures. But in order to understand how democratic politics serve this social end, we must start from the competitive struggle for power and office and realize that the social function is fulfilled, as it were, incidentally – in the same sense as production is incidental to the making of profits.[8]

But the most important quasi-economic aspect of Schumpeter's theory was the comparison and analogy between political and economic competition. His actual definition of democracy has been viewed as an implicit analogy of free-market economic competition for consumers' spending: 'just as firms compete for business in market systems, would-be political leaders compete for votes'.[9] The analogy with the market was also used to qualify his definition of democracy and make it more 'realistic'. After pointing out that imperfect competition was commonplace in the economy, he argued in favour of a realistic conception of democracy that would not exclude even cases of imperfect competition that are 'strikingly analogous' to what in the economic sphere is labelled unfair, fraudulent or restraint of competition.[10]

The most surprising quasi-economic feature of Schumpeter's theory is its use of some notion of 'collective action'. For example, his chapter on the 'classical doctrine' of democracy refers to it as the classical doctrine of collective action.[11] But he was not foreshadowing Olson's *The Logic of Collective Action*; Schumpeter was using a less rigorously rationalist notion of collective action than the economic concept that Olson used in his seminal contribution to the rational-choice approach to political science.[12] Yet some of Schumpeter's attacks on this classical doctrine of democracy and collective action were what might be expected of an economist, even if the target of his attacks might not have been recognised by political theorists as the 'classical' doctrine of democracy. By this he meant an eighteenth century conception of representative democracy which he defined as 'that institutional arrangement for arriving at political decisions which realizes the common good by making the people itself decide issues through the election of individuals who are to assemble in order to carry out its will'.[13] In contrast, his theory of 'realistic' democracy assumed that 'the deciding of issues by the electorate [is] secondary to the election of the men who are to do the deciding'.[14]

Yet although he vigorously attacked the classical doctrine of representative democracy as unrealistic, he acknowledged that such a form of representative democracy might well be appropriate for countries, such as the Switzerland of his day, that were not yet industrialised and were still faced with simple and stable public-policy problems.[15] He also acknowledged that the 'rule of the people' might be possible in cases of direct democracy, such as the Greek city-state assembly or the New England town meeting, but noted that it required a sufficiently small and locally concentrated population and that even then there might still be difficulties – certainly 'the psychologist of collective behaviour would still have something to say about leadership'.[16]

Schumpeter's emphasis on leadership is the key feature of his quasi-economic theory of collective action. He argued that the acceptance of leadership is 'the dominant mechanism of practically any collective action which is more than a reflex' and that 'collectives act almost exclusively by accepting leadership'.[17] Such leadership occurs both in a direct-democracy assembly, where behavioural/psychological factors are crucial, and also in the large political communities that have relied upon the non-classical, leadership form of representative democracy to bring about orderly and coherent collective action. In both situations the leadership involves the institutional or structural role of giving direction – a lead – to the political community on a formal or informal basis. Although Schumpeter did not provide an explicit definition of leadership, his notion of political leadership is clearly similar to the definition provided in the early 1980s by Tucker in *Politics As Leadership*, namely that political leadership means giving direction to a political community.[18]

As will be shown in the next section, Schumpeter actually presented a leadership model of democracy during his critique/replacement of the classic theory of democracy and collective action. This model has been overshadowed by the quasi-economic dimension of his theory, especially his use of market analogies, and his leadership model has also suffered from the tendency of a later generation of theorists of democracy to overlook or underestimate the role played by leadership. A 2005 Schumpeter-influenced article on representation in 'leader democracy' noted that in recent decades the role of leadership had received little attention from theorists of democracy.[19] Such a trend is all the more surprising when it is considered, as it will be later in the chapter, that Schumpeter's emphasis on leadership was continued in the 1950s–60s by two of political science's seminal theorists of democracy, Downs and Schattschneider.

The leadership dimension of his theory

Although Schumpeter's theory of democracy is best known for its quasi-economic features, its emphasis on leadership is almost as distinctive. More than twenty years earlier Max Weber had pioneered this approach to democracy in espousing a leadership or plebiscitary type of democracy, which on occasion he described as *Fuehrerdemokratie* (leader democracy).[20] Initially Weber believed that a plebiscitary type of leadership could be produced by parliamentary democracy through the post of Prime Minister but later he became convinced that a directly elected President with extensive powers was the only way in which Germany's new democracy could be provided with a plebiscitary leader.[21] However, Weber's emphasis on leadership was quite different from the Nazis' *Fuehrerprinzip* (leader principle), which espoused rule by an absolutist and personally responsible leader.[22] The Nazis said nothing about democratic (electoral) choice and accountability of leaders, and they sought to expand the number of leadership positions throughout state and society by replacing bureaucratic as well as committee/assembly forms of authority and administration. This campaign included an attempt at leaderising Germany's civil service, which Weber had taken as his model of modern, bureaucratic administration. The Nazi regime sought to convert some of these model bureaucrats into 'administration leaders', who would be trained to take on more responsible and creative duties than had previously been given to civil servants.[23]

Schumpeter's emphasis on leadership is much closer to Weber's than to the Nazis' views. It is true that Schumpeter displayed some sympathy towards the Nazi regime until the end of the Second World War,[24] despite having emigrated to America in 1932, and his attack on rule by committee or assembly was as sharp as anything that might have come from an exponent of the leader principle. 'Every parliament, every committee, every council of war composed of a dozen generals in their sixties displays ... a reduced sense of responsibility.'[25] But he viewed bureaucracy in a positive light, arguing that a European-style bureaucratic civil service was one of the conditions for successful democracy.[26] More importantly, he shared Weber's commitment to a democratic form of leadership, and in fact appears more democratic than Weber in emphasising competition for leadership and specifying that this leadership be attained through free competition for a free vote. Furthermore, he acknowledged that the holder of a formal leadership position may lack leadership qualities and may actually fail to provide a lead.[27]

Nonetheless, the theory of democracy that he presented in *Capitalism, Socialism and Democracy* is certainly one of leader democracy. He declared that 'collectives act almost exclusively by accepting leadership' and that propositions 'about the working and the results of the democratic method that take account of this are bound to be infinitely more realistic than propositions which do not'.[28] This assertion was followed up by a series of passing remarks that revealed the leadership dimension of his theory of democracy: free competition for a free vote is 'the kind of competition for leadership which is to define democracy'; the 'acceptance of leadership is the true function of the electorate's vote'; the electorate's role of producing government 'practically amounts to deciding who the leading man shall be'; the democratic method is 'free competition among would-be leaders for the vote of the electorate'; and the 'theory of competitive leadership has proved a satisfactory interpretation of the facts of the democratic process'.[29] Schumpeter had therefore presented a leadership perspective on democracy that viewed it merely as a particular way of deciding who is to be leader (by free competition for a free vote) and of accepting leadership by that individual.

As was described in the Introduction, the leadership dimension of his theory includes (1) authoritative and deliberative types of leadership and also (2) analogies with both the firm and the market. The analogy with the firm is more implied or latent than explicit but is evident in his comments about the autonomy of the elected leaders who form the government or 'executive'. He noted that the 'insincere word "executive" really points in the wrong direction. It ceases however to do so if we use it in the sense in which we speak of the "executives" of a business corporation who also do a great deal more than "execute" the will of stockholders'.[30] He also suggested that a democratic government may well – and quite appropriately – carry out policies that its people had not thought of and would not have approved of beforehand: 'Precisely in the best instances, the people are presented with results they never thought of and would not have approved of in advance'.[31]

This emphasis on the executive autonomy of management and government may seem similar to Burnham's *The Managerial Revolution*, which was first published in 1941. It had noted that in the 1930s there had been much discussion in the US of 'the separation of ownership and control' in big business and of 'management-control' of large public corporations.[32] Burnham had actually presented the rise of the non-owning, salaried managers as a peaceful and gradual version of a Marxist-style social revolution; it was creating a new ruling class of managers which was supported by a managerial and technocratic ideology that envisions running society 'efficiently and productively'.[33] However, Schumpeter did not go as far as Burnham in downplaying the power of shareholders and their voting rights; in his implicit analogy with the firm its managers' autonomy or 'control' was limited by their competition for votes.

Such analogies with the firm are now used more explicitly and have become something of a cliché. Recently they have even been used in textbook contrasts of democracy with non-democratic regimes, which are depicted as cases of either monarchical family-ownership of the state or dictatorial theft of state power through military coup or a misappropriation of power by elected public officials. In contrast, democracies are cases of public ownership of the state:

> [T]his means viewing the people as a collective principal (as are a royal family or a ruling organization) that in this case comprises millions of individual members. Each of them is entitled to an equal say in the principal's collective decisions in much the same way as equal shareholders in a public company, except that in this case the shareholders are owners of the state and its public offices/powers. Furthermore, the key collective decisions are made in the same manner as those of shareholders in a public company, by a majority vote, except that in this case the collective decision and voting involves the choosing – through competitive elections – of political agents who will hold public offices and use their public powers to make political decisions on behalf of the people.[34]

In this use of an analogy with the firm there has also been some use of the principal–agent approach employed by institutional economists to analyse the relationship between shareholders and managers. Elsewhere there have even been comparisons with economists' principal–agent analyses of how managers 'shirk' their responsibilities to shareholders and of how shirking by a firm's managers is countered by 'across-market competition' from 'would-be managers' of the firm – which is strikingly similar to Schumpeter's description of competition by 'would-be leaders' for public office.[35]

Nonetheless, he was clearly using an analogy with market competition when describing this electoral competition. It is a case of deliberative leadership, in which the would-be leaders compete by 'selling' leads to voters – who may prefer to 'buy' a different lead or none at all.

However, the selling–buying analogy is being used here as a heuristic device for distinguishing deliberative from other types of leadership; Schumpeter himself did not go beyond the standard giving–accepting formula when discussing leadership, and was not tempted to extend his analogy with market competition into the more complex area of market exchange. Some later political scientists have taken this step, though, and by the end of the 1960s Scott had developed an economic model of the US political system that was based on market exchange as well as competition. His *Competition in American Politics: An Economic Model* was based on the assumptions that any candidate 'seeking office tries to "sell" himself, his party and a set of programs' and that when 'a constituent "buys" the program offered by a candidate and supports him a transaction may be said to have taken place' – this constituent 'has exchanged his support for the products offered by the candidate'.[36] Schumpeter had preferred not to take the market analogy so far and instead to focus on market competitiveness and the importance of competition in a democratic political system, especially the competition associated with the market-like deliberative type of leadership.

But he made no mention of the other type of market-like leadership – the prophetic, visionary type of leadership. This is particularly surprising because Weber and Freud had already made some famous analyses of prophetic leadership that were probably known to Schumpeter. In the 1920s Weber's famous theory of charismatic legitimacy and leadership had included not only religious prophets but also the case of a communist political leader in Germany who had enjoyed some 'demagogic success'.[37]

In the 1930s Freud, too, had pointed to the important historical role performed by prophetic leaders. His book on prophet Moses' leadership of the Jews out of Egypt and towards the Promised Land was not published until the end of the decade but Freud had published similar ideas in his well-known book *Civilization and Its Discontents*. In it he had pointed to the role of leadership in the cultural development of human civilisations, namely 'the impression left behind by the personalities of great leaders – men of overwhelming force of mind or men in whom one of the human impulsions has found its strongest and purest, and therefore often its most one-sided, expression'.[38] Freud suggested that Jesus Christ was the best example of such a leader and of the tendency for the leader to be 'mocked and maltreated by others and even despatched in a cruel fashion'.[39] The same point could have been made about the role of leadership in the political-cultural development of political communities, with perhaps Abraham Lincoln being the best example of such a leader and of the tendency for the leader to be assassinated (the other obvious example, Mahatma Gandhi, was assassinated several years after Schumpeter constructed his leadership model). *Civilization and Its Discontents* also contained an argument that was similar to Schumpeter's views on the collective's need for leadership. Freud referred to 'the psychological poverty of groups' and noted that this psychological poverty is particularly likely when a group's social bonds are mainly derived from 'the identification of its members with one another, while individuals of the leader type do not acquire the importance that should fall to them in the formation of a group'.[40] So it is surprising that no influence from Weber or Freud – or any other writer on prophetic, visionary leadership – is evident in Schumpeter's descriptions of leadership.

On the other hand, the two other types of political leadership, the deliberative and the authoritative, are often implicitly described in Schumpeter's analysis of democracy. For example, both types appear in his disparaging account of the electorate's failings and its subsidiary role in a democracy. Voters could hardly complain about his famous formula that the primary role of the electorate is to produce a government and that the electorate's deciding of issues is secondary to its electing of the individuals who are to do the deciding.[41] He also maintained, however, that the electorate was incapable of deciding issues in an informed, rational manner and was at the mercy of groups with an axe to grind, such as politicians, idealists or exponents of an economic interest.[42] Within wide limits these groups can actually manufacture 'the will of the people' by methods that are analogous to commercial advertising but are even more influential because they are selling something that the public cannot readily test and reject.[43]

Presumably it was because of the danger of a manufactured will of the people that Schumpeter in one notorious instance argued that the electorate should be prohibited from attempting to influence the decisions of the individuals that they have elected.[44] It is true that in other instances he expressed much less authoritarian and elitist views about the nature of democracy, such as pointing out that freely competitive elections will normally mean considerable freedom of the press and considerable freedom of discussion for all citizens.[45] Furthermore, 'effective competition for leadership requires a large measure of tolerance for difference of opinion', if only because all would-be leaders must be allowed to present their cases to the electorate.[46] But this still implies that the people's participation in politics is limited to choosing between the alternatives presented to them by the individuals competing with one another to become the formal leaders of the country.

In Schumpeter's conception of democracy, electoral competition *for* formal leadership of the country is competition *by* political leaders who are also leaders *of* the people's electoral deliberation and choice. He argued that election issues are partly politician-manufactured even when based upon such genuine volitions as the unemployed's will to receive unemployment benefit.[47] 'Even if strong and definite they remain latent, often for decades, until they are called to life by some political leader who turns them into political factors ... by working them up and by including eventually appropriate items in his competitive offering'.[48] Often there is not such a genuine basis for the election issue that a political leader has raised as his competitive offering; he is instead seeking to manufacture a will of the people from out of thin air. But Schumpeter acknowledged that there were limits to what political persuasion could achieve. For example, political arguments had to be connected to voters' preconceived ideas and had to 'twist existing volitional premises into a particular shape'.[49]

Downs and Schattschneider

Downs expressed similar views about the limits on electoral leadership, which he defined as 'the ability to influence voters to adopt certain views as expressing their own will'.[50] The leadership aspect of Downs's seminal economic theory of democracy has been overshadowed not only by his rigorously rationalising, economics style of analysis but also by his focus on parties, not party leaders, as the competitors for votes and public office. However, the leadership aspect is clearly evident in his book's second-stage, more complex theory of democracy, which took into account the effects of uncertainty – the lack of knowledge about the course of actual or hypothetical events.[51]

> We assumed in Chapter 3 that voters' tastes in government were fixed, because they were simply rational deductions from the voters' views of the good society. However, in an uncertain world, roads leading toward the good society are hard to distinguish from those leading away from it. Thus, even though voters have fixed goals, their views on how to approach those goals are *malleable and can be altered by persuasion.* Consequently, *leadership can be exercised on most policy questions,* because nearly all policies are means to broader social goals rather than ends in themselves.[52]

Like Schumpeter, he viewed voters as being malleable but within the limits or bounds of having to address their existing ideas (about the good society). Both viewed leadership in terms of a limited or bounded ability to persuade voters to accept a lead on policy questions. It may be true that what has been called 'the Downsian tradition' views political parties' competition for votes as parties merely reacting to the preferences of the electorate rather than seeking to affect those preferences.[53] But Downs himself was in that sense not a Downsian, and he actually went further than Schumpeter in regarding any sort of persuasion of voters as a form of leadership. It could involve not only politicians and parties but also interest groups and those subtler forms of leadership that 'insinuate themselves into the reporting of news, the setting of political fashions, and the shaping of cultural images of good and evil'.[54]

So the second-stage theory of democracy that Downs presented in *An Economic Theory of Democracy* was actually a leadership model using economic concepts, notably a concept of rational choice, and economic analogies with the market and the firm. Downs's theory is better known for using a market analogy when analysing the competition between parties than for using an analogy with the firm, which is more obvious in the presentation of his first-stage theory of democracy – even if he prefers to talk of government rather than the state.[55] He defines democratic government as a party or coalition being 'chosen by popular election to run the governing apparatus', with a party being a 'team' of individuals who seek to control the governing apparatus by gaining office through popular election.[56] The state-as-firm analogy is discernible not only in terms of a management team being chosen by shareholders to run their firm but also in terms of how a shareholder decides which management team to vote for. Downs describes a voter's choice of party as being based upon the different 'utility incomes' he/she expects to receive from each party's policies and performance if it becomes the governing party, and with the voter focusing particularly on how well the incumbent party is doing – 'how good a job' – in providing the voter with utility income.[57]

In Downs's second-stage theory more prominence is given to parties' competitive marketing of issues of policy or performance – and at this stage he also introduces the notion of leadership persuasiveness and his version of a leadership model of democracy. With such an emphasis on the persuasive and competitive marketing of issues, the theory seems to have diverged from Schumpeter's assumption that a 'realistic' theory of democracy will consider that the electorate's deciding of issues is secondary to its choosing of the individuals who will do the deciding. However, Schumpeter occasionally implied that in reality there was some link between deciding to vote for a particular party leader and deciding issues of policy or performance. He implied that the two decisions were linked in the sense of voters choosing a leader who espoused their interests and ideals, because such an individual could be expected to make policy decisions that would be in accord with the voters' interests and ideals.[58] This is similar to the link that Downs described in his second-stage theory, where voters are depicted as choosing which candidates to support by taking into account the candidate's ideological or partisan *attitude* to present, past or future issues. Downs acknowledged that voters would find it difficult to decide whether to vote for a party on the basis of its past record in government because they 'do not know in great detail' (1) what policy decisions it has made and what were the consequences of those decisions and (2) what policy decisions it *will* make if it wins the election, as voters cannot 'know in advance what problems the government is likely to face in the coming election period'.[59] He argued that voting according to party ideology – supporting the party whose ideology is most like the voter's – is a rational response to this uncertainty and also is a rational short cut that saves a voter the cost of becoming informed about a wider range of specific issues.[60] Thus he assumed that there is a category of voters, the 'dogmatists', who look at ideological doctrines rather than at issues when deciding which party to support; in comparison, the category he labelled 'loyalists' deal with uncertainty and information costs by the less troublesome method of habitually voting for the same party.[61]

Only a few years after Downs's seminal work was published another leadership model appeared in another modern classic of political science, Schattschneider's *The Semisovereign People: A Realist's View of Democracy in America*. Although his 'realist's view' of democracy lacked the rationalist rigour of Downs's economic theory of democracy, Schattschneider used Schumpeter-like economic comparisons or analogies, such as describing political organisations as being 'in the business of manufacturing' the alternatives that the people will choose to vote for or against.[62] And his actual definition of democracy was similar to Schumpeter's in emphasising the role of competition in democracy:

> Democracy is a competitive political system in which competing party leaders and organizations define the alternatives of public policy in such a way that the public can participate in the decision-making process. ... [Democracy] is a political system in which the people

have a choice among the alternatives created by competing political organizations and leaders.[63]

More importantly, Schattschneider's theory of democracy shares a similar concern with leadership. He declared that the greatest democratic concepts are 'liberty and leadership' and that the essence of democracy is 'responsible leaders and organizations' exploiting the public's involvement in politics.[64] In a manner reminiscent of Schumpeter, he described American democracy's problem of organising a political community of 180 million as being a problem of 'leadership, organization, alternatives and systems of responsibility and confidence'.[65]

Schattschneider's theory was therefore at least in part a leadership model of democracy and, like Schumpeter's and Downs's leadership models, one that used economic analogies with the market and the firm. The market analogy may be more implicit than explicit but is very evident in his definition of democracy and in his argument that competition 'provides the people with the opportunity to make a choice. Without this opportunity popular sovereignty amounts to nothing'.[66] However, the distinctive feature of Schattschneider's leadership model is his use of the analogy with the firm. For example, he described the long historical process of extending the suffrage and the electorate's influence over the Presidency and Senate as being an extension of ownership rights, with the people coming to believe that they *own* the government and therefore, like 'all great proprietors', not being interested in excuses or details but only in *results*.[67] He also came close to the modern conception of a collective principal dealing with shirking agents when he described the public as being 'like a very rich man who is unable to supervise closely all of his enterprises. His problem is to learn how to compel his agents to define his options'.[68]

Furthermore, Schattschneider highlighted the fact that the owners of states, like the owners of firms, may well be interested in results and options related to the world that lies beyond the boundaries of a state or a firm. His theory of 'the primacy of foreign policy' referred specifically to the situation facing US democracy in the 1950s–60s but can also be applied to other eras or countries and to situations where the external pressures are not so intense and demanding.[69] It is a reminder that the results and options which political leaders provide for the voters/owners are often related to the external world or environment, and indeed the state's external relationships and policies seem particularly analogous to a firm's relationships and activities. For example, the state's international relationships with other states are strikingly analogous to a firm's relationships with other firms, which are cooperative and/or competitive relationships that range from the equivalent of formal business alliances to the equivalent of price wars aimed at driving a firm out of a market or even out of business.

But the most significant aspect of Schattschneider's analogy with the firm was its institutional dimension, for institutions constitute the underlying, skeletal framework of his and other leadership models of democracy. Schumpeter had pioneered this institutional application of the analogy with the firm when he pointed to the autonomy of government and management executives, and the institutional framework of his leadership model had been very evident in his description of British parliamentary democracy and comments about US presidential democracy. However, he had been much less explicit than Schattschneider in describing the role of institutions. Schattschneider emphasised the importance in politics of 'the structure of institutions' that delineates acceptable and unacceptable forms of conflict – just as the game of American football has rules that discriminate between acceptable and unacceptable forms of violence – and he pointed out that these 'rules of the game' also determine what is required to be successful in politics, such as what resources will be sufficient for success.[70]

In fact his account of institutions bears comparison with Elgie's description in the 1990s of the institutional basis of political leadership in democracies. He described institutions as defining the rules of the game, affecting the degree and direction of the pressure that leaders may exert and providing them with potential leadership resources.[71] Thus 'by mapping the institutional structure of a particular country, it is possible to indicate the fundamental pattern of that country's decision-making process' and the 'distinctive pattern of political leadership' in that country.[72] Furthermore, the institutional structure and pattern of leadership also vary over *time*, during the history of a particular country, as Elgie would have acknowledged and as Schumpeter recognised half a century earlier.[73]

Schattschneider, too, had recognised that democratic institutional structures vary not only from country to country but also during their historical evolution within a country. For example, he explored the historical changes in the US electoral/party system from the 1890s to 1930s as well as arguing that elections had played a less important role in the American political system than they had in the British political system.[74] However, like Schumpeter, he was less interested in the rules of the game than in the wider question of how the players were actually playing the game. And therefore Schattschneider's model of democracy, like other leadership models, was more concerned with the leadership processes than the institutional structure of the political system.

His leadership model of democracy continues to be influential and, for example, clearly influenced Kriesi's recent 'realistic theory' of direct democracy in Switzerland. Swiss democracy is known for its frequent use of referendums and initiatives but apparently Schattschneider's realism is applicable to these elements of direct democracy as well to the country's processes of representative democracy. 'In line with Schattschneider, the emphasis is on the role of leadership and organization in the democratic process', for his definition of representative democracy 'also applies to direct-democratic processes. The alternatives of the choice are defined by the political elites, here, too'.[75] Although Schattschneider's theory is much more applicable than Schumpeter's to these direct-democracy processes of referendum and initiative, Kriesi notes that Schumpeter produced the classic model of representative democracy and 'an extraordinarily influential theory'.[76]

For example, he appeared in a recent comparative study of modern democracies' tendency towards 'presidentialization of the executive' and specifically presidentialisation of the 'chief executives, whether presidents or prime ministers':

> In one sense, presidentialization seems to hark back to elitist models of representative democracy. Schumpeter's classic *Capitalism, Socialism and Democracy* (1942) emphasizes several features which resonate with the political phenomenon described in these pages, including the competitive struggle for power between rival political elites, the centrality of political leadership to this struggle and to government, and the prescription of a relatively limited role for citizens, as voters who periodically choose leaders but are largely passive beyond this.[77]

In their concluding summary Webb and Poguntke suggested that there is now a 'neo-elitist model' of democracy that goes beyond the Schumpeterian model in having a plebiscitary element that is a 'double-edged sword'.[78] The presidentialised chief executives' claim to have a personal mandate from the public is providing them 'with an additional power resource through which to bypass collective decision-making bodies' but is also leaving these pre-eminent leaders 'more susceptible to the fickle mood swings of public opinion', for 'the credibility of this mandate is continuously monitored by opinion polls, and any serious downturn undermines their claim to leadership'.[79]

This continuous monitoring of a leader's public standing is the key difference from Schumpeter's era. As will be seen in the next section, Schumpeter was well aware of how a Prime Minister might become an above-party leader of public opinion and thus overshadow Cabinet as well as parliamentary colleagues. He pointed out that as long ago as 1879 Gladstone had won a parliamentary election for his party through a public-speaking campaign that placed him 'on the crest of a wave of popular enthusiasm *for him personally*'.[80] But such pre-modern presidential Prime Ministers as Gladstone or Lloyd George did not have to deal with continuous feedback from opinion polls and the constant pressure to make policy decisions that would prove immediately popular. Their contemporary equivalent is therefore plagued to a greater degree by the problem of politics-versus-policy that Schumpeter identified when noting that the policy decision 'that a government decides on with an eye to its political chances is not necessarily the one that will produce the results most satisfactory to the nation':

> Thus the prime minister in a democracy might be likened to a horseman who is so fully engrossed in trying to keep in the saddle that he cannot plan his ride, or to a general so fully occupied with making sure that his army will accept his orders that he must leave strategy to take care of itself.[81]

Yet this was only one of the leadership problems that a Prime Minister faced between elections and that restricted his power as the pre-eminent leader.

Competition for leadership between elections and within government

Schumpeter acknowledged that the competitive struggle for the people's vote continues indirectly between elections, in the well-known sense of the government having to pay attention to the electoral implications of its legislation and policies.[82] But in describing his British-based model of democracy he identified a form of between-elections competition for leadership that occurs *within the government* and ensures that the country's primary formal leader does not become an elected dictator.

His theory of democracy provided an illustrated model of democratic government by presenting a Schumpeterian interpretation of the British system. He declared that 'thus far the logic of democratic government has worked itself out most completely in the English practice though not in its legal norms'.[83] The reference to the *logic* of democratic government was a warning that his account of what he referred to as the English practice would be closer to an economist's schematic model than to a historian's description or a political scientist's analysis.

Arguably it would have been better to have used the American practice as his model of democratic government. The directly elected Presidency comes closer than any aspect of parliamentary democracy to his notion of the electorate producing a government by deciding who the leading individual shall be. As he acknowledged, the American President is directly elected by the people to be, in Schumpeter's words, the 'sole minister' of the government; the Cabinet Secretaries 'are really no more than the word "secretary" conveys in common parlance'.[84] This is quite similar to Lijphart's description of the difference between presidential and parliamentary types of executive. The parliamentary type is a collegial Cabinet of Ministers who are 'more or less coequal participants' in its executive power, but the presidential type is a one-person executive whose Cabinet Secretaries are only 'advisers to the president'.[85]

The American system also has a mechanism for between-elections acceptance (or rejection or modification) of presidential leadership by representatives of the people. The President shares 'the power to decide' with an independent legislature composed of the people's elected representatives. If a majority of the people's legislative representatives refuse to accept a presidential lead, the President will usually be unable to lead the country in this direction. In fact Schumpeter argued that although a President's 'leadership is [legally] independent of his having a majority in Congress', in practice 'he is checkmated if he has none'; he is unable to move in any direction.[86] Moreover, an independent legislature composed of the people's elected representatives is more than just a convenient means of holding a referendum on each presidential lead. The people's representatives are able to enact a yes-but response that modifies a presidential lead to make it more acceptable. The President, too, is able to use his personal leadership capacities to convince or impress legislators in private discussions or negotiations that may result in the legislature's acceptance of policies that, as Schumpeter put it, the people 'never thought of and would not have approved of in advance'.[87]

The congressional legislature also acts as an auxiliary or supplementary source of leadership for American democracy. As was noted earlier, Schumpeter was well aware that not all occupants of a formal leadership post carry out their basic responsibility of providing a lead. If a President fails to fulfil this responsibility, the legislature can take on a leadership role and use its law-making power to set a direction for state and society. In fact there is good self-interested reason for legislators to take the lead in some areas of policy, partly because of competitive electoral pressures and partly because of internal competition for leadership within the legislature. On the other hand, the presidential right to veto legislation means that a President cannot be forced to accept such a lead unless it has an unusually large degree of support, a two-thirds majority, within the elected legislature. Thus the American system uses competition for leadership between executive and legislature to ensure both that there is sufficient leadership and that such leadership does not get out of democratic control between elections.

But in Schumpeter's time the US was the only good example of presidential democracy and therefore could hardly have been presented as a model example of democracy in general.[88] Instead Schumpeter based his model upon an example of parliamentary democracy, majoritarian rather than consensual, that did not too starkly reveal the anomalous features – from a Schumpeterian perspective – of the parliamentary form of democracy.[89] Perhaps the most obvious anomaly was that the British electorate, as in any parliamentary democracy, did not elect – and thus produce – a government. Schumpeter had to declare that the electorate actually 'devolves' the 'government-producing function' to 'an intermediate organ, henceforth called parliament'.[90] Instead of the people directly electing a government, they elect a parliament that on their behalf elects or chooses some of its members to form a government.

Another obvious anomaly was that the British government, like any parliamentary government, was a collective group of Ministers. In addition to lacking a Schumpeterian 'leading man' chosen by the voters, it could therefore be expected to suffer from the disadvantages that Schumpeter ascribed to all forms of collective rather than individual leadership. But he dealt with this problem by depicting Britain's formally collective Cabinet government as in practice a virtually one-person, prime-ministerial government. For the collective government of Ministers 'in all normal cases acknowledges an individual leader', the Prime Minister, who is already leader of their party in parliament and in the country and may well become a leader of public opinion beyond party lines – attaining a national leadership that is to some extent 'independent of mere party opinion'.[91] The Prime Minister can readily attain a national, non-partisan leadership of public opinion because the holder of this office, as the government's primary spokesperson, is the formal leader who publicly sets a direction for state and country.[92]

Schumpeter argued that the position of Prime Minister had not been given its due importance by other theorists of democracy because there was simply no room for leadership in the classical approach to democracy.[93] In contrast, his theory's emphasis on leadership seems to give the position of Prime Minister more than its due – as when he refers to the Prime Minister's 'rule'.[94] He appears to be presenting an extreme version of what decades later would be termed the 'prime ministerial government' thesis about the British practice of democratic government.[95] However, he also recognised that competition within the collective Cabinet government served to restrain prime-ministerial leadership and prevented its becoming a form of between-elections dictatorship.

Schumpeter depicted a Prime Minister's Cabinet colleagues as a group of powerful careerists who were willing and able to compete with the Prime Minister for governmental leadership. He described the Cabinet Ministers as 'an assemblage of subleaders' that can act like 'a miniature Parliament', which meant that the Prime Minister had to 'shape his program so that his colleagues in the Cabinet will not too often feel like "reconsidering their position" '.[96] And a Prime Minister has to view the Cabinet as 'an assemblage not only of comrades in arms but of party men who have their *own interests and prospects* to consider'; any Cabinet Minister 'steers a middle course between an unconditional allegiance to the leader's standard and an unconditional raising of a standard of his own'.[97]

The Ministers' concern for their career interests and prospects may well result in a few of them privately competing with the Prime Minister for formal leadership of the government – to take over the office of Prime Minister.[98] More importantly, their careerism will certainly result in widespread private competition with the Prime Minister for informal, personal leadership of particular *areas* of government. For Schumpeter noted that the Cabinet's function of 'intermediate leadership' involved individual Ministers being appointed to departments of state, such as the Treasury, 'in order to keep the leading group's hands on the bureaucratic engine'.[99] And as later analysts have pointed out, a Minister's political reputation and career prospects will depend very much upon how well he or she performs as a specialised, departmental Minister.[100] Cabinet Ministers therefore have good careerist reason to compete with the Prime Minister for direction-setting leadership of their specialised areas of government, whether or not they have any present ambitions to compete for formal leadership of the government.

Prime Ministers therefore have to tread carefully if they are not to provoke Ministers into a careerist reconsideration of how much allegiance they owe to their leader's standard. Just as the Ministers steer a middle course between unconditional allegiance and outright rebellion, so:

> the leader in turn responds by steering a middle course between insisting on discipline and allowing himself to be thwarted. He tempers pressure with more or less judicious concessions, frowns with compliments, punishments with benefits. This *game* results, according to the *relative strength* of individuals and their positions, in a very *variable* but in most cases considerable amount of freedom.[101]

Schumpeter's use of the 'game' metaphor was probably influenced by Cambray's *The Game of Politics: A Study of the Principles of British Political Strategy*.[102] Von Neumann and Morgenstern's seminal work on game theory had not yet appeared, and in any case it would have been difficult to apply game theory to Prime Ministers. Their preferred payoff in a game might differ from one individual to another because, having attained the highest public office, their career goals are likely to vary according to how they wish their careers to be viewed in retirement and in the verdict of history As Asquith famously pointed out, the office of Prime Minister 'is what its holder *chooses* and is able to make of it'.[103]

The Asquith adage is also a reminder that prime-ministerial leadership involves a mixture of subjective and objective factors. A Prime Minister's particular range of policy interests and ambitions is an obvious subjective factor and can vary markedly between different holders of the office.[104] Style of leadership is another subjective factor that varies between Prime Ministers. One observer has suggested that every Prime Minister has a different style; another has suggested that there is almost a pendulum tendency for new Prime Ministers to adopt a contrasting style to their predecessor's.[105]

But if subjective factors include personal qualities as well as inclinations, they will also affect what a Prime Minister is *able* to make of the office. For such personal qualities as intelligence and integrity are an important part of a Prime Minister's personal leadership capacities to convince and impress. As is described in the next chapter, Schumpeter regarded these capacities to convince and impress as characteristic of the political form of leadership, as when they act as power-multipliers for a political leader who holds a prominent public office. They are particularly important in the case of the office of Prime Minister because it is so weak in formal powers (party as well as constitutional) when compared to the constitutional powers of the Presidency in a presidential system. In fact the Prime Minister's personal leadership capacities have been termed 'informal powers', which 'matter as much for a Prime Minister as the formal powers' and vary 'not only between Prime Ministers but also within their terms of office'.[106]

However, one reason for this variation within a holder's term of office is that often personal leadership capacities involve an objective element that is beyond the leader's control. For example, public popularity increases the leader's capacity to convince and impress but can be subject to marked fluctuations caused by events beyond the leader's control.[107] Similarly, the increased prestige – and thus capacity to impress – that is enjoyed by a Prime Minister who leads a winning election campaign may be owed largely to such fortuitous factors as the bungling or disunity of his electoral opponents.[108]

Perhaps the most important objective factor affecting the Prime Minister's intra-Cabinet leadership capacities is whether the other Ministers in Cabinet have any outstanding personal qualities and leadership capacities. For example, Prime Ministers may well be more able to dominate Cabinet if they are more intelligent, aggressive, determined or experienced than other Ministers,[109] but this also depends on the relative lack of intelligence, aggression, determination or experience among the other members of the Cabinet. In a Cabinet of luminaries rather than mediocrities the Prime Minister's personal leadership capacities may even be overshadowed by those of other members of the government. If so, these colleagues will likely be more open and effective competitors with the Prime Minister for leadership of the government and/or the particular areas of government assigned to them as specialised Ministers. How openly and strongly they will compete, and how damaging this will be to the Prime Minister's position, are some of the many variables that the leader has to take into account when playing the game of collective government.

When the variables are in their favour, Prime Ministers have often tried to adjust the rules of the game, and their successful attempts at doing so have illustrated how much flexibility is built into the office of Prime Minister.[110] But just as the electoral, public competition for leadership guarantees considerable freedom of expression and discussion, so the within-government private competition for leadership results in considerable freedom from personal rule by the government's leader. As Schumpeter concluded, 'the competitive element is of the essence of democracy'.[111]

However, he would also have contended that the leadership element is of the essence of government, whether democratic or any other variety. Formal and informal leadership provides the context for the competitive element and for his model of democratic government. The next chapter will explore a further aspect of the role of leadership in democracy: bringing about change. The entrepreneurial-style, pioneering kind of leadership pursues innovation, while the standard, adaptive kind leads a democracy into more prosaic and predictable changes.

2
Pioneering and Adaptive Leadership

The (missing) analogy with entrepreneurship

One of the questions that are begged by Schumpeter's theory of democracy is why he did not draw an analogy with entrepreneurship in either the quasi-economic or leadership dimension of his theory. Considering how important a role entrepreneurship played in his economic theorising, this was a glaring omission from the quasi-economic aspect of his theory of democracy. And it was also a puzzling omission from the leadership dimension of the theory, not only because it was such an obvious economic analogy for him to use but also because in the economic chapters of *Capitalism, Socialism and Democracy* he had described entrepreneurs as economic leaders. He had viewed their entrepreneurial role as 'another form of individual leadership acting by virtue of personal force and personal responsibility for success'; it is a type of economic leadership provided by merchants and industrialists 'as far as they are entrepreneurs' and even though a 'genius in the business office may be, and often is, utterly unable outside of it to say boo to a goose'.[1]

Furthermore, since Schumpeter's time some political scientists *have* used the analogy with entrepreneurship, as was described in a chapter of the first edition of this book.[2] The analogy with entrepreneurship was made very explicit by the use of such terms as 'political entrepreneur' or 'policy entrepreneur', which also added a new concept to theories of politics or policy making.[3] It is true that these concepts were not part of an overall leadership theory or model of politics and that often they were not using Schumpeter's conception of entrepreneur. But it still begs the question of why he apparently overlooked an economic analogy that political scientists who lacked his expertise in economics have recognised and used to good effect.

Another part of the puzzle is that if Schumpeter was willing to use implicit analogies with the market in the leadership dimension of his theory, why not also include some implicit analogy with entrepreneurship? It has been argued that Schumpeter's description of electoral leadership did in fact implicitly use this analogy even if without ever mentioning entrepreneurship by name:

> [For] he argued analogously that professional politicians *at times* do not act merely according to a fixed behavior rule but actually create new combinations, innovative party programs and platforms that exploit long-standing political opportunities, and unmet preferences and needs ... Schumpeter even argued notoriously that this innovation amounted to creating and manipulating a 'Manufactured Will'.[4]

But will-manufacturing can also occur when raising a relatively familiar issue, just as it can occur in the economy when introducing a new but not innovative consumer product. Schumpeter did not draw a distinction between truly innovative and relatively familiar issues, such as the marginally new or the revival of such old favourites as the crime issue.

He came closest to an analogy with entrepreneurship when he drew a distinction between careerist and non-careerist *motivation* rather than between innovation and the lack of innovation. Schumpeter's emphasis on the motivation of politicians involved in a democracy's political institutions is another of those areas in which he pioneered approaches that are now taken for granted. According to Przeworski, modern political economy arose from the mid-1970s argument that 'the state is populated by the same [sorts of] actors as the market', for this argument forced political economists 'to ask not just what the state needs to do but what rulers will want and be able to do'.[5]

Yet in the 1940s Schumpeter was already depicting the democratic state's political institutions as populated by politicians pursuing their careerist self-interest. He actually described democracy as the 'rule of the politician', pointed out that in a modern democracy 'politics will unavoidably be a career' and argued that politicians' careerist 'professional interest' usually overrides any loyalties to class or group interests.[6] (Like Przeworski and other political economists, Schumpeter was using a broad definition of state institutions that includes not only the rules of the game but also the organs and organisations that make and enforce the rules, such as cabinets, legislatures and bureaucracies.)

Furthermore, he foreshadowed the present awareness among political economists that state actors' motivations are behaviourally no less complex than the motivations of actors in a market. As Przeworski pointed out, the state's institutions are 'populated' by actors pursuing various interests and even in the case of judges and central bankers 'the people who populate such institutions are not different from anyone else. Some have an ideological ax to grind, some favour the interests of the rich, some seek publicity, some rents'.[7] Similarly, Schumpeter was well aware that careerist self-interest was not politicians' only motivation and was simply the standard motivation for their political activity in the same sense that profit-seeking was the standard motivation for the economic activity of businessmen in a market. He noted that a few individuals, such as 'instances of the crusader type', compete for votes and raise election issues but do *not* have the standard, careerist motivation; they are 'deviations from the standard practice' because they are not 'harboring any wish to start in on a normal political career'.[8]

By acknowledging these non-careerist deviations from the standard careerist motivation, Schumpeter was providing a more comprehensive and accurate depiction of political leaders' motivation than when he had compared vote-dealing politicians with profit-seeking businessmen (see Chapter 1). It is true that his theory of democracy and model of political leadership would have had more 'rigor' if it had included only careerist motivations and had adopted something like Downs's basic assumption or axiom that politicians seek public office as an end in itself and never as a means of carrying out a particular policy.[9] On the other hand, by presenting a less rigorous but more comprehensive view of motivation Schumpeter gained the opportunity to make a two-pronged comparison between political and economic motivations. In addition to the comparison between the standard motivations of careerist politicians and profit-seeking businessmen, there would also be the comparison between the non-standard motivations of (1) non-careerist politicians and (2) entrepreneurial businessmen. The latter comparison has much to offer, as will be seen in the next section of this chapter, and it also opens up the broader analogy with economic entrepreneurship – including the similarities between entrepreneurship and innovative political leadership.

Yet for some reason Schumpeter did *not* take this opportunity to make a comparison with entrepreneurs and open up the broader analogy between entrepreneurship and a particular kind of political leadership. What makes this omission all the more perplexing is that in Schumpeter's early work, *The Theory of Economic Development* (see Appendix), he had described entrepreneurship as the economic version of a special kind of leadership that is also found in politics and which many years later Olson aptly labelled 'pioneering'.[10] Such pioneering leadership is needed because most people have difficulty in going beyond the boundaries of ordinary routine and because there is actual resistance to anyone wishing to introduce something new.[11] This resistance to change can involve much more than the social pressure against deviation from custom that is found in traditional societies; the resistance can take the form of political or even legal impediments, and in the case of economic change it also involves the difficulty of winning over the consumers.[12]

Pioneering leaders have the intellectual will power to overcome psychological habits of thought, and the emotional will power to overcome social resistance.[13] Schumpeter emphasised that it is not the pioneering leader's function to find or create new possibilities but rather to make the possibilities a reality. New possibilities are 'always present' and it is 'doing the thing' that is so important.[14] To illustrate this point he argued that there had been a ready possibility of preserving Louis XVI's monarchical regime (and thereby preventing the French Revolution) but nobody had seized the opportunity. That Schumpeter used an example from political rather than economic history is further evidence that he was describing a kind of leadership that occurs in politics as well as economics, even if the political version seems in shorter supply than the economic!

However, the economic and political versions of pioneering leadership differ markedly in capacities and resources. The economic entrepreneur is a pioneering leader in the sense of leading the means of production into new channels and drawing other producers into these new channels.[15] But as the other producers are competitors who will bring an end to the profits the entrepreneur has won from his pioneering, this leadership was described by Schumpeter as being in a sense 'leadership against one's own will'. More importantly, it is not leadership 'by convincing people of the desirability of carrying out his plan or by creating confidence in his leading in the manner of a political leader – the only man he has to convince or impress is the banker who is to finance him'.[16] With this finance the entrepreneur is able to buy the resources he needs to transform a possibility into reality. The economic entrepreneur is therefore more independent and self-sufficient than a pioneering political leader, who secures his needed public-sector resources by using his capacity to convince or impress people. On the other hand, Schumpeter suggested that this is also why the entrepreneur does not fit the popular image of leadership, and why his economic leadership has none of the glamour that is associated with political leadership.[17]

But another reason why the entrepreneur lacks the appearance and glamour of leadership is that he lacks a formal leadership position like those held by a democracy's elected public officials. It is true that an entrepreneur who heads a major firm may be regarded as a leader of business and of a sector of the economy. But this recognised position of leadership is comparatively informal and more like the special attention that a parliamentary democracy gives to the leaders of political parties during an election campaign or whenever else they are acting as the party's spokesperson. Moreover, many budding entrepreneurs are better compared to policy advocates who lack an interest-group post that would give them some recognised position of leadership in their area of policy expertise. To become a pioneering political leader within this area of public policy they will have to rely solely on their personal capacities to convince and impress.

The pioneering policy advocate or party leader faces a more difficult challenge than any form of economic entrepreneur. As Schlesinger pointed out in his essay on democracy and leadership, winning democratic consent for innovation 'requires leaders who possess not only a personal vision but the capacity to communicate that vision to their age', and he believed that resistance to innovation made this 'art of fostering and managing innovation in the service of a free community' a very difficult task.[18]

It may not be so formidable a task for *top-down* pioneering leaders, who use their powers as one of the country's formal leaders to instigate an innovation that has not been raised as an election issue. In a sense top-down pioneering is similar to an entrepreneur's use of capacities and resources, because pioneering formal leaders' use of their public powers to command the resources of the state is almost as impersonal as economic entrepreneurs' use of money to buy the resources that they need. But the Schumpeterian model of democracy acknowledged that there are severe constitutional and political restraints upon a democracy's formal leader. A top-down pioneering leader will therefore still require the personal leadership capacities of convincing and impressing to extend and strengthen the formal powers of a public official to the degree required for top-down pioneering leadership.

Entrepreneurship and its pioneering political equivalent

Although there are significant differences between the economic and political versions of pioneering leadership, some of Schumpeter's account of entrepreneurship is also applicable to the political version of pioneering leadership. He argued that entrepreneurship cannot be incorporated into (classical) economic theory's rationalistic forms of description and explanation, for entrepreneurial aptitudes differ in kind as well as degree from those of 'mere rational economic behavior', and the entrepreneurial choice of new methods cannot be explained simply by 'the concept of rational economic behavior.'[19] In particular, entrepreneurs differ markedly from (classical) economic theory's conception of 'economic man', whose economic activities are assumed to arise from 'balancing probable results [in terms of consuming goods and services] against the disutility of effort'.[20] Instead the Schumpeterian entrepreneur is motivated by such desires as (1) founding a private kingdom; (2) wanting to fight, to conquer, or to prove himself superior to rivals; or (3) seeking the pleasure of creating, of exercising energy and ingenuity, or of just getting things done. Such motivations are unlikely to be included in even the modern cost-benefit explanations of economic behaviour that have replaced the classical cost-benefit notion of balancing probable results against the disutility of effort. And these entrepreneurial motivations seem to have survived into modern times, considering the apparent motivations of the two most famous entrepreneurs of the 1970s–80s IT economic revolution. One apparently has viewed as his life's work the creation of a company that would 'sell software to the masses until the end of time', while the other apparently 'wants to tell the world how to compute, to set the style for computing' and 'doesn't care what the odds are against his success... Nor does he have to *win*, if, by losing the mother of all battles he can maintain his peculiar form of conviction'.[21]

There are some obvious similarities with the political version of pioneering leadership, which has displayed similarly 'non-rational' motivations and aptitudes for pioneering new things. And such entrepreneurial-style, pioneering political leaders have played an important enough role to be worth a mention – and an analogy with entrepreneurs – in a leadership model of democracy, especially if it is also using analogies with the market and/or firm. However, a leadership model may be too rigorously rationalist to include the analogy with Schumpeterian entrepreneurs. For example, Downs's model was based on a rigorous conception of political rationality that includes efficiency, a consciously selected political goal and an office-seeking selfishness.[22] It assumes that such rational self-interest is limited only by politicians' law-abidingness and team solidarity with party colleagues,[23]and also by the limits on rationality arising from the problem of uncertainty – 'any lack of sure knowledge about the course of events' – that Downs added to his second-stage, more realistic model of democracy.[24] A third-stage model, even more realistic and less rigorously rationalist than the second, would have to be added if entrepreneurial-style, pioneering leadership were to be included in the Downsian leadership model.

Even Schumpeter's leadership model would have some problems accommodating an analogy with such a multi-faceted and distinctive concept as the Schumpeterian notion of entrepreneurship. For example, the economic function of this entrepreneurship is the carrying out of not merely new but *revolutionary* new combinations of factors. The entrepreneurs bring about revolutionary new (1) methods of production, (2) consumer goods, (3) markets, (4) sources of supply, and (5) ways of organising an industry.[25] Furthermore, as is described in the Appendix, such revolutionary changes are brought about through the entrepreneur's spontaneous use of *initiative* – another distinctive feature of Schumpeterian entrepreneurship.

It is true that in his later writings Schumpeter paid less attention to the spontaneous, initiative aspect of entrepreneurship. In *Capitalism, Socialism and Democracy* his analysis of entrepreneurship was focused on the creative-destructive economic revolutions instigated by entrepreneurs. Several years later his essay on 'the creative response in economic history' described entrepreneurship in terms of a reaction to external change, as a creative (innovative) response, not as the spontaneous pursuit of innovation.[26] On the other hand, he emphasised that the actual content of the creative response cannot be predicted beforehand – it is still a truly innovative rather than routine or marginally new change.[27]

The entrepreneur's creative response is therefore an incomplete or partial form of pioneering economic leadership. Schumpeter had always recognised that some entrepreneurs come closer than others to the ideal. For example, his theory of economic development had pointed to the captain of industry as exhibiting the entrepreneurial function with 'particular purity', especially as entrepreneurs increasingly tended to be only managers rather than owners of industry.[28] Moreover, he emphasised in his essay on the creative response that such creativity may involve only a quite humble innovation. The entrepreneur's creative new thing 'need not be spectacular or of historic importance', and entrepreneurship occurs 'even in the humblest levels of the business world'.[29]

In *Capitalism, Socialism and Democracy* he had indicated that entrepreneurial innovation ranges in degree from the revolutionary to the quite humble:

> We have seen that the function of entrepreneurs is to reform or revolutionize the pattern of production by exploiting an invention or, more generally, an untried technological possibility for producing a new commodity or producing an old one in a new way, by opening up a new source of supply of materials or a new outlet for products, by reorganizing an industry and so on. Railroad construction in its earlier stages, electrical power production before the First World War, steam and steel, the motorcar, colonial ventures afford spectacular instances of a large genus which comprises innumerable humbler ones – down to such things as making a success of a particular kind of sausage or toothbrush.[30]

So it would seem that, depending upon the complexity of change and its economic effect, the degree of innovation can be anything between the revolutionising of an industry and the modification of a toothbrush design, such as introducing the angled-head kind of toothbrush.

But there are obvious problems in describing individuals as being entrepreneurs merely because they have brought about an innovation of however humble a degree. Schumpeter remarked in his theory of economic development that just as an entrepreneur usually does not spend all his career being entrepreneurial, so an ordinary businessman usually behaves entrepreneurially, 'to however modest a degree', at least once in his career.[31] If entrepreneurial behaviour is as common as Schumpeter suggests, the title of 'entrepreneur' would have to be reserved for that elite few who have carried out either a revolutionary innovation or an unusual number of humbler innovations. In his theory of economic development Schumpeter argued that entrepreneurial aptitudes, notably economic initiative, are distributed among a population in the usual bell-curve distribution pattern.[32] And in *Capitalism, Socialism and Democracy* he confirmed that only a small percentage of the population possessed these aptitudes in sufficient quantities to undertake major or frequent innovations.[33]

He also emphasised that the entrepreneurial function and aptitudes are all about 'getting things done' rather than inventing anything. Entrepreneurs need not be – and often are not – the actual inventors of their innovations.[34] Indeed 'to carry any improvement into effect is a task entirely different from the inventing of it, and a task, moreover, requiring entirely different kinds of aptitudes'.[35] But it is a scarcely less important task than invention. Scientific or technological inventions that 'are not carried into practice' are 'economically irrelevant'.[36]

Most of these points about how to define and distinguish entrepreneurship could also be made about its political equivalent – entrepreneurial-style, pioneering leadership. There is the same need to expand the definition to include the partly pioneering, creative response; there are the same sort of differences in degrees of innovation; and there is the same problem of distinguishing the true pioneer from the standard leader who indulges in an occasional or once-in-a-lifetime bout of modest pioneering. Moreover, in politics as much as economics there are marked differences – in the task and the appropriate aptitudes – between inventing a new idea and actually carrying it out. And the distribution of political initiative is probably similar to Schumpeter's assessment of the distribution of economic initiative, particularly an individual's psychological ability to go beyond the boundaries of routine.[37]

However, unlike in the economy, pioneering leadership in politics seldom brings about truly revolutionary innovations. Instead political pioneering tends to bring about either only modifying changes or complex changes that do not have a major effect on a sector of the democracy's political system. There seems to be nothing comparable to the cycles of creative-destructive economic revolutions that Schumpeter described in *Capitalism, Socialism and Democracy* (and will be discussed in Chapter 3). Thus when a recent study of US sub-national policy entrepreneurs argued that 'we should think of the policy entrepreneur as a figure embodying both creative genius and the ability to lay waste to outmoded governance structures', no examples of such a creative-destructive figure were offered.[38] France at least provides the example of De Gaulle's 1958 destruction of the Fourth Republic's parliamentary system of democratic government and creation of the more presidential system that characterises the Fifth Republic.[39] But the historical prominence of this case suggests that it is an exception which proves the rule that democracy tends to avoid truly revolutionary political or policy changes.

Some might also argue that it is an example of how democracies' innovations are not necessarily improvements. At the time there was by no means unanimous support for De Gaulle's change of constitution, and during the 1960s his opponents on the left did not accept the strongly presidential system he had built upon the new constitution. France's change from a two-ballot to a proportional-representation system for the 1986 parliamentary elections was even more controversial as it appeared to be a case of 'partisan self-seeking' aimed at improving the government's electoral prospects.[40]

But the most relevant example of a controversial innovation comes from Schumpeter's own time and country, as his dislike of President Roosevelt's New Deal may well explain why his theory of democracy made no mention of entrepreneurial-style, pioneering leadership. The New Deal policy programme was the nearest thing to an entrepreneurial-style revolutionary policy change to have occurred in the democracies of Schumpeter's era. And he argued that the extent and rapidity of these innovations actually had a negative impact on the economy's prospects for recovery from the Depression. He argued that 'so extensive and rapid a change' will adversely affect production and can account for 'the fact that this country which had the best chance of recovering quickly was precisely the one to experience the most unsatisfactory recovery'.[41] In another passage he criticised the actual content of the New Deal, specifically its labour legislation and attitude to labour problems, but again emphasised that change had been 'crowded into so short a time'.[42]

The New Deal experience also highlights another possible explanation for his not mentioning entrepreneurial-style, pioneering political leadership in his theory of democracy. Medearis has shown that Schumpeter viewed the pro-labour policies of the New Deal not only as a threat to capitalism but also as part of a threatening historical process of social and economic democratisation, whose earlier effects on Europe had inspired him to develop a 'transformative' conception of democracy that differed markedly from the theory of democracy that he would later present in *Capitalism, Socialism and Democracy*.[43] His fear of transformative democracy may in fact explain why his later, more publicised conception of democracy paid so little attention to the possibilities for democratic innovation:

> Although there were clear tensions, even contradictions, between the two conceptions of democracy he developed throughout his life, the conceptions were also connected to each other, both practically and politically. It is because Schumpeter believed that democracy could be transformative, that it had the potential to threaten the

conservative institutions and hierarchies he cherished, that he theorized a form of elite-dominated democratic politics in which democratic change could be stifled.[44]

Whatever the reason or reasons for Schumpeter's wariness about discussing the political equivalent of economic innovation, this reticence had left an unresolved tension within the theory of democracy presented in *Capitalism, Socialism and Democracy*. The tension has been described by Medearis as the 'combination of equilibrium and non-equilibrium aspects', with the former depicting politicians' behaviour as 'specified responses to specified environmental changes' and the latter implicitly acknowledging 'an internal source of change' – entrepreneurial-style political innovators.[45] It could also be described as a combination of two different kinds of political change and leadership. The standard kind is the adaptive response and involves careerist leadership by the political equivalent of profit-seeking businessmen; the other kind is the creative response or pioneering initiative and involves entrepreneurial-style, pioneering leadership, with its non-rational motivation and behaviour. This chapter has been mainly concerned with the pioneering kind of leadership and change but the next section will focus on the standard, adaptive kind of leadership and its incremental or innovative adaptive responses.

Adaptive leadership versus entrepreneurial-style pioneering

The standard kind of political leader, the politically rational careerist, provides a democracy with the leadership to carry out the standard kind of political change – the adaptive response. It is the equivalent of the standard kind of change in the economy described by Schumpeter as 'adaptations which common business experience suggests in the face of conditions that change under the influence of external factors'.[46] In the case of the political adaptive response, the 'external factors' that have changed the conditions facing political leaders are events that have occurred in other parts of the political system, in the economy, the society, or even other countries. Then the 'internal' factors of careerist self-interest and political competition ensure that political leaders respond to these events by providing sufficient leadership, such as by raising issues or proposing policies, to supply not only their individual careers but also their democratic political community with an adaptive response to the changed conditions. Whereas economic adaptation involves competing firms supplying themselves and the economy with adaptive responses, political adaptation involves competing leaders supplying their careers and their democracy with adaptive responses.

Schumpeter's notion of a democracy's adaptive response seems to have included a broader view of adaptation than simply an enhancing of the democracy's survival prospects. His definition of democracy's success included not only survival – 'that the democratic process reproduce itself steadily' – but also the capacity to deal with 'current problems in a way which all interests that count politically find acceptable in the long run'.[47] So presumably a response might be considered adaptive either if it enhanced the democracy's survival prospects *or* if it dealt with a problem in a way that no politically significant interest found unacceptable in the long run.

When leaders supply their democracy with adaptive responses, these issues or proposals typically involve only routine or marginally new changes – not innovations. In *The Theory of Economic Development* Schumpeter depicted economic adaptive responses as (1) only small variations at the margin and (2) as the economy's continual adaptation through continuous small steps (see Appendix). This view of economic adaptation as an incremental rather than innovative response also appeared many years later when he contrasted the adaptive and creative responses as two different kinds of reaction to external change. The creative response is an unpredictable innovation; it is 'something outside the range of existing practice' and 'cannot be predicted by applying the ordinary rules of inference from pre-existing facts'.[48] The adaptive response, by contrast, produces a change that is within the range of existing practice or can be predicted by applying the ordinary rules of inference, such as assumptions about economically rational behaviour.

The *political* adaptive response, too, typically involves only incremental change that is within the range of existing practice and can be predicted by applying assumptions about rational behaviour – in this case politically rather than economically rational. But some political adaptive responses have been more innovative than incremental and have certainly gone beyond the range of existing practice, even if in a predictable manner that distinguishes them from a creative response's innovation. A striking example occurred in Schumpeter's lifetime when innovations in economic and social policy were introduced as an adaptive response to the outbreak of a 'war of survival' or 'total war', such as the Second World War. These innovations were clearly adaptive in the sense of being required for the survival of democracy, perhaps the state itself, and were going far beyond the range of existing practice but were also predictable and indeed varied predictably from one country to another according to differences in the level of threat and the nature of society, such as the mobilisation of women for 'war work' being more extensive and coercive in Britain than in the US.[49] A less obvious and clear-cut example of Schumpeter-era adaptive innovations are the new policies and institutions that the US and other democracies introduced in response to the economic and social crisis brought by the Depression. Although Schumpeter may have viewed the New Deal innovations as entrepreneurial, some of them are better explained as adaptive innovations (as they are in the Conclusion). The New Deal era was another of those times when the adaptive innovation has been so prevalent and significant that it has overshadowed the merely incremental adaptive response.

In recent decades it has become apparent that some economic adaptive responses, too, are more innovative than incremental – and that adaptive innovations have become an increasingly important feature of the modern economy. As long ago as the 1980s Drucker published an influential work, *Innovation and Entrepreneurship: Practice and Principles*, that was intended to be the innovation-focused equivalent of his celebrated works on the theory and practice of management. His book also uses the term 'entrepreneur' and, like Schumpeter, emphasises that entrepreneurship requires will power and a commitment of time and effort: 'innovation becomes hard, focused, purposeful work making very great demands on diligence, on persistence, and on commitment. If these are lacking, no amount of talent, ingenuity, or knowledge will avail'.[50] But Drucker's notion of entrepreneurship also lacks the distinctively Schumpeterian features of revolutionary change and entrepreneurial initiative. He emphasises that innovations which 'in themselves constitute a major change' are fairly uncommon exceptions and that successful innovations are mostly 'far more prosaic' and 'exploit change'.[51] In Schumpeterian terms they are not only humble rather than revolutionary innovations but also are produced by opportunist responsiveness rather than entrepreneurial initiative. Similarly, Drucker's definition of the entrepreneur and entrepreneurship describes an individual who 'always searches for change, responds to it, and exploits it as opportunity'.[52]

Furthermore, this opportunist innovation is clearly an adaptive rather than creative response to change. Not only does the innovativeness lack creative innovations' unpredictability but also the opportunism lacks the economically non-rational motivation that is a distinctive feature of Schumpeterian entrepreneurship, even when engaged in the only partly pioneering innovation of a creative response rather than an entrepreneurial initiative. Although Drucker does not emphasise the profit-seeking, economically rational motivation for opportunist innovation, he notes that innovation is 'the proper and profitable course' when the opportunity exists.[53] Another indication that he envisages an economically rational opportunism is his downplaying of the element of risk. According to his experience, successful innovators do not have a propensity for risk-taking, and indeed are successful because they define and confine risks, whether dealing with opportunities 'of small and clearly definable risk, such as exploiting the unexpected or a process need, or opportunities of much greater but still definable risk, as in knowledge-based innovation'.[54]

The adaptive aspect of opportunist innovation is also evident when Drucker warns that it is risky *not* to innovate, for Schumpeter pointed out that adaptive responses may well be 'forced' upon firms (as is described in the Appendix). Drucker warns that 'defending yesterday – that is, not innovating – is far more risky than making tomorrow', and he points out that in 'a period of rapid change the best – and perhaps the only – way a business can hope to prosper, if not to survive, is to innovate'.[55] Such innovation is clearly a forced adaptive response, which the firm must make in order to survive or to enhance its survival prospects. And the forced adaptation may well require innovative change in not merely pricing or product development but also a firm's actual structure and culture. A prominent example of such institutional change is the way that IBM secured its future in the mid-1990s by a 'total commitment to change. The old IBM was forever dead'.[56]

Institutional change is rarely found among political adaptive innovations, which are more likely to be a new issue or policy, and in fact any form of adaptive innovation is less common in politics than in the economy. Modern political systems are not as subject to rapid change as modern economies have become in recent decades. And there is no longer any need to make adaptive innovations in response to a 'total' war of survival or in response to a Depression-like economic crisis, as both these dramatic types of external change have been extinct for generations.

In addition, modern democracies are more subject than modern economies to the effects of 'rigidity' – a resistance to adaptation. The economic version was mentioned by Schumpeter in *Capitalism, Socialism and Democracy*: 'Rigidity is a type of resistance to adaptation that perfect and prompt competition excludes' but that otherwise 'spells loss [to the community] and reduced output'.[57] Politics' version of rigidity is so prevalent that a democracy's adaptive response is usually something less than what would have been optimal for that political community. A suboptimal but useful response is therefore usually the realistically 'appropriate' adaptive response and is the best that reasonably can be expected of democracies with normal amounts of political rigidity.

Political rigidity takes several different forms, such as vested interests or unconscious biases (as is described in Chapter 3). In the case of vested interests, a careerist political leader may refuse to support the optimal adaptive response or even a useful response because these policies are opposed by vested interests. If there is insufficient political competitiveness to neutralise vested interests' resistance to an appropriate adaptive response, careerist political leaders may believe that it is not an appropriate adaptive response for their career – it is an issue or policy proposal to be ignored or opposed.

This is all the more likely to occur when the appropriate adaptive response is innovative rather than incremental. The innovative adaptation usually involves a higher cost and risk for both a political career and a political community. When the effects of rigidity are added to these costs and risks, there is a strong tendency to avoid innovative adaptive responses or to delay them until a crisis forces an innovative adaptive response. An insider's view of this drift-into-crisis tendency was provided by a former British Prime Minister, James Callaghan, when replying to a question about whether the British government had missed an opportunity in the mid-1960s to take action that might have averted the violence which plagued Northern Ireland for decades to come:

> I think it was like so many things in politics. It took a crisis to enable us to take the action that was necessary. It is like so many things that you cannot really act [on] even though you know it is logical to act and you ought to be able to act, until circumstances are right that permit you to do so. This is why probably we shall enter the European currency, because it will be seen that it is inevitable and must be done, and this happens all the time in politics.[58]

If the crisis is produced by a threat to national security, the likelihood of an innovative response seems to increase with the acuteness and immediacy of the threat.[59] Polsby's study of political innovations described how two national-security crises from the Truman era produced innovative responses in foreign policy – the Marshall Plan and the Truman Doctrine. He depicted the Marshall Plan economic aid as a 'corrective response' evoked by warnings about impending economic collapse in Western Europe and the likelihood of social disorders.[60] The Marshall Plan can therefore readily be categorised as a forced adaptive innovation, with President Truman concluding that his other, less innovative policy options would be unable to counter this threat of Western Europe being lost to communism (and his career being blighted by a major failure in national-security policy).[61]

However, the Truman Doctrine seems a less forced and adaptive innovation than the Marshall Plan. Polsby described it as a response to the problem posed by an impending British withdrawal from the eastern Mediterranean at a time when Greece and Turkey seemed to be threatened by internal or external communist pressure.[62] But the resulting Truman Doctrine seems a disproportionate and even extravagant response, as it offered military and economic aid not just to Greece and Turkey but to *any* country, anywhere in the world, which was resisting communist insurgency or pressure from communist states. In fact President Truman was criticised by the left for launching a crusade against communism and encouraging the division of the world into East–West blocks, and even historians favourably disposed towards the Truman Doctrine have acknowledged that 'Truman's rhetoric was exaggerated and created an "ideological straightjacket" for later policy'.[63] The exaggerated, Cold War rhetoric can be explained by the need to win congressional and public support for the notion of giving aid to Greece and Turkey, which required this regional policy change to be framed as part of a more momentous and far-reaching innovation – a global campaign against the spread of communism.[64] But the Truman Doctrine was such an ambitious and risky commitment, in terms of Truman's career and his country's foreign policy, that it seems more like the non-rational and unpredictably innovative response of a leader who is supplying a partly pioneering, creative response to a problem.

As is often the case with creative responses it was riskier as well as more ambitious than an innovative adaptive response to the problem. The riskier nature of the creative response is reminiscent of the age-old definition of entrepreneurs as risk-takers. Schumpeter argued against defining entrepreneurs as risk-takers, and preferred Say's almost as ancient definition of entrepreneurs as combiners of productive factors.[65] But the greater risk-taking of the entrepreneurial, creative response is clearly one of the features that distinguish it from the non-entrepreneurial, adaptive innovation. And the risk-taking involved in creative responses is illustrated by how often they have failed or been controversial. They are potentially more advantageous than an incremental or innovative adaptive innovation but also potentially a less useful and perhaps even disastrous response. Careerist leaders have good reason to avoid such high risks to their careers and to leave it to crusaders and others with non-rational motivations to propound and support the creative response.

Yet the Truman case suggests that a careerist leader may make a creative response at least once in his career. As was mentioned earlier, Schumpeter argued that just as an entrepreneur usually does not spend all his career being entrepreneurial, so an ordinary business-man usually behaves entrepreneurially – however humble the innovation – at least once in his career. Clearly the same applies to political careerists and entrepreneurial-style, political pioneering but there is also the similar problem of how to distinguish the true pioneer from the careerist who occasionally engages in pioneering. A similar solution would be to reserve the title of 'pioneer' for the elite few who have propounded revolutionary innovations or an unusual number of humbler innovations. However, this category would have to include (1) crusaders and others who give a higher priority to pioneering than to having a political career, (2) realists and others who pursue their careerist self-interest in order to be more effective pioneers, such as seeking powerful public office in order to engage in top-down pioneering, and (3) any careerist who engages in an unusual (for careerists) amount of pioneering, whether by proposing revolutionary initiatives or responses or by propounding an unusual number of humbler pioneering innovations.

Another key variation among political leaders is how averse they are to innovation of any kind – *adaptive* as well as pioneering. The innovation-averse leaders prefer to deal with only incremental adaptations or with the forced adaptive innovations that arise from a drift into crisis. As was noted earlier, an innovative adaptation usually involves a higher cost and risk than an incremental adaptation. And the innovation's careerist costs and risk escalate when the leader goes beyond raising an innovative issue or presenting an innovative policy proposal and actually strives to keep the issue alive or to convert the proposal into public policy. It is hardly surprising that so many careerist leaders so often assess this cost in time, effort and other resources (such as the political capital of personal prestige) as too high a cost to pay for the prospect of some career benefits that may or may not accrue from this relatively risky investment. In addition, there is the 'opportunity cost' of what these scarce resources might achieve for a leader's career if they were instead invested in less costly and less risky political activities.

Nor is it surprising that political leaders tend to be more innovation-averse than their business counterparts. Politics has not experienced anything like the routinisation of innovation which has occurred in business and which led Schumpeter to prophesy in the 1940s that the entrepreneur would become redundant. Entrepreneurial 'personality and will power must count for less in environments which have become accustomed to economic change – best instanced by an incessant stream of new consumers' and producers' goods – and which instead of resisting, accept it as a matter of course'.[66]

Political environments have not become accustomed to political innovation and certainly do not accept it as a matter of course instead of resisting it. Schlesinger noted in his 1980s essay on democracy and leadership that the resistance to innovation described by Schumpeter in his theory of economic entrepreneurship could (still) be analogously applied to politics, where his description 'illuminates the difficulties of political leadership'.[67] Not much has changed since Schlesinger wrote that:

> In whatever form, vested interest refuses lines of thought that are unsettling to the person, the discipline, the institution or the existing power arrangements ... Given the power of gravity, custom and fear, the dead weight of inertia, of orthodoxy and of complacency, the tasks of *persuading majorities to accept innovations remain forever formidable*.[68]

He was describing the resistance to innovation that occurs when a leader is striving to convert an innovative policy proposal into public policy by persuading a majority of voters or legislators to accept the proposal. However, resistance to innovation may well be 'formidable' even when a leader is merely *presenting* an innovative policy proposal or is merely raising an innovative issue rather than striving to keep the issue alive. And the resistance is faced by any leaders who are not innovation-averse, whether pioneering or adaptive leaders, because it includes rigidity's resistance to an *adaptive* innovation. Both kinds of resistance, the anti-adaptive and the anti-pioneering, create what Schlesinger described as 'forever formidable' tasks for leaders who are not averse to innovation.

What is more, these tasks are performed not only by elected leaders but also by individuals who occupy leadership positions in other parts of the political system, such as the state bureaucracy. When Kasza investigated the organisational tools that have been used 'to break down the barriers' to innovation in state bureaucracies, he discovered that these tools merely offered an opportunity for innovative action.[69] The 'crucial role' was 'played by the individuals who create and manage these structures'; it was 'the role of bureaucratic leadership' that was crucial in bringing about innovation.[70] Even in this formally 'apolitical' part of the political system some leadership was required to bring about adaptive and pioneering innovation.

The role of innovative leadership, however, is only one aspect of the overall processes of change – and leadership for change – in a democratic political system. In his magisterial work on bureaucracy Wilson noted that it is difficult to develop a useful theory out of the 'chance appearance of a change-oriented personality', even if these individuals are 'enormously important in explaining change'.[71] The exceptionally change-oriented personalities, those who would be categorised as pioneering leaders, are especially difficult to incorporate in a theory of change. At least adaptive change-oriented leaders can be included alongside their innovation-averse counterparts in a theory or model of democracy's standard, adaptive kind of leadership for change – leadership which supplies adaptive responses that normally involve only incremental change but occasionally are more innovative. In contrast, pioneering change-oriented leaders have to be incorporated in a theory or model that has room for not only their exceptional, pioneering kind of change but also the standard, adaptive kind. However, such a wide-ranging model of leadership for change can be developed if the leadership dimension of Schumpeter's theory of democracy is updated and his missing analogy with entrepreneurship is added to form an adaptive/pioneering model of leadership in democracy.

Towards a leadership-evolutionary model of democratic politics

This Schumpeterian adaptive/pioneering model will have an evolutionary aspect added in Chapter 3, will be presented in Chapter 4 as the leadership-evolutionary model and will be used in Part II to assess the prevalence of entrepreneurial-style, pioneering leadership. It incorporates both (1) the standard, adaptive leadership whose selling of leads is analogous to standard market activities and (2) the exceptional, pioneering leadership whose selling of leads is analogous to economic entrepreneurship, whether a creative response or an entrepreneurial initiative. It also provides the context for an assessment of the prevalence of entrepreneurial-style, pioneering leadership within a democracy – in other words, to what extent is it an 'entrepreneurial democracy' – and for making comparisons with the prevalence of pioneering in other periods of the democracy's history and/or in other democracies elsewhere in the world.

This adaptive/pioneering leadership model is Schumpeterian in more ways than just its inclusion of both adaptive and pioneering leadership. In particular, it follows Schumpeter's approach of using the British and American democracies as its model examples. Both are influential as well as famous examples of democracy; many former British colonies have copied the institutions of Westminster parliamentary democracy, and many Latin American countries have copied the institutions of US presidential democracy. But another important feature of these two model examples is that they are very long-established democracies that have experienced many decades of democracy uninterrupted by coups, revolutions or other sorts of non-democratic interlude. Similarly, when the chapters in Part II occasionally use examples drawn from other democracies, they are usually drawn from long-established rather than recent democracies and certainly not from countries undergoing democratisation or experiencing only *semi*democracy.[72]

Drawing examples from only clear-cut and long-established democracies may appear a very narrow selection when compared to Schumpeter's unusually broad interpretation of what constitutes democracy. For instance, his definition of democracy does not exclude the property or gender limits on the franchise that are now categorised as semidemocratic and indeed as a premodern form of semidemocracy. In modern times the semidemocracies and even one-party states have automatically adopted universal suffrage for their version of elections. Similarly, any modern theory or model of democracy, such as an updated Schumpeterian model, views universal suffrage as one of the obvious, taken-as-read elements of modern democracy.

Another instance of Schumpeter's broad interpretation of democracy is that he seems to view democracy solely as a matter of elections – and not necessarily elections of a high standard. His conception of democracy has been described by Przeworski as 'minimalist' because it is 'just a system in which rulers are selected by competitive elections'.[73] And it was noted in Chapter 1 that Schumpeter had a distinctly 'realistic' or minimalist view of how competitive these elections needed to be to count as democratic rather than semidemocratic. Clearly he was content with a somewhat indiscriminate and very broad interpretation of what constitutes democracy and a democratic political community.

On the other hand, he implied that democracies might well be rated according to their durability – their ability to maintain democracy for long periods of time. Schumpeter's pessimism about a political community's chances of establishing and maintaining a successful democracy was revealed by his stringent set of preconditions for successful democracy:

> Among his preconditions were (1) the personnel factor of having politicians who are honest, reasonable and capable of providing inspiring leadership, (2) the institutional as well as personnel factor of having a strong and competent civil service and (3) the presence of 'democratic self-control' in the sense of (a) keeping political conflict within procedural rules, (b) keeping some issues out of the political arena and (c) being willing to compromise about any interests and ideals that politics involves.[74]

Considering that he defined 'successful' democracy primarily in terms of survival, presumably he would therefore rate a democracy highly if it had been able to survive for a long period of time – or in his words, had for a long time seen 'the democratic process reproduce itself steadily without creating situations that enforce resort to non-democratic methods'.[75] So it is quite compatible with Schumpeter's overall view of democracy to prefer examples drawn from long-established democracies rather than from relatively recent democracies or from those that have experienced a non-democratic interlude, such as a period of military rule, during their reproduction of the democratic process.

However, the leadership model presented in Chapter 4 differs markedly from Schumpeter's approach in its use of an evolutionary perspective on democratic politics – and therefore being titled a leadership-*evolutionary* (LE) model. Its evolutionary perspective will be developed in Chapter 3, which shifts from an evolutionary perspective on market economics to a similarly evolutionary perspective on change and continuity in democratic politics. Schumpeter did not adopt an evolutionary perspective or analogy in his theory of democracy, despite the fact that he used the term 'capitalist evolution' – and an analogy with biological evolution – in the economic chapters of *Capitalism, Socialism and Democracy*. It is true that he adopted the evolutionary perspective's environmental approach when arguing that local 'environmental conditions' affect the success of political systems and that therefore any propositions about the working of democracy must refer to 'given times, places and situations'.[76] But he did not accompany this environmental approach with any equivalent of the evolutionary perspective and analogy that he had used in his economic analysis. Here again, as with the missing analogy with entrepreneurship, he missed an opportunity for intellectual pioneering. Although many economists and some political scientists have used evolutionary perspectives or analogies, few social scientists have used them to analyse *both* economics and politics.

A relatively recent and very prominent example was North's 2005 work on *Understanding the Process of Economic Change*. The evolutionary perspective's environmental approach is not very evident but the book certainly highlights the historical variations that, along with geographical variations, produce local environments that change from one time to another as well as from one locality to another. In fact North argues that an underlying aspect of these historical variations, namely that the human environment is not ergodic (constant and timeless), is one of the reasons why the social sciences have only a 'very limited' understanding of the human environment:

> the world we live in is non-ergodic – a world of continuous novel change; and comprehending the world that is evolving entails new theory, or at least modification of what we possess. In consequence, there is no implication that 'we have it right'.[77]

As the book's title indicates, its other uses of the evolutionary perspective and analogies are usually related to economic change and in fact the book is catalogued as 'evolutionary economics'.[78] But occasionally North applies the evolutionary perspective to politics and political change. Indeed political markets, political organisations, polities, nation-states and political institutions are all described as evolving.[79] He also describes a case of political rigidity, in which vested interests provided successful resistance in 1990s Japan to the prospect of a policy change that would have restructured the country's capital markets, and he points out that 'adaptation is much less likely to be forthcoming' when 'the polity becomes the battleground for those who believe they would be adversely affected by the rule changes'.[80] There is even a description of political entrepreneurs as well as economic entrepreneurs occasionally producing something more than merely incremental change: 'the occasional radical and abrupt institutional change [which] suggests that something akin to the punctuated equilibrium change in evolutionary biology can occur in economic change as well'.[81] This is not very different from the evolutionary perspective that will be developed in Chapter 3 and included in the leadership-evolutionary model presented in Chapter 4.

3
From Economic to Political Evolution

Entrepreneurs and capitalist evolution

Schumpeter's conception of entrepreneurship was closely linked to his evolutionary perspective on economics. As the Appendix describes, such evolutionary notions as the adaptive response had played an important part in his early theory of economic development. Later, in *Capitalism, Socialism and Democracy*, he explicitly used an evolutionary perspective, and in fact Nelson has declared that all later evolutionary theories of economic growth that he knows of have drawn inspiration from this book.[1] The term 'capitalist evolution' occurred quite frequently in its economic chapters and clearly had replaced Schumpeter's earlier concept of economic development. Moreover, all forms of (capitalist) economic change were accommodated within the concept of evolution, whether the change was gradual or revolutionary, was an adaptive response or a spontaneous use of initiative:

> Capitalism, then, is by nature a form or method of economic change and not only never is but never can be stationary. And this evolutionary character of the capitalist process is not merely due to the fact that economic life goes on in a social and natural environment which changes [and produces adaptive responses]. ... The fundamental impulse that sets and keeps the capitalist engine in motion comes from the new consumers' goods, the new methods of production or transportation, the new markets, the new forms of industrial organization that capitalist enterprise creates.[2]

These new forms of industrial organisation not only were created through the spontaneous initiative of capitalist enterprise but also involved 'revolutions' that 'periodically reshape the existing structure of industry by introducing new commodities, such as automobiles and electrical appliances, new methods of production', such as the mechanised and electrified factory, new forms of organisation, such as mergers, new sources of supply, such as American cotton, and new markets to sell in.[3] Schumpeter's best example of an industry undergoing such periodic revolutions was the history of transportation from the mail coach to the aeroplane.[4] He gave this revolutionary process the now famous title of Creative Destruction and declared that it was 'the essential fact about capitalism. It is what capitalism consists in and what every capitalist concern has got to live in'.[5]

In accordance with his explicitly evolutionary perspective, Schumpeter used a biological evolutionary analogy to describe this creative–destructive revolutionary process. It is the 'process of industrial mutation – if I may use that biological term – that incessantly revolutionizes the economic structure *from within*, incessantly destroying the old one, incessantly creating a new one'.[6] As is noted in the Appendix, his analogy with biological mutation can be made more precise and effective by specifying that this revolutionary process involves not ordinary mutations but *macro*mutations, and that these are complex rather than merely modifying macromutations (as in the case of a snake species merely increasing or reducing its number of vertebrae).[7]

Another possible biological analogy of a recurring revolutionising process is the *punctuated equilibrium* theory of evolution. According to this 1970s revision of Darwinism, evolution occurs 'not gradually but as episodes of calm punctuated by change'.[8] The calm of stasis (whether simply no change or minor fluctuations around a norm) is punctuated by sudden changes that arise when isolated local populations of a species undergo rapid change and then split or branch off as a new species.[9] But the sudden change is brought about by a series of relatively rapid ordinary mutations rather than by a single macromutation of large effect. Although these mutations take many generations to occur and take effect, the process appears distinctly rapid when compared to the stasis in the ancestral species and in comparison to the geological-time standards of the fossil record.[10]

Both the macromutation and the punctuated-equilibrium biological analogies are compatible with Schumpeter's description of creative–destructive economic revolutions as occurring 'in discrete rushes which are separated from each other by spans of comparative quiet'.[11] But biological evolution does not take the spiralling cyclical shape that he ascribed to the economy's experience and absorption of economic revolutions.[12] Nor is the economic equivalent of biological selection, namely the pressures of market competition, very apparent in the economy's revolutionary sectors, which were acknowledged by Schumpeter to favour oligopolistic imperfect competition.[13] He dealt with this problem by arguing that they were, nevertheless, experiencing effects similar to those of perfect competition. First, he pointed out that competition through new commodities, technologies, sources of supply and types of organisation is the form of competition that involves decisive cost or quality advantages – in order 'to escape being undersold, *every* firm is in the end compelled to follow suit'.[14] Second, he maintained that the effects of such competition could still be felt even in a monopoly situation:

> It is hardly necessary to point out that competition of the kind that we now have in mind acts not only when in being but also when it is an ever-present threat. It disciplines before it attacks. The businessman feels himself to be in a competitive situation even if he is alone in his field ... In many cases, though not in all, this will in the long run enforce behavior very similar to the perfectly competitive pattern.[15]

Political evolution and historical selection

Considering Schumpeter's liking for biological evolutionary analogies and comparisons, it is surprising that he did not use them in his theory of democracy. It would not have required much intellectual imagination to have developed a Schumpeterian evolutionary perspective on democratic politics as well as capitalist economics. Analogies or comparisons with biological evolution and mutation have quite often been used to describe political processes. As early as the nineteenth century such a famous political analyst as Bagehot could be found experimenting with Darwin's concept of natural selection, and even the revisionist Darwinian concept of punctuated equilibrium has been used in theories of the state and of agenda-setting.[16] Comparisons or analogies with mutation have been less common but Duverger's classic work on political parties used the term quite extensively and distinguished between two different forms of mutation.[17]

The term 'mutation' could well have been used more often as a neutral way of describing innovations, as it has none of the positive connotations that the marketing and advertising industries have attached to the word 'innovative'. Biological mutations are random errors that occur (rarely) when an organism is copying the genetic data carried in its DNA.[18] Any resulting structural or behaviourial changes experienced by the inheritors of mutant DNA are usually changes for the worse and therefore fall victim to nature's continual, permanent 'purge' of the disadvantageous.[19] Occasionally, though, a change can be for the better, in the sense of being useful in the biological struggle to survive and reproduce. Darwin pointed out decades before the scientific discovery of genetic-mutation forms of variation:

> But if variations *useful* to any organic being do occur, assuredly individuals thus characterised will have the best chance of being preserved in the struggle for life; and from the strong principle of inheritance they will tend to produce offspring similarly characterised. This *principle of preservation*, I have called, for the sake of brevity, Natural Selection. ... Amongst many animals, sexual selection will give its aid to ordinary selection, by assuring to the most vigorous and best adapted males the greatest number of offspring.[20]

Darwin's theory of evolution is therefore categorised as one of the 'variational' theories of change, as the selection and preservation of a particular variation within a population leads to that variation becoming increasingly prevalent over time.[21] In the Darwinian, biological case the increasing prevalence with and within each new biological generation of the population may eventually result in a new species.

A variational theory of change, even a specifically evolutionary theory, need not involve such random or undirected variations as biology's copying-error mutations. As an evolutionary economist has argued, the evolutionary approach to analysing change can take other forms than the biological, with less randomness in the variations: 'What matter are variety and selection'.[22] The discussions of economic and political selection in the Appendix and Chapter 2 involve a similar assumption, that evolutionary variations can be a set of directed but differing responses to an external change. In fact they become a 'population' of varied responses that have been evoked by a particular external change, and the selection of a useful (or the most useful) variation means that this one of the varied responses will over time become increasingly prevalent among the responses to that external change – becoming an actual as well as appropriate adaptation to change in the environment.

Another assumption of those discussions is that (sufficient) economic and political competition ensures that the variations that are selected as adaptations are useful to both the individual (businessman or leader) and the community. But it could be argued that in fact the pressure of external events plays a more important role than the pressure of competition in a democracy's evolutionary processes – and is much less predictable than the effects of competition. For it is external change that both evokes the new variations and in a sense determines which of these variations will be a useful response. Furthermore, when Chapter 2 highlighted the predictability of adaptive leadership, it was focusing on the *response* to external change and therefore did not look at the external changes themselves. These response-evoking and adaption-determining external changes form a much less predictable part of the overall evolutionary process of selecting variations for preservation. Such a wide range of events and influences in the international, economic, social and other environments can affect the process so much that it might be better described as historical selection than political selection – and certainly it is so unpredictable that it is best suited to a historical form of explanation. As Gould argued in the case of biological evolution, a historical form of explanation, focused on narrative rather than experiment, is required to cope with a contingent, unpredictable process.[23]

Riker's (1982) pioneering analysis of what he called the 'natural selection' of political issues acknowledged that political evolution was similar to biological evolution in offering little opportunity for predicting outcomes.[24] He also likened the issue-selection process to that of economic entrepreneurs offering new products: prospective political leaders entrepreneurially offer new issues and alternatives to the voting market in the hope that a majority will prefer one of them to previous issues or alternatives.[25] He was therefore also pioneering the combination of biological and economic analogies that could well have been introduced 40 years earlier in Schumpeter's theory of democracy.

Carmines and Stimson, too, noted in their (1989) *Issue Evolution: Race and the Transformation of American Politics* that the evolution of political issues is similar to biological evolution in being more suitable to historical than predictive forms of explanation.[26] They took a different tack from Riker in the way that they linked issue selection to political change, though they acknowledged that he had foreshadowed their approach by pointing out that a new issue might flourish to such an extent that it completely reshaped the environment in which it arose.[27] Their analysis of issue evolution was primarily concerned with the very few issues that have 'the ability to alter the party system from which they emerged', specifically 'replacing one dominant alignment with another and transforming the nature of the parties themselves'.[28] Carmines and Stimson compared this process to the punctuated equilibrium found in biological evolution, with the emergence of a transforming issue being the marked change, the punctuation point, that sets in motion a slower and continuous change that produces a new equilibrium.[29]

Like Riker, they looked at the overall population of issues in a democracy (not merely the population of issue-responses to a particular external change). From this perspective they argued that although there is an abundance of potential issues, the selective pressure of competition for public attention means that most do not survive long enough to develop and evolve.[30] Of those issues that survive into the development stage of their life cycle, few will go beyond it into the evolution stage; instead, they have a large but only temporary impact on the political system or they are of concern only to a section of the public who are particularly well informed and/or have a special interest in that particular issue.[31] But in the case of a select few issues, the development stage of their life cycle is followed by an evolution stage in which there is a process analogous to the biological 'local variation' process of species-evolution: a new species is created by an isolated population's adaptation to a local environment that is not shared by other members of its species.[32] In issue evolution this process takes the form of producing an 'offspring' issue that is so well adapted to its specialised or local context that it takes on a distinct identity and developmental path of its own, separate from that of the ancestral issue.[33] For example, a new species of race issue, 'racial conservatism', was created by local variation (associated with the increased prominence of conservative ideology) in the 1964 US presidential campaign and went on, as a case of punctuated equilibrium, to have a marked long-term effect on the two parties' electoral competition.[34]

Such an upheaval is also an example of the unpredictability of evolutionary processes. Gould once noted that the explainable but quite unpredictable outcomes of 'the Darwinian theory of evolution, and variational theories of historical change in general', may make them appear intellectually peculiar.[35] But the subject matter of political science may require such apparently peculiar theories. When Kingdon pointed to the similarity between his garbage-can model of policy making and 'models of complexity and evolution', he singled out the latter's historical contingency and 'inherent unpredictability'.[36]

Political development and evolution

Political science has tended to be more interested in developmental than evolutionary theories or models of change. The preference for developmental approaches may have been because the Darwinian conception of evolution is not progressive but rigorously neutral. 'It has *no built-in direction*, be it forward, backward or sideways' and indeed may result in 'degeneracy', which was defined in the nineteenth century as a descendant becoming 'far simpler or lower in structure than its ancestor'.[37] Although the notion of degeneracy has since been largely replaced by the less judgmental term 'simplification', the process remains a well-recognised aspect of biological evolution that Gould suggested might be as common as increased complexity.[38] In contrast, theorists of political development have viewed large-scale political change in terms of some kind of progress, such as a political system's increasing capability and modernity or its passage through a series of specified crises/stages of development.[39]

However, an important reason for preferring a developmental rather than evolutionary approach is that in biological terms an individual organism develops rather than evolves. (Analogies with biological development are in fact often viewed in terms of the stages of an individual's life cycle: conception, embryo, birth, infancy and maturation but seldom old age.) Consequently, any study of the political system as a single, individual entity would seem to require a developmental rather than evolutionary approach.

Yet clearly there are also ways of applying an evolutionary approach to a political system, as when Riker, Carmines and Stimson applied the evolutionary approach to a democratic political system's population of issues. A democracy's overall population of issues comprises not only several separate (sub)populations of issue-responses to particular external changes but also several older issues that have been preserved as adaptations – and perhaps one or two innovative issues that have been raised spontaneously by a pioneering political leader, as will be discussed in Chapter 5. In that chapter it will also be argued that some issues may have been preserved by being transformed into policies. This transformation could be considered a final stage in the democratic development of a response to an external change: the politicians have raised a set of varying issue-responses to the external change; electoral competition has resulted in one of them being selected as the appropriate response; and the government or legislature has enacted it as a law or other form of public policy – as a final stage in the life cycle of an issue-response.

The analogy with biological development has also been applied to policies and stages in policy making. For example, Price referred to the US Senate's incubating of policy proposals, and Polsby drew the analogy with incubation to describe the period when a policy idea that has originated with experts and staff is taken up and publicised by politicians but has not yet definitively entered the legislative process.[40] A biological analogy was also used in a British study of the Thatcher government's disastrous poll-tax policy, which was described as having its gestation in 1984–85 and birth in 1985–86 before going on to be enacted into law.[41] Other analogies with biological development have focused on the post-natal progress towards maturity, as when a recent study of the early twentieth-century US federal administration described how 'Fledgling experiments with dubious survival prospects at the turn of the century became, by the close of the 1920s, established policies.'[42] So even after enactment and implementation, these policies' preservation was still in doubt until, some years later, they finally matured into established policies.

A similar use of the analogy with post-natal biological development has occurred in descriptions of how new political or administrative tools develop into mature institutions. For example, an analysis of 'entrepreneurial issue parties' depicted these new parties as developing through birth-to-maturity phases on the way from 'inception in the mind of one person to complete institutionalization'.[43] Parties that failed to meet the needs of these phases would collapse (and presumably die) before being institutionalised.[44] Although institutionalisation seems to be analogous to attaining maturity, it can lead on to a further phase, a period of decline, that appears to be the party's equivalent of old age and ends in collapse or fading away.[45]

But the most well-known analysis of the life cycle of political institutions is to be found in Downs's work on bureaucracy and its administrative tools – the bureaus. He defined bureaus as (typically public-sector) organisations that are not evaluated in a market and have often been created by what he termed 'zealots' or 'spontaneous entrepreneurship'.[46] Their life cycle has several stages or periods: the bureau's birth as a new organisation; the fledgling period in which it is seeking to expand in size (and functions) and is engaged in a drive or struggle for autonomy; the passing of an initial survival threshold that seems equivalent to reaching maturity and institutionalisation; and finally the period in which the institutionalised bureau grows older and becomes more conservative and complex.[47] Although few bureaus ever achieve sufficient autonomy to become immune to threats to their survival, the most dangerous period in a bureau's life cycle is when the still fledgling organisation is approaching its initial survival threshold.[48] For here it is most vulnerable to being eliminated by rival organisations that are carrying out similar, competing social functions or are competing with it for public funding or other resources.[49]

Clearly competition and selection continue to affect policies and institutions long after their selection for preservation at the early, proposal stage in their development. On being enacted as a new policy or organisation they join a population of more established policies or tools/institutions that vary from one to another and are subject to an evolutionary process of selection for continuing preservation and development. Issues develop in a rather different way from policies and institutions but they, too, are subject to selection even after surviving the early stages of their development (such as being merely one of several competing issue-responses to an external change). In fact Riker described a case of the same party raising a succession of new issues over a period of decades and 'natural selection' resulting in the one that electorally worked gradually displacing the other issues that the party had tried out.[50]

However, it appears that a relatively established issue, policy or institution is more likely to be eliminated by evolutionary selection at some political times than at others. Downs noted that public bureaus rarely disappear after passing their initial survival threshold – reaching maturity and becoming institutionalised – but he also mentioned that bureaus are most likely to disappear 'when the particular government that created them is replaced'.[51] The replacement of its maternal government therefore constitutes another survival threshold and period of selection vulnerability that even a mature, institutionalised bureau must face. Moreover, the replacement of its maternal government may occur not only through electoral defeat but also through the rise of a new political generation within the governing party.

Both these forms of government replacement could be covered by Huntington's definition of a change in leadership generations as 'the replacement of one set of leaders by another set with significantly different organizational experiences'.[52] The new leadership generation may well be more likely to view some of the older institutions and policies, irrespective of which party had created them, as having outlived their usefulness in a changed economic, social or international environment. In other words, this seems to be a threshold where the older institutions and policies are more vulnerable than the newer ones. But the generational threshold is faced by all institutions and policies at the same stage not in their life cycles but in the life history of their political system – the coming to power of a new political generation of leaders. Although selection is historically continuous, it takes on special significance or thoroughness in a political system's periodic changes of leadership generation, when institutions and policies – and issues, too – are likely to experience an upsurge in competitive pressures on behalf of other variations.

But while some variations among the populations of issues, policies and institutions will be not be preserved, the many more that *are* selected for cross-generational preservation will have thereby been *inherited* by the political system from the previous political generation of leaders. For example, when the British political system experienced a change in leadership generations from the Thatcherite Conservatives of the 1980s to the New Labour of the 1990s, most of Thatcherism's new variations in economic policy were selected for cross-generational preservation and political inheritance: 'the long-term dominance of Thatcherite economics has been secured by Tony Blair accepting the market as the prime influence on economic policy'.[53] And although many marked policy changes had occurred during Prime Minister Thatcher's lengthy term of office, most pre-Thatcher policies had been selected by her government (if only by default) for cross-generational preservation and political inheritance. Nearly three quarters of the policy programmes in effect when she left office in 1990 had been in place when she took office in 1979.[54] The lack of change in *institutions*, especially the most powerful and/or symbolic institutions, is also quite striking in the British practice of democracy and in other examples of long-standing democracy.

Nonetheless, the changes in a political system's inheritance (in the populations of issues, policies and institutions inherited by each new leadership generation) are political evolution's nearest equivalent of the long-term and large-scale changes in the political system that are studied by theorists of political development. That Darwin's initial name for evolution was 'descent with modification' is an indication of how important a role inheritance and descent play in biological evolution.[55] And it seems only appropriate that any notion of the evolution of a political system as a whole should be viewed in terms of the modifications inherited by each new leadership generation.

Path dependency, rigidity and the need for pioneering leadership

The inheritance from previous leadership generations seems likely to create a political equivalent of biological 'path dependency'. The biological version was memorably described by Gould's 'panda principle', named in honour of his favourite example:

> When adaptation to a diet of bamboo required more flexibility in manipulation, pandas could not redesign their thumbs but had to make do with a makeshift substitute – an enlarged radial sesamoid bone of the wrist, the panda's false thumb. The sesamoid thumb is a clumsy suboptimal structure, but it works. Pathways of history (commitment of the true thumb to other roles during an irreversible past) impose such jury-rigged solutions upon all creatures.[56]

Path dependency has also been identified by some theorists of economic evolution and been built into models of technological-industrial evolution, such as the automobile industry and the petrol-powered engine. 'If the roll of the die early in the history of automobiles had come out another way, we might today have had steam or electric cars.'[57] So there is good reason to expect that path dependency also occurs in the political evolution of democracies.

However, it would be better to view such path dependency as one aspect of a wider concept – biological, economic or political *rigidity*. For rigidity is a type of resistance to adaptation that prevents or delays not only optimal but also *useful* adaptations, such as the suboptimal and jury-rigged panda's thumb. Furthermore, the non-biological, economic and political forms of rigidity incorporate consciously directed resistance to change as well as the less conscious ways in which adaptation is affected by what Gould called 'the pathways of history'. In fact the possibility of directed resistance to optimal or useful adaptation is a characteristic of economic and political forms of evolution.

In *Capitalism, Socialism and Democracy* Schumpeter discussed rigidity at some length, defining price rigidity as a price being 'less sensitive to changes in the conditions of supply and demand than it would if perfect competition prevailed'.[58] He made a long digression that downplayed the dangers of monopoly and the benefits of perfect competition, especially in relation to the process of creative destruction by successful innovators.[59] But as was described in the account of adaptive leadership in Chapter 2, he ended by acknowledging that price rigidity is a costly type of resistance to adaptation: 'Rigidity is a type of resistance to adaptation that perfect and prompt competition excludes. And for the kind of adaptation and for those conditions which have been treated by traditional theory, it is again quite true that such resistance spells loss [to the community] and reduced output.'[60] If rigidity extends to product as well as price changes, there will also be loss to the community from delays in making optimal or merely useful changes to products. For example, there was some loss to the US community from its automobile manufacturers' delays in producing more fuel-economic cars in the 1970s (though the competition from fuel-economic foreign imports limited the degree of product rigidity in the market and ensured that by the end of the decade the automobile industry was experiencing a punitive financial crisis).[61]

Rigidity occurs in political systems when issues, policies and institutions, not products and prices, are insensitive to changes in the conditions. The political form of rigidity can be defined as not responding to these external changes with the change in issues, policies or institutions (such as the altering of an existing example or the adding of a new one) that would have been made if perfect political competition prevailed. Rigidity's resistance to adaptation therefore obstructs optimal or merely useful adaptive responses to external changes. The resulting loss to the community can be more obscure or controversial than in the case of price rigidity but can also be much more severe.

Schumpeter came close to describing issue rigidity when describing how leaders of the main political parties may fail to raise an issue because either they fail to appreciate its political value or the issue is in fact of doubtful value.[62] In the former case, the typical reason for underestimating the issue is that it 'has never been tried out', while in the latter case 'technical difficulty' or the 'fear that it will cause sectional difficulties' are typical reasons why the main parties 'may tacitly agree to leave an issue alone in spite of their realizing its potentialities'.[63] The idea of an issue not being appreciated because it has never been tried out might be interpreted as a theory of issue evolution, with the political value of an issue being discovered by raising it as a new variation for selection. But it is more likely that Schumpeter was implying that these politicians' imagination is limited by their attachment to habitual ways of thought, as he had argued in one of his earliest works that there is a common psychological preference for the habitual.[64] In contrast, when politicians are aware of an issue's potential value but leave it alone because of technical or sectional difficulties, they are showing impressive professional expertise in judging what the electoral market will bear intellectually or in terms of the power of sectional interests. However, this also seems very like issue rigidity and indeed Schumpeter went on to show how it could be counteracted, as would be expected of rigidity, by the breadth of political competition. For issues that have not been raised by the leaders of the main parties 'may then be taken up by outsiders who prefer making an independent bid for power to serving in the ranks of one of the existing parties'.[65] He noted that this was perfectly normal politics and distinguished it from the abnormal politics that occurred when crusaders and their ilk focused upon an issue for its own sake rather than as part of pursuing a political career.[66] But clearly it was not perfectly competitive politics. The main parties enjoyed a competitive advantage over outsiders, and there would not be sufficient outsiders to produce a multitude of diverse competitors. Some issue rigidity and its type of resistance to adaptation would continue to exist.

The various forms of political competition (including competition among administrators and among policy advocates) have also been insufficiently competitive to prevent extensive *policy* rigidity in democracies, as was illustrated by Rose and Davies's study of policy inheritance in Britain.[67] Their book examined the inheritance and change of British policy programmes during the near half-century from 1945 to 1990, which had also seen the party in government replaced by its rival on six occasions.[68] But there had not been much replacing of policies, especially of the older programmes. While 102 of the period's 245 new policy programmes had been terminated by the time the period ended, less than one-fifth of the 115 programmes inherited from the pre-1945 era had been terminated – suggesting that 'novelty is a greater cause of failure than obsolescence'.[69] However, Rose and Davies pointed out that many of the new policies that had been terminated were actually designed to be only temporary. For more than one-fifth of all programmes were either planned-achievement or ad hoc programmes, such as (respectively) the privatisation of state-owned enterprises or the response to a foreign policy crisis.[70] They can hardly be viewed as cases of a programme being replaced by a new policy that is intrinsically better or is better suited to changing times. The true examples of replacement are to be found among the policy programmes that Rose and Davies categorised as trial-and-error adaptations. Such programmes typically arise from a politically pressured government attempting to meet a persisting concern or goal, often economic, in a turbulent policy environment of frequent and unexpected changes – which make it very difficult for a policy to be more than temporarily satisfactory.[71] The trial-and-error adaptations form only a small category of policies, comprising less than a quarter of all policy programmes and less than one-tenth of public expenditure, but these policies certainly show some sensitivity to changing conditions and some willingness to accept rather than resist adaptation.[72]

But the main category of policy programmes presents a striking contrast and serious circumstantial evidence of policy rigidity. More than half of all the period's policy programmes, comprising more than four-fifths of public spending, were categorised by Rose and Davies as examples of 'continuing-inheritance', about half of which had been inherited from the pre-1945 era.[73] Unlike the trial-and-error adaptations, the programmes in the continuing-inheritance category typically arise from measured policy making that is dealing with a relatively predictable rather than turbulent policy environment.[74] But another reason why they tend to be preserved rather than replaced is that they have had the opportunity to develop what Rose and Davies described as *political inertia*. A policy programme with political inertia can be terminated only by 'building a coalition that constitutes a greater force than the coalition of beneficiaries, officials and routines supporting it'.[75] To mix metaphors, this political inertia removes any prospect of competition taking place on a 'level playing field'. It is tilted in favour of competitors defending the policy programme against replacement, unfavourable alterations and even the creation of any new policy programme that might be a rival in terms of functions or resources (as Downs described in the case of administrative bureaus). This policy rigidity's resistance to adaptation will have obstructed many optimal and some merely useful adaptive responses to external changes, but there is unlikely to ever be an assessment of the costs to the community of such delays in adaptation.

Democratic political systems' institutions are no less prone than their policies to rigidity and its resistance to adaptation. Indeed Selznick's classic work on leadership in administration seems to suggest that protection from replacement or alteration is evidence that an organisation has been institutionalised. For he argued that administrative organisations develop from tool into institution by becoming infused with value above and beyond their technical value as administrative tools, thereby becoming less expendable and more likely to be preserved:

> The test of infusion with value is expendability. If an organization is merely an instrument, it will be *readily altered or cast aside* when a more efficient tool becomes available. Most organizations are thus expendable. When value-infusion takes place, however, there is resistance to change.[76]

Some organisations' value-infusion involves taking on a symbolic meaning for the whole community, which will therefore be more reluctant to cast aside the organisation for purely technical or economic reasons.[77] But a more common form of infusing value is through the creation of what Selznick described as 'vested interests'.[78] For example, when 'a government agency develops a distinctive clientele, the enterprise gains the stability that comes with a secure source of support'; now individuals and groups outside as well as inside the organisation 'have a stake in its continued existence'.[79] This creation of external and internal vested interests is similar to what Rose and Davies described as political inertia, and would similarly produce a degree of rigidity protecting against replacement, unfavourable alterations and the birth of any dangerous rival in terms of functions or resources. As in the case of policy rigidity, the conservative bias in selection for preservation will spell loss to the community from resistance to optimal or merely useful adaptive responses.

A generation after Selznick's work, March and Olsen noted that political parties and other political institutions preserve themselves in a variety of ways. In addition to resisting unfavourable changes, they develop their own constitutional rules, resource distributions and criteria of appropriateness and success.[80] Considering how much institution rigidity these protective measures would produce, it is no wonder March and Olsen argued that institutions do not instantaneously adapt to changes in their environment.[81] They also criticised any notion that political institutions 'evolve through some form of efficient historical process' in which competition results in the differential survival of institutions that are optimal.[82] In fact historical selection may be so distorted by institution-rigidity's conservative bias that not only optimal adaptations but also some very important useful adaptations are successfully resisted, spelling possibly severe loss to the community.

The most effective tactic associated with institution or policy rigidity's resistance to adaptation can be summed up by Schattschneider's adage that defining the alternatives is the supreme instrument of power.[83] For the conservative response to change (sticking with the existing policy/institution or making a favourable alteration to it) is the variation most likely to be selected if any new variations that are potentially too competitive can be formally or informally excluded from the range of possible responses at the variation stage – before selection has begun. However, a conservative bias in the defining of alternatives may sometimes be an unconscious form of rigidity and instrument of power. If Schumpeter was correct in arguing that there is a common psychological preference for the habitual, it could well result in an objectively quite obvious variation not even entering policymakers' minds as a conceivable proposal. For example, Mueller's book on the obsolescence of major war in the developed world noted that 'peace is most secure when it gravitates away from conscious rationality to become a subrational, unexamined mental habit'; war-avoidance becomes 'so habitual that war never comes up again as a serious option, even when it might have been objectively reasonable at least to consider it as a possibility'.[84] Mueller also made a more general point that could be applied to the unconscious exclusion of options in other areas of policy making, such as government intervention in the economy: 'An idea becomes impossible not when it becomes reprehensible or has been renounced, but *when it fails to percolate into one's consciousness as a conceivable option.*'[85]

A similar point could be made about issue rigidity and the unconscious exclusion of options that might have been raised as election issues. Indeed Schumpeter seemed to be implying something very like this unconscious habitual bias when he explained that the political value of an issue may be unappreciated because it has never been tried out. But he also mentioned that independently minded careerists – outsiders – may take up issues that the leaders of the main parties have failed to raise, and presumably this would include cases where the failure has been due to an unconscious bias that might be avoided by an independently minded individual. In fact these cases highlight the importance of high-quality adaptive leadership in providing the diversity and strength of competition that reduces rigidity and its resistance to adaptation.

But it was pointed out in Chapter 2 that not much in the way of innovation can be expected from adaptive leadership, which tends to be averse to innovation. As Schumpeter emphasised, innovation can arouse widespread resistance from society – a resistance that extends well beyond the vested interests threatened by this change. Even the leader of a dictatorial regime may well be deterred, unless he has established personal rule, by the amount of resistance there is likely to be to any truly innovative policy changes.[86]

Adaptive leadership in a democracy can therefore hardly be expected to pursue innovative adaptations. And certainly it is left to non-careerist, *pioneering* leadership to provide (1) the revolutionary (and potentially more advantageous) innovations involved in creative rather than adaptive responses and (2) the spontaneous innovations arising from the use of initiative rather than merely responding to external changes. The extraordinary level of resistance that pioneering leadership will encounter in bringing about revolutionary and/or spontaneous innovations was recognised by Schumpeter in his description of entrepreneurship as an economic version of pioneering leadership. As was pointed out in Chapter 2, he argued that it requires extraordinary motivation and capacities to overcome such resistance, and that *doing* the thing is therefore much more important than having an idea about the thing. This applied to any version of pioneering leadership, political as well as economic, and the same might be said of his distinction between inventing an innovation and putting it into effect and of his point that an invention becomes economically relevant only through the efforts of an entrepreneur. Indeed more than 40 years later it was argued by Kingdon that inventors of policy are less important than policy entrepreneurs and that 'the key to understanding policy change is not where the idea came from but what made it take hold and grow'.[87]

Schumpeter in one sense actually underestimated the resistance faced by pioneers, as he underplayed the fact that entrepreneurs often fail to bring their innovations to fruition. Although they can make an innovative variation economically or politically relevant in the economic or political marketplace, they cannot guarantee that this variation will be selected for preservation. As two anthropologists have pointed out, it is *selection* that determines the ultimate historical significance of any innovative act.[88] And two political scientists have suggested that politics may be as ruthless as economics in ruining the careless or premature entrepreneur.[89]

However, selection also prevents a ruthless or deluded political entrepreneur from ruining a democracy. It is just as well that morally repugnant issues and harebrained policy proposals are prevented from doing much damage. Such issues and proposals are usually not selected for preservation and continued development; usually they soon die out or become (often lunatic) fringe issues or proposals. Furthermore, in recent decades the risk to the community from pioneering innovations has been reduced by the new propensity for the 'policy transfer' of innovations from one country to another.[90] Not long before this practice became fashionable, Polsby noted that innovations which have been successfully introduced in other countries provide 'the certain knowledge that in some form or another they could work'.[91] But it is doubtful whether this reduction in the risk to the community has been accompanied by a similar reduction in the risk to the entrepreneurial-like political leader – for whom Weber's warning is still relevant:

> Certainly all historical experience confirms the truth – that man would not have attained the possible unless time and again he had reached out for the impossible. But to do that a man must be a leader, and not only a leader but a hero as well, in a very sober sense of the word ... with that steadfastness of heart which can brave even the crumbling of all hopes.[92]

4
The Leadership-Evolutionary Model

> We recognize that a costly change in NORAD's defense posture to deal with the danger of suicide hijackers, before such a threat had ever actually been realized, would have been a tough sell.
>
> *The 9/11 Commission Report*

Developing the leadership-evolutionary model

This chapter presents the model of democratic politics that has been foreshadowed in earlier chapters and will be used, often more implicitly than explicitly, in Part II's assessment of the prevalence of entrepreneurial-style, pioneering leadership. It is labelled a Leadership-Evolutionary (LE) model because it combines (1) the evolutionary processes of political change and continuity described in the previous chapter with (2) a leadership model of democracy that uses analogies with the market, firm and entrepreneurship, as described in the Introduction and the first two chapters. The key analogy is with the market because the deliberative, market-like type of leadership, with its selling/buying of leads, is the basic leadership activity depicted by the model and was also very evident in the leadership dimension of Schumpeter's theory of democracy, as when he argued that the 'mass of people' is not able on its own initiative to develop and articulate definite opinions but can only 'follow or refuse to follow such group leadership as may offer itself'.[1] The LE model also includes an institutional framework that might well have been presented as an analogy with the firm but this would have distracted attention from another, more important analogy – with entrepreneurship. In fact the LE model uses the term 'political entrepreneurship' rather than 'pioneering leadership' to highlight and rectify Schumpeter's failure to draw the analogy with entrepreneurship. When the model is applied in Part II, though, the emphasis will be back on 'pioneering' in order to avoid confusion with some political scientists' analogies with non-Schumpeterian concepts of entrepreneurship – the model's analogy with entrepreneurship is solely with the Schumpeterian conception of this exceptional and extraordinary form of economic leadership.

Another quasi-economic and Schumpeterian aspect of the LE model is that it stops short of the rigorously rationalist approach used by Downs's economic theory of democracy and by other rational choice theories. Schumpeter has actually been described as the founder of *ir*rational choice theory because his theory of democracy 'allows for the diverse irrationalities observable in really existing democracies', such as bounded rationality, satisficing and the various motivations of 'entrepreneurial rationality'.[2] The irrationality of the political entrepreneur's motivations, when compared to the careerist rationality of standard politicians, was emphasised in earlier chapters. But perhaps for this reason there was not enough attention paid to important imperfections in the careerist rationality of standard politicians. It was pointed out in Chapter 2 that Downs's economic theory of democracy acknowledged that a politician's office-seeking is affected by the problem of uncertainty: the lack of sure knowledge about the course of events. But at about the same time as his theory emerged, a more sweeping and detailed analysis of the cognitive limits on rationality was presented by Simon in his notions of bounded rationality and satisficing.[3] He argued that the bounds of human rationality are constricted not only by lack of knowledge but also by other cognitive limits – so that in reality an individual can pursue his or her self-interest only with 'bounded' rationality. Many years earlier Schumpeter had presented a similarly realistic view of rationality, arguing that assumptions about rational economic behaviour are a fiction but 'sufficiently near to reality, if things have time to hammer logic into men' and numerous precedents have 'eliminated unadapted behavior'.[4]

The LE model therefore includes the realistic assumption that politicians operate with bounded rationality. But this also means assuming that politicians' competition is limited by their failure to conceive of all the potentially competitive electoral issues and other opinion leads. (As was noted in Chapter 3, something as historically familiar as war or intervention in the economy may fail to percolate into policy makers' consciousness as a conceivable option.) A second way in which bounded rationality reduces the diversity of politicians' competing leads is in discouraging a politician from selling untried innovations that might blow up in his or her face. For it can be assumed that politicians are very aware of the problem of uncertainty and therefore tend to err on the side of caution when deciding how to pursue their careerist self-interest.

The LE model also assumes that another imperfection in standard politicians' careerist rationality is that they make satisficing rather than optimising choices. In other words, instead of looking for the best possible way to pursue their careerist self-interest, they are content with merely satisfactory progress. This reduces the competitive pressure that politicians exert upon one another, especially if their satisficing includes the choice of career *goals* as well as strategies. Research into satisficers' aspirations has indicated that they learn from experience to set themselves criteria of satisfactoriness that require them to make an effort but are realistically attainable.[5] If this is also true of satisficing politicians, then presumably the mediocre majority of them soon learn to give up any ambitions of winning the highest posts in their profession; they give up competing for the top prizes at quite early stages in the development of their perhaps long and satisfactory but not very ambitious careers. Satisficing would therefore severely limit the strength of competition among politicians at all but the earliest stages of their careers. Of course the limitation would be removed if even mediocre politicians suffered throughout their careers from the self-delusion that they have the ability and luck to make it to the top and do a good enough job to enjoy the self-satisfied retirement of a successful careerist. But it is unlikely that this bounded-rationality illusion is sufficiently prevalent among politicians to wholly prevent satisficing from exercising its 'irrational' negative effect on careerist competition.

However, the LE model's most obvious lack of rational choices is its lack of rational voters, which creates a striking contrast with what Kuran has described as the voter-centred economic theory of politics.[6] The model either ignores voters or views them from Schumpeter's seemingly irrational-choice perspective on the electorate (though some rational choice theorists would agree with some of his pessimistic views about the electorate).[7] For the model is based on a *leader-centred quasi-*economic theory of politics, and focuses upon the *competition* between political leaders that reaches its highly publicised peak at election time. As Santoro has pointed out, even if voters' electoral preferences are always to some degree manufactured by politicians, at least the competition between the manufacturers

> ensures that the electorate is not 'manufactured' by *only one* active ruling elite. ... [Voters] can be said to be 'independent' because

they may be manipulated by the other groups, too. These groups, in Schumpeter's view, do not necessarily consist of professional politicians or exponents of an economic interest. They can also be constituted by idealists of one kind or another.[8]

This competition for influence over the electorate is just one of the ways in which political leadership plays such an important, indeed defining role in the Leadership-Evolutionary model. Schumpeter did not provide an explicit definition of the political form of leadership. But clearly he viewed leadership from the institutional or structural perspective – of setting a direction by giving a lead – that has since been widely adopted by political scientists, such as by Tucker in *Politics as Leadership*.[9]

The LE model has to do more than simply follow in Schumpeter's footsteps when it applies this conception of leadership to various areas of the political system. For his theory explored only the electoral/ party and governmental (executive) sectors of a parliamentary democracy. A legislative sector has had to be added to the LE model so that it can cover the forms of political leadership, particularly the political entrepreneurship, that occur in the congressional legislatures of American-style presidential democracies. Indeed Chapter 8 is based on the quite large body of literature about legislative entrepreneurship in the US Congress, including the link between this entrepreneurship and the competition for leadership posts in Congress. However, the LE model's coverage of the governmental sector retains the Schumpeterian bias towards the parliamentary form of democratic government, with its collective government by a Cabinet of Ministers led by the Prime Minister, and this bias is also very evident in Chapter 6's largely British-based assessment of governmental political entrepreneurship. The presidential, one-person form of government can be fitted into the model only as a special case that lacks some of the normal features or that has them in an only analogous and shadowy form (as when Schumpeter suggested that key members of Congress may be analogous to Ministers in a collective government headed by the President).[10]

Adding a legislative sector is not the only way in which the LE model has to extend the Schumpeterian map of leadership in democracy. For some form of political leadership and indeed entrepreneurship occurs in areas of the political system, such as the civil service, that are commonly thought to be uninhabited by political leaders. However, Schumpeter would likely have approved of adding an administrative sector to the LE model, as he himself emphasised the important role played by a skilful and dutiful, Weberian-style bureaucracy in ensuring the success of democracy. He viewed these bureaucrats in a much more optimistic light than have public-choice economic theories of bureaucracy,[11] and there is also an obvious contrast with his realistic view of politicians as careerists engaged in a competitive struggle to gain powerful public offices. The LE model removes this anomaly by assuming that civil servants, too, are self-interested careerists, 'searching for career paths which leave them favourably placed to reach an appropriate rank in a suitable sort of agency'.[12] They engage in a private form of careerist competition that is similar to the competition among Ministers in a Cabinet government that was described in Chapter 1, such as the competition to be the leader of a specialised area of government.

The model's administrative sector contains only the 'influential policy making ranks' of the civil service: the policy-level senior officials who are usually numbered only in the hundreds rather than thousands.[13] Even when responding to the directions of their political masters, these high-ranking administrators have room to display some adaptive leadership. American researchers have shown that bureaucratic responses to what they termed 'stimuli' from government and legislature are not simply a matter of carrying out orders:

> Some responses are immediate and completed very quickly; others are delayed, gradual, and distributed through time in various causal patterns with different speeds of adjustment. The image produced is one of complex, dynamic bureaucratic adaptation.[14]

More importantly, high-ranking administrators have some policy-making powers devolved to them and have some influence on the government's policy-making decisions and legislature's law-making decisions. They have ample opportunity to provide direction-setting leadership within a specialised policy area, even if they and their proposals are quite unknown to the wider public. As will be seen in Chapter 9, there have also been some quite public and famous cases of entrepreneurship by senior administrators, perhaps most notably the development of the FBI through the administrative entrepreneurship of J. Edgar Hoover.

But adding an administrative sector to the LE model is a much more Schumpeterian step than the final, radical extension of the model's map of leadership in democracy. Schumpeter's 'vision of democracy leaves out that enormous range of individual and organizational activity' carried out by 'voters and interest groups in the lengthy periods between elections'.[15] This omission reflected his concern about the activities and political influence of economic interests and others with an axe to grind, which threatened the elected political leaders' freedom of political action that he considered one of the conditions for successful democracy.[16] It would have been more realistic for Schumpeter to have acknowledged that interest-group leaders and other varieties of policy advocate provide a form of political leadership – however unknown to the public – in their particular, specialised areas of policy expertise. Some have provided a form of political entrepreneurship, too, most publicly and famously in the case of consumer advocate Ralph Nader. And Chapter 10 will describe the important role that he and other policy-advocate entrepreneurs have played in American democracy.

The policy advocates' sectors are not based on particular institutions, such as the legislature, but on particular areas of public policy, such as social welfare or national security. Each of a democracy's hundreds or thousands of policy advocates operates in at least one of these many policy-based sectors, selling policy proposals related to this narrowly specialised area of policy. The policy advocates have much more varied career paths than politicians or administrators, and their careers may well involve a dramatic sideways move into a new path. For they are employed (whether as policy advocates or as policy experts who have a part-time advocacy role) by a varied range of not only interest groups but also think tanks, universities and media organisations. Competition between policy advocates, too, ranges from being as public as an electoral campaign to being as private as the competition in the administrative sector. Like the latter, it is usually competition to be the informal leader of a particular, specialised area of policy but is not so closely linked to a career path of ranks and departments.

The notion of policy-based sectors dominated by policy advocates is similar to Sabatier's concept of 'policy subsystems' dominated by 'advocacy coalitions'. There is a similar emphasis on the individuals (rather than organisations) who participate in a subsystem/sector, and on how they include not only the multitude of policy advocates employed by interest groups but also the various researchers, analysts, journalists, public administrators and legislators who specialise in this policy area.[17] However, Sabatier's concept of advocacy coalitions depicts these policy specialists as grouped into coalitions of individuals who share a particular belief system of values, causal assumptions and problem perceptions and seek to translate their beliefs into public policies – showing 'a non-trivial degree of coordinated activity over time'.[18] In contrast, the LE model assumes that it is individual advocates rather than coalitions who do the competing and selling/buying of policy proposals. But it later acknowledges that in reality the policy-based sectors have a tendency towards 'cartelisation', which is similar to Sabatier's argument that most policy subsystems have a predominant or monopoly advocacy coalition.[19]

Another comparison begged by the notion of policy-based sectors is the comparison with 'policy networks', especially Marsh's use of the term as a generic category or continuum that extends from the loosely knit 'issue network' to the tightly knit and exclusive 'policy community'.[20] The LE model's use of the cartelisation analogy is similar to this continuum but avoids the problem of where to draw the line between an issue network and a policy community.[21] A more serious and apparently more common problem associated with policy-network models is avoided by the LE model's quite explicit linking of the policy-based sectors to the overall policy-making process.[22] They are linked to the institution-based sectors and to the evolutionary policy processes that play such an important, indeed defining role in this model of the political system.

The evolutionary dimension of the Leadership-Evolutionary model has already been covered in earlier chapters and needs no introduction. All that remains is to tie the evolutionary more closely to the leadership dimension by suggesting that the evolutionary process of selecting variations for preservation also applies to leaders and their careers, as Schumpeter himself implied:

> the democratic method selects not simply from the population but only from those elements of the population that are available for the political vocation or, more precisely, that offer themselves for election. All methods of selection do this of course ... the competitive struggle for responsible office is, on the one hand, wasteful of personnel and energy. On the other hand, the democratic process may easily create conditions in the political sector that, once established, will repel most of the men who can make a success at anything else. For both these reasons, adequacy of material is particularly important for the success of democratic government. It is not true that in a democracy people always have the kind and quality of government they want or merit.[23]

But if the notion of leadership in democracy is expanded to include not only the electorally competing politicians but also the expert administrators and specialised policy advocates, there does not seem to be such a danger of the people failing to have 'the kind and quality of government they want or merit'. For the conditions in the administrative and policy-based sectors are not so likely to repel capable individuals. Nor are the forms of competition as wasteful of personnel and energy as those in the electoral/party sector. The people are fortunate that much of the leadership in a democracy occurs 'backstage' or 'off camera'.

The LE model of the democratic political system

This model of the democratic political system has been labelled a Leadership-Evolutionary model largely because it assigns such important roles to political leadership and to evolutionary processes of selection and adaptation. The role of leadership includes not only the ever-present competition for leadership but also the 'selling' of leads, such as by raising issues or presenting policy proposals, which are 'bought' by voters or by other leaders. In addition, the leaders' various forms of competition and of selling/buying leads are part of the evolutionary processes of selection and adaptation that occur in the various sectors of the political system. Sector's adaptive responses (to changes in their environment) are made through the selection of variations/leads that are provided by competing leaders as their careerist adaptive responses to the changes.

In rare cases political leaders show some entrepreneurial initiative by spontaneously selling an innovative lead. But these spontaneous initiatives rather than adaptive responses do not escape the evolutionary process of selection, and indeed entrepreneurial variations often fail to be preserved. The other cases in which leaders show some entrepreneurship, when selling a creative rather than merely adaptive response, are also subject to selection and, like adaptive responses, are reactions to changes in a sector's environment. Often these external changes have occurred outside the political system, in its economic, social or even international environment. But many external changes occur in a sector's *political* environment, frequently in the form of another sector's adaptive response to external change. For example, when a change in the economic environment produces an adaptive response in the governmental sector's economic policies, this response becomes a change in the political environment of the administrative sector, which will in turn have to make an adaptive response in its implementation of economic policy.

The model assumes that a democratic political system has several core, institution-based sectors and many peripheral, policy-based sectors.

The core sectors are based on the state institutions used: (1) in the competitive struggle for votes that determines who shall have the power to decide (electoral machinery); (2) in exercising that power to decide (government and legislature); and (3) in implementing and informing those decisions (the civil service bureaucracy). But in addition to the electoral, governmental, legislative and administrative sectors, there is a group of very important non-state political institutions: the political parties. They help the state's constitutional regulations link and coordinate the several core sectors, so that these sectors can operate as subsystems of the political system, and the political parties also play an important part in the internal workings of the legislative and electoral sectors. In fact the competitive struggle for votes is so much a matter of competition between party politicians that it is more realistic to describe the electoral sector as a combined, electoral/party sector. Much of the party component of the sector continues to operate after election day, as the political competition for voters' support continues between elections – and ensures that the prospect of future elections does not lose its influence over those who have been elected to power.

The electoral/party sector's free competition for a free vote is what distinguishes a democracy from other types of political system. But even this sector is dominated by political leaders: the individuals who set a direction for the political community by giving it a lead on political topics and decisions. The political leaders' domination arises from the public's tendency not to develop and articulate definite political opinions on its own initiative but instead to choose from the opinion leads presented to it by publicly recognised political leaders. The electoral/party sector's competing politicians present the public with opinion leads about any topic of political interest (or any topic a politician wishes to be of political interest) and then hope that the direction they have set is more appealing to the public than the directions set by their competitors. For the public may reject an opinion lead not because it is unacceptable but because they prefer one of the competing leads. Indeed when members of the public accept or reject a particular lead, their decision is analogous to them buying or refusing to buy a product that is being sold to the public in competition with other, comparable products. The economic analogy also applies to the supply side, with politicians attempting to sell a consumer product to a mass market. They use methods that are analogous to not only commercial advertising but also market research: assessing what is likely to sell and how to sell the product as effectively and efficiently as possible. It may be the same old product, simply reaffirming or reemphasising a well-known direction, or it may be a new product, setting a direction that is some-what new or perhaps even a real innovation.

The competition between politicians to lead public opinion is most intense and publicised when they are raising issues during an election campaign. This is the time, too, when it is most evident that they are not only selling a lead but also selling themselves to the public as some-one who ought to be entrusted with formal leadership of the country. For at election time the public is making its most important accept/reject decision about the political goods on offer: the formal voting decision in favour of some political leaders rather than their competi-tors. Voting for leaders means accepting their claim to be worthy (or more worthy than their competitors) of being entrusted with a formal leader's power to decide upon and set directions that the people will be *obliged* to accept because these are authoritative leads framed as law or public policy and are enforced by the state. (Of course formal leaders also have a responsibility to set a direction for the country by espousing their policy programmes and rhetorically inspiring the people with a sense of direction in times of crisis, but it is the formal leaders' power to decide on an obligatory direction that best distinguishes them from the many other forms of political leader.) The democratic operation of the electoral/party system can therefore be described as political leaders freely competing for formal leadership through a competitive leading of public opinion – the raising of issues – that culminates in the voters freely choosing whom to accept as their formal leaders.

The political leaders are raising issues that they hope will be more successful vote-winners than their competitors' issues, and this political competition also forces them to make adaptive responses to changes in their political, economic, social or international environment. It may be sufficient merely to reemphasise or reintroduce an old issue, but often a new issue will have to be raised – and occasionally even a truly innova-tive issue will be appropriate. However, raising an innovative issue as an adaptive response is quite different from making the creative response of selling an issue that is *more* innovative than is required to meet the external change and the competition within the sector. Such political entrepreneurship is quite rare, and even more rarely will a leader show some entrepreneurial initiative by seeking to sell an innovative issue quite spontaneously, not as any sort of response to external change.

Political entrepreneurship's innovations are not motivated by the careerism that motivates standard politicians and their adaptive leader-ship. The entrepreneur either is not a careerist politician or is not being motivated in this instance by his or her usual careerism. The standard politicians' political choices are usually based upon the rational pursuit of careerist self-interest, albeit with a bounded rationality and with a satisficing approach. Their career goals include not only winning election to public office but also attaining one of the highest posts in the (parliamentary) government or (congressional) legislature, followed by the venerable and self-satisfied retirement that caps off a successfully completed career. Of course politicians are by no means the only careerists within the political system. A similar careerism is also the standard motivation of public administrators and of policy advocates, though they have different career goals and paths than politicians' and engage in a very different form of career competition than what occurs in the electoral/party sector. The careerist competition among administrators and among policy advocates is usually kept from the public's view and involves quietly competing for an *in*formal leadership, within specialised policy areas, that only indirectly results in sought-after jobs. However, this is quite similar to politicians' careerist competition within the governmental and legislative sectors, where they privately or quietly compete with their own party colleagues for sought-after jobs within a collective government or congressional legislature.

Such competitive careerism also motivates their competitive selling of leads, as the formal leaders of the country, in the collective governmental sector or the congressional legislative sector. (The model's conception of the governmental sector is based on the British Cabinet and its conception of the legislative sector is based on the US Congress.) In these sectors a politician sells leads not by raising issues that may win him or her public approval but by presenting other formal leaders with proposals about new laws, public policies or administrative tools. It is always a competitive form of selling because even when proposals are not opposing or overlapping each other, they are competing for a place on the agenda and usually also for budget resources. But if a proposal is successfully sold to other formal leaders, it produces a momentous result: a decision to promulgate it as an authoritative lead, in the form of a law or government policy, that is binding on the whole political community.

A formal leader's selling of leads to other formal leaders is more analogous to inter-firm selling of producer goods than to the selling of consumer goods to a mass market. Both inter-leader and inter-firm selling are aimed at relatively few buyers and may involve some complex and often secret sales negotiations about altering the proposal/product to make it more appealing or about side deals relating to other proposals/products. In the legislative sector it is likely to be a case of some member of Congress selling a bill to colleagues on his or her subcommittee, as the first in a series of sales to other legislators that will have to be negotiated before the bill becomes law. In the governmental sector it is likely to be a Minister selling a policy proposal to Cabinet colleagues. In both sectors it is usually some form of proposed adaptive response to an economic, social or other external change, with the careerist competition among the formal leaders ensuring that an appropriate adaptive response is made to the change. But occasionally it is not a case of adaptive leadership but of political entrepreneurship: an innovative bill or policy proposal being sold in creative response to an external change or through a spontaneous use of initiative. The idea behind this innovation may have already appeared – and even been successfully sold – in some other part of the political system. For example, it may have already appeared in the form of an innovative election issue that has been unsuccessfully sold to the public within the electoral/party sector. But the first attempt to sell it within the legislative or governmental sector, whether as an entrepreneurial initiative or creative response, is still a case of legislative or governmental entrepreneurship. (As will be argued in Chapter 6, though, if the innovation has won a democratic mandate as a successful election issue, its selling in the legislative or governmental sector will be a case of forced adaptive response.) For the various forms of political entrepreneurship, such as the electoral, legislative or governmental, occur when an entrepreneur makes an innovative idea politically relevant within that particular *sector* of the political system by attempting to sell it as a new issue, bill, or policy proposal.

Another sector in which political leaders, albeit civil servants rather than formal leaders, sell proposals to one another is the administrative sector. It is based on an array of departments and bureaus that in most cases have completed their development from merely administrative tool to mature institution, and in fact have become the institutional base of a separate subsector within the overall administrative sector. The careerist competition among their senior administrators ensures that proposals are being sold in this sector in a similarly competitive fashion to the selling in governmental or legislative sectors. The senior administrators are obviously a very different form of political leader from those involved in government, the legislature and the competitive struggle for the people's vote. The people rarely recognise the name of even the most prominent administrators, let alone recognise them as some form of political leader. Nonetheless, when selling their proposals, senior administrators are setting a direction for the political community in their specialised areas of policy expertise, even if only informally and in the privacy of their own department or bureau. Often an administrator is proposing only a new administrative policy, whose sale can be negotiated with other administrators and, if required, with the government Minister or congressional legislators who participate (as predominantly buyers rather than sellers) in this administrative subsector. But the administrator may well be proposing new legislation or government policy, which the subsector's Minister or congressional legislators will have to be prepared not only to buy but also to 'on sell' within Cabinet or Congress as a legislative bill or proposal for government policy. Although administrators are usually selling their proposals as adaptive responses, occasionally they try selling an innovation that is not merely an adaptive response but an entrepreneurial (creative) response or spontaneous initiative.

Similar processes also occur in the political system's many *policy-based* sectors. Each of these sectors is based on a particular, specialised area of public policy, with proposals relating to this area of policy being competitively sold by policy advocates as adaptive responses or entrepreneurial responses/initiatives. Policy advocates are similar to senior public administrators in being expert specialists who engage in careerist competition. But instead of being state employees they are lobbyists for interest groups (including public-interest groups and charitable organisations) or they are employed by universities, think tanks or the media as experts who are encouraged to sell as well as buy new policy ideas. A policy advocate is a form of political leader even if, like a civil servant, he or she is anonymous to the public and is selling specialised, often esoteric leads in a manner analogous to inter-firm selling. A few policy advocates may become publicly recognised as a sectional form of political leader because they also sell opinion leads to the public on behalf of consumers, trade unions and other newsworthy groups. But most policy advocates usually sell their proposals only to other advocates and to public administrators and/or congressional legislators who have a career interest in a particular policy area and participate (predominantly as buyers rather than sellers) in the relevant policy-based sector. These administrators and legislators are often 'in the market' for a policy lead that they can develop into an administrative policy proposal or a legislative bill and then on-sell as an adaptive response or entrepreneurial response/initiative.

The successful selling of a lead, in any sector, means the selection of a variation for preservation. Often it means preservation for further development, as when an advocate's policy proposal is developed into a legislative bill. On the other hand, one variation's success is often other, competing variations' failure and elimination. Among them may well be an existing issue, policy, law or even institution, which is being replaced by the proposed new variant, but most elements of the political system will show a successfully strong urge to self-preservation. This also highlights the problem of rigidity, the lack of sufficient competition, that affects all real-world democratic political systems.

Imperfect competition and entrepreneurial democracy

Any realistic model of democracy would have to acknowledge that its political competition is far from perfect. Careerist competition among the leaders ensures that the selected variations are useful adaptive responses or an advantageous entrepreneurial innovation. But such factors as bounded rationality and satisficing career choices mean that often a political leader's issue, proposal or bill is faced with too little diversity and strength of competition from other leads to satisfy even a realistic democrat. The ramifications of overly imperfect competition include high levels of issue, policy and institution rigidity, with the resulting costly delays in making appropriate adaptive responses.

An example of the overly imperfect competition that plagues democracies is the tendency towards cartelisation in the policy-based sectors.[24] A cartel of policy advocates may establish a monopoly and prevent new sellers entering the market. Or, more commonly, there is some degree of competition between rival cartels but one of them is predominant and has an effective monopoly because most (or the most powerful) legislators and administrators are committed to buying its proposals. Both forms of monopoly usually involve not only preserving a basic policy – defending it against challenges from outside or inside the sector – but also making minor changes aimed at improving the basic policy's implementation.[25] In fact members of a cartel may compete among themselves by selling different versions of a secondary variation, and the dominant cartel may even buy a secondary variation from policy advocates of a rival cartel. But these are still inherently monopolistic situations that (as will be seen in Chapter 10) can provoke frustrated entrepreneurs into 'hawking' their policy proposals around the political system in search of uncommitted buyers.

Another example of imperfect competition's effects is that its presence in the electoral/party sector not only increases rigidity but also reduces a democracy's capacity to provide its citizens with a political education. A competitive struggle in the electoral/party sector to win the people's vote enables the people to make better informed and shrewder political judgments than those made by the subjects of non-democratic regimes. Although Schumpeter highlighted the political ignorance of a democracy's citizenry, he also acknowledged that 'given time the collective psyche will evolve opinions that not infrequently strike us as highly reasonable and even shrewd'.[26] This achievement of democracy is somewhat analogous to what Schumpeter described as the historic achievement of capitalism, namely enabling the masses to enjoy standards of consumption that were once the privilege of the elite.[27] Similarly, one of the historic achievements of democracy has been to enable the masses to enjoy standards of political education that were once the privilege of the elite – enabling the masses to 'evolve' political opinions that are 'highly reasonable and even shrewd'. However, just as capitalism's historic achievement has required a competitive economy, so too has democracy's achievement in political education required a competitive electoral/party sector. As Stokes has pointed out, the people's 'policy opinions – general and vague as they may be – would be even more general and vague were we not subjected at repeated intervals to the competitive rhetoric of campaigns'.[28] And overly imperfect competition may well reduce this electoral education about policy options. Ware noted that if the competition is between only two parties, they may choose to downplay the policy aspect of this competition:

> Rather than being drawn into intense competition with each other over policy, the parties may choose instead to compete over such matters as the 'image' of their leaders, or through campaign advertising that is non-political in content.[29]

He made this point when applying an economic theory of market oligopoly to two-party competition, which economists would describe as an extreme case of market concentration and power.[30] In fact a textbook definition of market competitiveness may actually be phrased in terms of the sellers' power to influence the market – the less the power, the more competitive the market.[31] So by analogy a case of overly imperfect competition in the electoral/party sector would mean that the parties have a deal of power to influence the electoral 'market', such as by focusing the attention of the market on the competing leaders' 'images' instead of on policy matters.

Although Schumpeter was apparently unconcerned about imperfect competition in the electoral/party sector, this was only because he favoured a broad or tolerant interpretation of his *definition* of democracy as electoral competition. It was when arguing against any 'unrealistic ideal' of democratic competitiveness, that he pointed out that in the economic sphere 'competition is never completely lacking, but hardly ever is it perfect'.[32] If he had been focusing on the actual *operation* of a democracy's electoral/party sector, an economist of Schumpeter's stature would doubtless have pointed out that lack of competition means that the parties will have more power to influence the electoral market, that there will be more rigidity in the electoral/party sector and that there will be other serious implications for this democracy's political community – including the demise of political education and other historic achievements of democracy that require sufficient competition in the electoral/party sector.

Competition in this sector is also a crucial means of overcoming rigidity in policy-based sectors. Parties and individuals who compete successfully in elections have the power to decide in any area of public policy, no matter how important and/or technical, and so are the ultimate weapon for dealing with rigidity in any policy-based sector, from family law to foreign policy. These parties and individuals can introduce new ideas or override vested interests and compensate for the effects of cartelisation in a policy-based sector. Thus overly imperfect competition in the electoral/party sector helps maintain rigidity throughout the democracy as well as in its own sector of the political system.

Overly imperfect competition in the electoral/party sector can occur not only when there are more than two competing parties but also when the competition is reduced by what the economists describe as 'artificial factors'.[33] A sophisticated economic example is investing in high levels of advertising in order to increase new entrants' set-up costs – an artificial barrier to entry that is more difficult to prohibit or control than most other anti-competitive practices.[34] Such artificial factors can also be found in the electoral/party sector of democracies. In fact there has been an economic analysis of the US Congress's use of government-subsidised advertising to strengthen the barriers to entry that protect incumbent members of Congress.[35] And some well-established European party systems have been accused of a tendency to 'collusion and cooperation between ostensible competitors' that had gone so far as the 'formation of a cartel' that favoured only limited inter-party competition and the state-resourced survival of all its parties.[36] A critic of this theory of cartelisation pointed out that European democracies' party systems had not shown any evidence of reduced inter-party competition or of new parties being prevented from entering the electoral market, but he acknowledged that cartelisation had long existed in several consociational European democracies – where all the major parties had cooperated and enjoyed governmental status.[37]

There may be good reasons why a democratic political community accepts such markedly imperfect competition in its electoral/party sector. And there are certainly good reasons why any democracy would be cautious about establishing near perfect competition in that sector, as is illustrated by Israel's experience in the 1980s–90s.[38] A pure system of proportional representation with a 1 per cent threshold encouraged as many as 30 parties to seek representation in parliament, and helped about a dozen of them to win seats, but the costs in terms of policy-making immobilism and potential government instability were so severe that in 1992 Israel became the first parliamentary democracy to introduce a directly elected Prime Ministership.

However, there seems no reason why a democracy should not encourage political entrepreneurs to perform a similar role in the electoral/party sector to what they do in cartelised policy-based sectors – countering imperfect competition. Political entrepreneurs would perform this role in the electoral/party sector not by hawking innovative policy proposals but by raising innovative issues or at least posing an ever-present threat of doing so. They would be analogous to the economic entrepreneurs whom Schumpeter depicted as enforcers of competitive-like behaviour upon firms in oligopolistic and monopoly sectors of the economy. As was noted early in Chapter 3, Schumpeter argued that the kind of competition arising from new commodities, new technologies and other forms of innovation has a disciplining effect on these firms even when they are facing only an ever-present *threat* of this kind of competition, which will 'in the long run enforce behavior very similar to the perfectly competitive pattern'.[39] In the long run these firms will be constrained from exploiting their huge market power; their prices, products and adaptive responses will eventually be very similar to those that would have been forced upon them by a perfectly competitive market. For they fear a kind of competition that involves creative–destructive innovation and that presumably is motivated not by the businessman's economic rationality but by the comparatively irrational motives that would lead an entrepreneur to take on the challenge of entering an oligopolistic market despite the presence of artificial, firm-created barriers to entry and of various other anti-competitive practices. Apparently the only sure way of deterring entrepreneurs is to conform to such 'perfect' behaviour in pricing, products and adaptive responses that an entrepreneur will have nothing new to offer this market.

The same argument can be made about how the threat of competition from *political* entrepreneurs affects party leaders in an oligopolistic or cartelised electoral/party sector. Merely the threat of a political entrepreneur raising an innovative issue that they have ignored or overlooked will in the long run constrain these party leaders' use of their power over what will or will not be sold to the public. They will be forced to raise the sorts of issue that otherwise would have emerged only in a perfectly competitive electoral/party sector. Such an issue may be only drawing attention to a problem rather than suggesting an innovative way of solving it. But even problem-identifying innovative issues can be used to such creative–destructive effect by entrepreneurial competitors that careerist party leaders are forced to raise them to ensure that they do not fall into the hands of political entrepreneurs. An ever-present threat of entrepreneurial competition can therefore compensate to some extent for that lack of perfect competition which allows issue rigidity to occur and to produce costly delays in adaptation. But Schumpeter warned that entrepreneurial competition's counteracting of imperfect competition will occur only in the long run; its counteracting effect cannot be expected to prevent some delays in adaptation and the losses that they cause the community.

More importantly, imperfections in the standard, careerist form of political competition can be counteracted only if there is indeed some actual or threatened entrepreneurial competition. Many democracies do not show much evidence of issue entrepreneurship, nor of innovative issues that may have been introduced by careerist political leaders because of the threat of entrepreneurial competition. Of course this may be because there is sufficient entrepreneurship in other sectors of the political system to compensate for its absence in the electoral/party sector – an abundance of innovative policy proposals and legislative bills can compensate for the lack of innovative election issues. But even if all the sectors of the political system are taken into account, many democracies would still show little evidence of actual or threatened entrepreneurial competition.

For political entrepreneurship is not an essential, defining component of democracy but only a secondary aspect, the entrepreneurial aspect of democracy. It is found in varying degrees among the many past and present cases of democracy, and only rarely is it found in sufficient degree to justify describing a particular case as an 'entrepreneurial democracy'. In fact there may be even fewer entrepreneurial democracies than participatory democracies. But the entrepreneurial aspect of a democracy may well be a means of counteracting and compensating for deficiencies in what *is* an essential, defining component of democracy – competition. The search for the presence of political entrepreneurship in Part II will therefore be implicitly asking some questions about the state of democracy as well as about the nature of leadership in democracy.

Assessing the prevalence of pioneering leadership in the 1960s–90s

In Part II the focus shifts from theoretical questions and problems to analysing and assessing actual cases of entrepreneurial-style, pioneering political leadership. But it cannot wholly escape theoretical matters because the researchers and analysts who have already identified these cases have often applied some notion of entrepreneurship to them and usually it is not a Schumpeterian conception of entrepreneurship (see Chapters 8, 9 and 10). This different notion of entrepreneurship also means that usually they are applying the term to a wider range of examples, some or many of which would not qualify as examples of Schumpeterian, pioneering entrepreneurship. Consequently, Part II will emphasise the pioneering nature of Schumpeterian entrepreneurship and will usually be referring not to 'political entrepreneurship' but to 'entrepreneurial-style' or 'entrepreneurial-like' pioneering leadership or simply 'pioneering'.

The cases of entrepreneurial-style, pioneering leadership that will be analysed and assessed are not case studies or illustrations, as the underlying theme of Part II is to assess whether this unusual kind of leadership has become more prevalent in recent decades. The period chosen is the 1960s–90s, as this is longer than a biological generation, includes several leadership generations and incorporates the apparently change-oriented decade of the 1960s, which will act as a benchmark for the later decades in the period. The five chapters each cover particular sectors of the political system in which innovative issues, policies, laws or even institutions are pioneered: election issues in the electoral/party sector; government policies in the governmental sector; laws in the legislative sector; tools/institutions in the administrative sector; and public policies in the policy advocates' various policy-based sectors.

The chapters are primarily concerned with two very long-established democracies, the British and the American, which also have distinctive claims to special attention. The British case was Schumpeter's model example and the American case is the best example of an entrepreneurial democracy. In fact the chapters on administrative and policy-advocate pioneering are almost solely concerned with American examples simply because the US political system offers either the only or the most numerous group of examples of administrative and policy-advocate pioneering to be found in any democracy. Similarly, the chapter on legislative pioneering is solely concerned with US examples not only because the model's conception of the legislative sector was based upon the US Congress but also because it offers the only or at least most numerous group of examples of legislative pioneering. Although the chapter on presidential pioneering, too, is solely concerned with US examples, this chapter is only a supplement to the main chapter on governmental pioneering and is largely concerned with foreign policy. The main chapter on governmental pioneering is confined to British examples because not only the LE model's but also Schumpeter's conception of the governmental sector was based on the British Cabinet.

These British and American examples, and political scientists' analyses of them, will provide the basis for a *prima facie* assessment of whether there is a tendency for pioneering to become more prevalent. Although the assessment of prevalence is only impressionistic, it should be able to identify any obvious historical tendencies in the prevalence of pioneering leadership – both within the 1960s–90s period and from a longer historical perspective. It should also be able to identify tendencies within the various sectors of the political system, such as whether pioneering has become more prevalent in the legislative sector but less prevalent in the administrative sector. In fact it is possible that the overall amount of pioneering in a democracy does not change very much over the decades and that a decline in pioneering in one or more sectors is compensated for by increases in other sectors. Similarly, any cross-national comparisons of the prevalence of pioneering in different democracies would have to take into account all the various sectors of the political system, not just the highly publicised electoral/party sector. And such an overall, multisector assessment would also of course be an assessment of the degree of entrepreneurial democracy in that country.

Part II

Assessing Entrepreneurial-Style, Pioneering Leadership

5
Electoral Pioneering

Parties as innovative electoral tools

Although this chapter is focused on innovative election *issues*, it is as well to begin by acknowledging that the electoral/party sector has also been the scene of innovation in electoral *tools*, namely political parties, that may also become important political institutions. The democratic political party is an organisational tool for winning the competitive struggle for the people's vote. As Duverger argued, its having an organisational structure is what distinguishes a party 'in the true sense of the word' from a mere faction or a parliamentary group, such as the Jacobins of the French Revolution.[1] If a particular party is successful enough for a long enough period, it is likely to be institutionalised and be viewed as one of its democracy's important political institutions rather than just a tool for winning elections.

Arguably the world's very first political party was pioneered by Jefferson in the newly independent United States of the 1790s, more than half a century before political parties began to appear in Europe.[2] The early development of parties in the US has been linked to the early enfranchising of a mass electorate.[3] And it seems that the Jeffersonian (Democratic-) Republicans were the first group to use the organisational capacities of a true political party to mobilise support within this mass electorate. Although Jefferson was not the inventor or creator of the party,[4] he made it politically relevant by becoming its leader, apparently for non-careerist reasons, and (very effectively) introducing it into the electoral sector. Epstein's only doubt about its credentials as the first-ever party was that after winning a near monopoly it began to disintegrate.[5] But this means only that it could also claim to be the

first-ever party not to survive long enough to become a political institution rather than just an electoral tool!

By the twentieth century a range of new types of political party was
beginning to emerge, and these new types would often be created by an
individual founder-leader. (However, the two most famous examples,
Lenin's revolutionary-elite communist party and Mussolini's paramili-
tary fascist party, were new types of tool not for winning elections but
for taking power through non-electoral means.) During the 1960s–90s
the most innovative new type of party was created by a business entrepreneur. The Forza Italia (FI – 'Come on Italy') party established in
1993–94 by business magnate Berlusconi has actually been described as
a 'business firm masquerading as a party'.[6] Various parts of his Fininvest
conglomerate were mobilised to perform the key functions required by
a party competing in modern elections: opinion-polling, selecting candidates, political advertising, manipulation of the media, and providing a territorial network of party organs or officials.[7] Thus Diakron, an
opinion-polling agency, provided the FI party with poll data on what
messages and policies would attract voters; Publitalia, the conglomerate's commercial advertising branch, not only recruited, selected and
trained FI candidates but also constituted a territorial network of party
representatives; Programma Italia, a mutual-funds branch, used its
nationwide sales team to set up a network of thousands of FI Clubs;
and Mediaset's television channels provided advertising opportunities,
biased news coverage, politicised games shows, and professional expertise in presenting an attractive image of Berlusconi to the public. The
party adopted a more normal structure a few years later, with a mass
membership electing a network of provincial assemblies that in turn
elected delegates to the party's first Congress.[8] But during its brief existence as an innovative political tool, this must have been structurally
the ultimate 'business' party.

In most other cases the pioneering party-founder has simply imported
a new type of party that has been invented and used in other parts
of the world. For example, Brechtel and Kaiser applied Schumpeter's
notion of creative response entrepreneurship to the introduction
of a new, coalition-oriented type of party, apparently modelled on
Germany's FDP, into New Zealand politics after that country changed
its British-style electoral system to a German style of proportional representation.[9] Before the country's first election (1996) under the new
system, an already well-known politician split from his party and
founded a new party, New Zealand First (NZF), whose strategy was to
establish itself as the centre-coalition party in the new, German-style

party system that was expected to arise from the change in electoral system.[10] After the election the NZF party and a larger party did indeed form a coalition government in which NZF's leader held the posts of Treasurer and Deputy Prime Minister. But before this can be described as a straightforward case of (partly) pioneering a new type of party, there are several questions to be asked about the predictability of the response, the careerist opportunism of the pioneer, and his career prospects of attaining as high a public office if he had stuck with his party of origin instead of founding a party of his own. As in many other cases of innovation, there is at least a suspicion that this may have been an adaptive innovation rather than a case of pioneering or partly pioneering leadership.

Looking for innovative election issues

It might be expected that there would be many more examples of pioneering electoral issues than pioneering electoral tools. But such issues seem to have been rather scarce during the 1960s–90s, even if the search is expanded to include *any* innovative issue, with no questions asked about whether it is adaptive or pioneering, and even if the search is not too particular about whether an issue is truly innovative or merely (marginally) new.

Electoral competition seems to be predominantly a matter of candidate personalities, various other non-issues and the saliency strategy of raising and emphasising a few old-hat issues that are likely to be electorally advantageous. The old-hat issues take such different forms as 'permanent' issues, 'threshold' issues and 'hardy perennials'. In the British case, Macfarlane argued that there are bound to be some seemingly permanent issues because they relate to permanently important and broad areas of social policy, such as housing and education, that have given rise to a series of issues about more specific problems and policies.[11] And he pointed out that there are also 'some issues, such as the level of prices and unemployment, which only come to the fore when certain well understood objective conditions are met', such as abnormally high levels of inflation or unemployment.[12] These might be called 'threshold' issues because they are predictable adaptive responses by parties to external changes that have raised inflation, unemployment and the like above their thresholds of possible voter attention and concern (though these thresholds would vary from one society to another and from one historical period to another). A similar type of issue is what Kingdon has described as hardy perennials in American politics, such as complaints about taxes and proposals for health-care reform.[13] These may be partly threshold issues, in the sense of being partly linked to levels of taxation and demand for health care, but are more likely to be the product of less specific changes in society and of new strategies in the competitive struggle for votes.

One reason for the lack of innovative issues may be the oligopolistic lack of competition in the electoral/party sector (that was described in Chapter 4). If the major parties long ago established a virtual duopoly, as in the British and US cases, then the party leaders may have had sufficient market power to ensure that some innovative issues have not been sold to the public – have never been raised as election issues. Macfarlane noted that 'some issues bitterly disputed in the country, such as abortion and immigration, do not become election issues because the parties do not take a firm stand on them'.[14] The same occurs in the US, as Downs pointed out in a well-known article on the public's discovery of problems and attention to issues. The media, dramatic events and policy advocates draw the public's attention to practical problems that have (apparently) arisen in society, converting them into *public* issues.[15] But politicians avoid taking a stand on some of them, such as racism and poverty, because it is not in their electoral self-interest to raise them as election issues.[16] The fact that some public issues are not developed into election issues would suggest that there are insufficient entrepreneurial-like, pioneering leaders to do the job or even to pose a threat that forces careerist politicians to raise these issues, eventually, to prevent them falling into the hands of political pioneers.

Another reason for the lack of innovative issues was provided by Downs in his economic theory of democracy. He assumed and argued that 'political tastes are fixed. Even though these tastes often change radically in the long run, we believe our assumption is plausible in the short run, barring wars or other social upheavals.'[17] If the electorate's political tastes change radically only in the long run, it would be reasonable to expect that only seldom, at long intervals, would careerist politicians raise a radically new election issue – in adaptive innovative response to one of these seldom-seen changes in the electorate's tastes. What is more, even some entrepreneurial-like, pioneering leaders might well be deterred from raising innovative issues during the long periods between radical changes in the electorate's tastes.

On the other hand, it was pointed out in Chapter 1 that later in his theory Downs acknowledged that there was some room for a leader to change voters' views by persuading them that there are better ways of attaining their goals. A prominent example of this views-changing leadership was identified by Dunleavy when using the analogy with Schumpeterian entrepreneurs to describe party leaders who anticipate or lead public opinion, initiate a new political project, or respond dynamically to changing conditions.[18] One of his examples of how a politician can lead public opinion, or 'shape voter preferences', was Reagan's 1980 use of supply-side economics to increase voters' expectations of what was economically feasible, namely that it was feasible to cut taxes while also boosting defence spending and preserving core welfare programmes.[19] In other words, Reagan was raising an innovative issue by claiming that there was a comparatively effortless way of attaining voters' economic, defence and social-welfare goals. Successfully selling supply-side economics to the voters was one of his more remarkable feats of persuasion.

Raising such an innovative issue was by no means typical of US presidential elections. Page had pointed out a few years earlier that innovative policy ideas were 'rarely brought forward' in presidential elections and had tended to be raised by third parties or by candidates outside the political mainstream, such as Goldwater and McGovern, who had captured a major party's nomination.[20] There had been only a few occasions when regular major-party candidates had 'come up with important new ideas': Truman with civil rights and national health insurance; Stevenson with ending both the peacetime draft and atmospheric nuclear testing; and Kennedy with the Peace Corps – apart from these instances, 'it is not so easy to find examples'.[21]

Nor did Reagan's supply-side innovation begin a new trend towards innovative issues in the presidential elections of the 1980s–90s. Even Perot's independent candidature in 1992 and Reform Party candidature in 1996 were not as issue innovative as some third-party campaigns of the past, though his innovative emphasis on balancing the budget may have forced the major-party candidates to pay more attention to the budget issue than they would have without his entrepreneurial-like competition. Clinton's most significant issue, health-care reform, was a Democratic hardy perennial that was first raised in Truman's 1948 campaign. The Republicans' only significant post-Reagan innovation came not from a presidential candidate but from a House Minority Whip, Newt Gingrich, when he put together a ten-point 'Contract with America' that most Republican candidates endorsed before their successful 1994 mid-term elections.[22] This ten-point platform may not have included many innovative issues in its wide range of topics: constitutional amendments for term limits, balanced budgets and presidential line-item vetos; defence policy changes to reinstate a missile defence system and ban US troops serving under foreign UN command; and various changes in criminal, family, welfare and tax legislation. But Gingrich was doing something truly innovative in presenting a congressional party programme, comparable to presidential candidates' programmes and British party leaders' election manifestos.

Although the 2000 presidential campaign lies outside the 1960s–90s assessment period, it should be noted that the entrepreneurial-like competition from two new minor-party candidates failed to provoke the two main candidates into issue innovation. In 2000 consumer-advocate Nader fronted the Green party's first serious presidential campaign, and paleoconservative ex-Republican Buchanan took over the presidential campaign of a divided and seemingly irrelevant Reform party.[23] Yet this does not appear to have forced the major-party candidates to be more issue innovative than they would otherwise have been, perhaps because Nader's and Buchanan's support fell far short of the levels that Perot had achieved in the 1990s. On the other hand, their revival of the threat of entrepreneurial competition might have forced the 2004 major-party candidates to be more innovative if that election had not been dominated by the electoral adaptive response to the 9/11 attack. In the 2008 campaign the novelty of Obama as a candidate obscured the lack of issue innovation. Even Obama seemed to be merely continuing the Democratic strategy, so successful with Carter and Clinton, of offering intelligent policy analysis and problem solving by a nice guy who is also seeking the health-care reform that was left as unfinished business by the New Deal (see Conclusion).

In comparison to American presidential elections, British parliamentary elections seem quite well endowed with innovative issues in the later stages of the 1960s–90s period. For example, in the 1979 election the Conservative party introduced monetarism as an election issue, and would continue to raise innovative issues in its series of election victories of the 1980s–90s (though these issues were typically an electoral selling of a top-down policy innovation that was already under way). In the 1997 election the Labour party raised the innovative issue of sweeping constitutional reform. The new Labour government's implementation of this election commitment, such as the introduction of Scottish and Welsh devolution and reform of the House of Lords, made it 'utterly and unarguably different from all its predecessors', with 'no precedent since 1688 for such a concentrated and deliberate rebuilding of the constitutional architecture'.[24] But there is a marked contrast in the role played by the respective party leaders in the raising of these innovative issues in the 1979 and 1997 elections. The Conservative party's leader, Margaret Thatcher, had indeed been an instigator of the shift to a monetarist stance after she defeated the centrist leader of the party in a 1975 leadership vote by Conservative MPs seething with revolt.[25] Her comparatively right-wing beliefs had not been the basis of her leadership victory, and even after being elected to government in 1979 she would struggle to have her government implement the party's election-manifestoed and democratically mandated policy of monetarism (see Chapter 6). In contrast, the Labour party's innovative constitutional issue was not instigated by its 1997 leader, Tony Blair. It was under his predecessor, John Smith, that the party had committed itself to constitutional reform and to key elements of the package that was presented to the electorate under Blair's leadership. Although his first-term government's 'major achievement would be the wide range of constitutional reforms', it has been suggested that Prime Minister Blair and his publicists underplayed these reforms partly because of his 'lack of interest in pledges largely made by his predecessor'.[26]

The hunt for issue innovation and pioneering should also include those issues that merely *identify* a problem rather than suggesting how to solve it. Identifying a problem means setting a direction, selling a lead, for the public to accept or reject. And Page noted that presidential candidates sometimes draw voters' attention to a problem and try to persuade them that something should be done about it, even though the candidates have no specific policy suggestions.[27] He pointed to the cases of Kennedy drawing attention to the suffering in depressed areas of the US and the Third World, of Johnson drawing attention to the problem of the less fortunate throughout American society, of Goldwater drawing attention to the problem of urban crime, and of how 'McGovern in 1972 opened, for the first time in decades, the question of redistribution of income and wealth'.[28] McGovern's raising of the long-defunct redistribution issue may seem a case of what Nadel termed a 'resurrected' issue but he specified that any issue reintroduced more than 30 years after it had last appeared should be viewed as a new issue.[29] However, a long-defunct issue that has been reintroduced is not quite the same as a wholly new issue and might be better distinguished from a resurrected issue by being viewed as a 'reborn' rather than new issue.

The fact that McGovern and Goldwater again figure in a not very impressive list of issue innovators might suggest that innovative issues are more likely to arise in presidential campaigns through pioneering than as an adaptive innovation. Otherwise, more mainstream candidates than McGovern and Goldwater would have been just as likely to have raised these issues, and these two innovators would not have suffered electoral defeats of historic proportions. They seem typical cases of pioneers failing to sell their innovative issues to the voters, who have preferred the more familiar leads being sold to them by mainstream candidates. On the other hand, it could be argued that the failure to win election is not necessarily evidence that the candidate was engaged in issue pioneering rather than selling an adaptive innovation that the candidate's mainstream competitor had overlooked or avoided (see Chapter 3), for the candidate may have lost because of voters' overall appraisal of his worthiness to be the country's most powerful formal leader. In the case of Goldwater, his hawkish attitude towards nuclear weapons may have lost him the support of many voters who bought his innovative lead regarding the problem of urban crime – which soon became a mainstream issue and then a hardy perennial.

Perhaps the most clear-cut case of losing an election through unsuccessfully pioneering an innovative issue occurred in Australia rather than the US or Britain. In the 1993 parliamentary elections the leader of the opposition Liberal party, John Hewson, raised the innovative issue of reforming the tax base by introducing a goods and services tax (GST). He was 'a strong personal advocate of GST and initially appeared to relish the prospect of *attempting to sell* the introduction of this new tax to the electorate'.[30] As GST was the issue that received most attention during the campaign, the Liberals' failure to defeat the governing Labor party was commonly blamed on Hewson's new issue.[31] And indeed 'the *difficulty of selling* a complex new tax system from opposition to an electorate confronted with a barrage of negative messages about it from the government clearly rated in the assessment of party members as the major obstacle they had faced in the campaign.'[32] Although Hewson for a time retained his position as leader of the Liberals, GST was quickly removed from the party platform and seemed to be dead and buried as an election issue. In the 1998 elections the new Liberal leader and by then Prime Minister, John Howard, resurrected the issue of GST-based tax reform and won an election that, like the 1993 election, was to some extent 'a referendum on the GST' (especially as the government had not yet developed its ideas into public policy).[33] But Howard had the informational selling advantages of a Prime Minister seeking reelection and, more importantly, he was raising a resurrected issue rather than pioneering a new or reborn issue.

The life cycle of issues

One of the factors that complicate the study of issue pioneering is this complex 'life cycle' that allows issues to be resurrected or reborn. A famous example is given in Carmines and Stimson's book on the evolution of the race issue in America. The issue of race emerged after the Civil War's resolution of the slavery issue and became the focus of much public concern during the post-war era of Reconstruction in the defeated south.[34] But the ending of Reconstruction in 1877 also transformed the issue of race into a predominantly regional, southern issue: its 'life as a national political issue was only sporadic and inconsequential'.[35] It was reborn in 1948 when Truman raised the issue of race by calling for civil rights legislation. Although it soon seemed to be fading away again, it was revived or resurrected in the early 1960s and became a key public and election issue. In fact Carmines and Stimson have argued that presidential candidate Goldwater, by opposing the 1964 Civil Rights Act, played a crucial role in bringing about the 'critical moment' in the evolution of the race issue.[36]

His continuing opposition to the Civil Rights Act is also an example of how a policy decision may leave an issue unsettled by transforming it into a contentious policy. As Macfarlane pointed out in his work on British political issues, a policy decision does not necessarily settle or close an issue if another party opposes the new policy.[37] In the US, opposition to a new policy has taken such subtle forms as the issue of race continuing to live on into the 1980s through opposition to policy implementation. Despite Goldwater's landslide election defeat, the race issue was 'every bit as much alive in the politics of the 1980s as when the issues were squarely confronted'.[38] But as advocacy or defence of racial segregation was no longer a reputable political stance, the politicians with conservative views on race had gone underground. They were sending out subtle cues that would not capture public attention but would be picked up and understood by the political activists in the electorate. That these politicians 'now support the goals of affirmative action and oppose effective implementation' shows how an issue that has been transformed into a policy can thereafter be opposed through politicising matters of policy implementation, such as affirmative action, instead of taking an open stand against the policy.[39]

Clearly the life cycle of issues is much more complex than that of policies or institutions.[40] Even if an issue develops into an unopposed policy, it may well become the focus of a policy-based sector, as was described in Baumgartner and Jones's (1993) work on agenda setting.

As Downs had suggested that a resolved public issue can live on in the new form of policies or institutions created to deal with the issue,[41] Baumgartner and Jones described as 'Downsian' those mobilisations of public enthusiasm for an issue that leave behind an institutional and/or policy legacy, often in the form of a 'policy subsystem', that continues to exist long after the public enthusiasm has faded away.[42] The members of the policy-based sector may actually enjoy a cartel-like monopoly over the issue's policy legacy. But a monopolistic policy-based sector is vulnerable to an issue-expanding, 'Schattschneider' type of mobilisation of public enthusiasm (see Chapter 10) that 'leads either to the dissolution of the policy subsystem or to protracted conflict'.[43]

Ways of issue innovating: (1) heresthetical and (2) reframing

Issues not only have a complex life cycle but also have been the subject of some complex theorising about ways and means of issue innovation. The most well-known theoretical work relating to issue innovation is Riker's theory of the manipulation of dimensions of political alignment. He had already presented a theory of issue evolution that used the slavery issue to illustrate both the natural selection of issues and the importance of agenda manipulation.[44] For by raising the new issue of slavery, the political losers of the 1819–60 era were able to manipulate the agenda and transform themselves into political winners.[45] They had previously introduced other issues aimed at manipulating the agenda but these had not succeeded: 'The slavery issue gradually displaced these others by a kind of natural selection. It worked and the others did not.'[46] Riker would use the same example in his (1986) book on heresthetic to illustrate the manipulation of *dimensions* rather than the agenda. In this book he coined the term 'heresthetic' to celebrate the 'art of manipulation', and pointed to the manipulating of dimensions as one of the three kinds of heresthetical event or manoeuvre.[47] It occurs (successfully) when a politician or party that has won only a minority of the votes introduces a new issue that splits the opposing majority by introducing a new dimension of political judgement and alignment – as when the issue of slavery was introduced in nineteenth-century US politics to split the Democratic party's vote.[48]

Riker described heresthetical politicians as innovators and opportunists, who have to be clever enough to find a new dimension that will upset a particular political equilibrium.[49] This goes beyond simply increasing the number of dimensions of political alignment; the new dimension has to be salient enough to turn opponents into allies. In fact politicians who win victory through manipulation of dimensions 'have set up the situation in such a way that other people will want to join them – or will feel forced by circumstances to join them – even without any persuasion at all'.[50] But it is unlikely that these innovating politicians will be pioneering. Riker described them as opportunists, not entrepreneurs, and they seem to be careerists introducing an adaptive innovation that has been forced upon them by their unsuccessful competition in the electoral/party sector. It is true that at least one example of non-careerist heresthetical innovation has been identified. The British parliament's Repeal of the Corn Laws in 1846 was apparently due not only to a heresthetical opening up of a new dimension (the preserving of public and social order) but also to non-careerist leadership by politicians who 'brought down their own political careers' by leading the campaign within parliament for Repeal.[51] However, this was a case of *legislative* rather than electoral pioneering, and was carried out by politicians who had already won the competition for leadership of the government and parliament.

Heresthetical electoral pioneering seems most likely to occur when a *new* competitor enters the electoral/party sector with a perhaps unintentionally heresthetical issue. If the new entrant is a crusader or has some other non-careerist motivation, this would be a case of pioneering initiative or creative response (even if the heresthetical innovation is socially dangerous rather than advantageous). Examples of this 'new entrant' version of heresthetic pioneer might be found in the 1980s–90s wave of new parties set up by political leaders who sought to exploit the anti-immigration race/ethnic issue, such as Le Pen's National Front in France and Hanson's One Nation party in Australia.[52] On closer examination, though, many of them might well prove to be outsider careerists (as described in Chapter 3) who were opportunistically exploiting the anti-immigration issue as part of an intentionally or unintentionally heresthetic electoral strategy.

A quite different sort of issue innovation occurs when an existing issue is *reframed* into a new and innovative issue. The effect produced by different ways of 'framing' a decision or choice has been elegantly compared to the effect produced by alternative perspectives on a visual scene, as when the relative height of peaks in a mountain range varies with the viewer's vantage point.[53] But the most influential notion of framing was put forward in Goffman's (1974) book *Frame Analysis: An Essay on the Organization of Experience*. He described a 'frame' as the principles or basic elements that organise individuals' experience of a social event; their subjective 'definitions of the situation' are constructed in accordance with these framing principles or elements.[54] Goffman's approach emerged from the interactionist–sociology tradition and its notion of defining the situation, which emphasised that definitions organise experience.[55] Tucker has argued that defining the situation authoritatively for a group is in fact the initial part of a leader's function of setting a direction for the group.[56] But *re*defining the situation may in itself set a new direction, indeed give a quite innovative lead, in similar fashion to identifying a problem without suggesting a solution. Although Goffman's book did not use the notion of *re*framing, it provided a set of categories to describe the shifting or transformation of a frame.[57] The closest to reframing seems to be the notion of fabrication, which applies to cases of inducing someone to have a false belief about what is going on.[58] Although the reframing of an issue cannot be viewed in terms of an objective truth or falsity, reframing may well involve convincing people that this new view of an issue is 'truer' than the older view.

The importance of changing how an issue is defined was noted by Baumgartner and Jones in their work on agenda-setting. They argued that changes in issue definition are more common than might be imagined and that 'fresh definitions of old issues' are often the way that new alternatives reach the decision-making stage of the political agenda, as with the redefinition of the pesticides issue to include damage to health and the environment.[59] They ascribed to policy entrepreneurs this role of redefining issues to appeal to the apathetic, to alter people's understanding of issues and to convince them that the entrepreneur's view of the issue is truer than opposing views of it.[60] But electoral issue pioneers, too, may benefit from the fact that 'when issues are redefined to bring in new participants', there is 'the potential for mobilizing the previously disinterested'.[61] Whether the pioneering politicians have themselves reframed the issues or have been sold them by pioneering policy advocates, a reframed electoral issue offers the potential for mobilising previously uninterested voters.

New entrants in the electoral/party sector seem particularly likely to engage in issue reframing. For example, in the 2000 US presidential campaign Nader reframed the issue of corporate power by talking of an 'apartheid economy' that served only the wealthy's interests, and Buchanan reframed the anti-abortion issue by denouncing the 'commissars' on the Supreme Court.[62] Further afield, the dog breeder and the tax lawyer who respectively founded the Progress parties of Norway and Denmark in the early 1970s reframed their anti-tax and anti-bureaucracy message into a populist issue: that the political establishment of professional politicians was unresponsive to the people's desire for less taxation and red tape.[63] In fact their founding of anti-establishment parties opposed to 'the politicians', 'the political boys' and the 'established politicians' gives them some claim to be pioneers of electoral tools as well as issues.[64]

6
Governmental (Executive) Pioneering

While Chapter 5 was focused on the selling of innovative election issues, this chapter and the next two look at the selling of innovative leads within the governmental and legislative sectors by the *winners* of the electoral competition for power. The electorate has entrusted them with a formal leader's power to decide, to give a lead that others are obliged to accept and follow, which enables them to engage in a *top-down* form of entrepreneurial-style, pioneering leadership. But these pioneering leads often must first be sold by formal leaders to one another, in the shape of legislative bills or proposals for government policy, before they can become authoritative leads that all citizens are obliged to accept and follow. The selling of bills within a congressional legislature will be examined in Chapter 8; the present chapter looks at the selling of policy proposals within a parliamentary democracy's government (executive).[1] Schumpeter described this collective, Cabinet form of government when presenting his 'English practice' model of democracy, as was discussed in Chapter 1, and so the more recent history of British Cabinet government seems the appropriate place to look for and assess 1960s–90s examples of the selling of pioneering leads within the governmental sector – the selling of innovative policy proposals in creative response to external change or through a spontaneous use of initiative.

However, such governmental pioneering does not include proposals to carry out an innovative measure that the government's party had already proposed during its successful electoral competition for power. For the government not only can therefore claim to have an electoral mandate for the measure but also has a politically self-interested, careerist motive to carry it out. In fact the carrying out of electoral commitments might well be described as a form of forced adaptive response to events in the electoral/party sector. Downs's theory of democracy long ago argued that a political party must maintain a reputation for reliability in carrying out electoral commitments or else the party will lose its electoral competitiveness: 'the struggle for votes compels all parties to be reliable'.[2] A substantial body of research has confirmed that party manifestos and other election pledges are good indicators of what policies an elected government will pursue.[3] And some recent theorising on electoral mandates noted that politicians are frequently faced with an obvious political incentive to carry out their electoral commitments: 'Voters may punish them if they don't.'[4] Cabinet Ministers' careerist rational self-interest can therefore be expected to stimulate them to carry out election commitments within their respective areas of government and to support one another's proposals to do so. A classic study of British Cabinet Ministers' executive leadership pointed out that Ministers may support a colleague's electorally mandated policy proposal 'even against their better judgement' because 'it is a question of honouring an election pledge'.[5] So there is ample reason to define governmental pioneering as not including policy proposals that have been foreshadowed in the government's party manifesto or other election pledges.

Furthermore, this chapter's assessment of the prevalence of governmental pioneering will focus on the *leader* of a Cabinet government – the Prime Minister. As was described in Chapter 1, Schumpeter focused on the Prime Ministership when presenting his British-based model of democracy, and even referred to the 'rule' and the 'programme' of the Prime Minister.[6] The next section of the chapter will provide an updated analysis of a British Prime Minister's potential for instituting a personal programme that includes entrepreneur-like, pioneering policy proposals. (Of course there are good careerist reasons why they might choose not to engage in pioneering, but that is a different question from whether they are able to do so and with what degree of difficulty.) Then the chapter examines the pioneering credentials of the two most powerful and important Prime Ministers of the 1960s–90s era: Thatcher and Blair. The former was the dominating leader of the most innovative government of the era and the latter seemed to institutionalise his dominance through a structural centralisation of government that may have significantly enhanced the prime-ministerial potential for pioneering leadership.

The British Prime Minister as potential pioneer

Schumpeter's 1940s account of the Prime Minister's role in British government has at least not been overtaken by later developments and become seriously outdated. In the mid-1990s the Prime Minister's 'potential influence and the repertoire of roles open to him or her' had probably not changed much 'from 30 or even 60 years ago'.[7] And the Blair centralisation of the late 1990s would appear to have made Schumpeter's prime-minister-centred account of British government all the more relevant.

However, there must be doubts about the validity and internal consistency of Schumpeter's account, as when he described the British Prime Minister as having a *programme*. He could not have thought that this was equivalent or comparable to the programme of a US President. The Bureau of the Budget had already institutionalised the notion of the 'programme of the President', and the Bureau's centralised clearance process for civil service departments' and bureaus' requests for legislation would decide whether the proposed bill was in accord with the President's programme, consistent with his objectives, or at the very least not opposed by him.[8] In contrast, there has never been an even informally recognised 'programme of the Prime Minister'; the nearest British equivalent to a President's programme is the election manifesto of the government's *party*. The party manifesto could in practice be virtually the Prime Minister's personal programme if, as leader of the party, he or she had played a dominant role in deciding its contents. But as governmental pioneering does not include policies that are merely fulfilling electoral commitments, the pioneering aspects of any prime-ministerial programme would by definition have to come from some other source than an election manifesto. Whatever that source might be, Schumpeter acknowledged that for a Prime Minister to be 'in a position to impose measures about a political issue which he has created himself' is a 'case of the most brilliant achievement'.[9]

This remark is also an instance of the striking contradiction between Schumpeter's reference to prime-ministerial *rule* and his acknowledgements of the Prime Minister's lack of power. As was described in Chapter 1, Schumpeter's model of democratic government contained an acute analysis of the competitive careerist pressures that forced a British Prime Minister to adopt a conciliatory attitude towards Cabinet Ministers and would deter him or her from personal policy initiatives that might be viewed by Ministers as competing with them for leadership over their particular areas of government. His model's analysis presents a very different picture from a study of innovative policy leadership during the Thatcher era that pointed to her skill in 'selecting able lieutenants' and dealt with 'the question of how much of Thatcher's government's impact can be attributed to her' by assuming that 'policies (innovative or otherwise) for the decade of her reign bore Thatcher's impress'.[10] But such key lieutenants of the early 1980s as Tebbit, Howe and Lawson have also been described as 'powerful allies-cum-rivals' with whom the Prime Minister eventually fell out – and who fell or were pushed out of Cabinet.[11] After she and her allies had won the early 1980s dry/wet factional struggle within Cabinet, she saw these allies become her rivals for leadership of the government or of a specialised area of government, as in her conflict with Foreign Secretary Howe and Chancellor Lawson over their belief in joining the EU's Exchange Rate Mechanism.[12] Furthermore, her two antagonists' departure from Cabinet proved to be a costly victory that, according to conventional wisdom, weakened her leadership of the party and government and thereby contributed to her failure in 1990 to be reelected party leader on the first ballot.

So it seems that any Prime Minister would find it problematic to sell entrepreneurial-like, pioneering policy proposals to Cabinet colleagues. Prime Ministers who sell policy proposals to their colleagues have lowered themselves to the position of an ordinary Minister, for whom the Cabinet has traditionally been 'a forum in which he fights for his department's policy proposals, for Treasury money and for Parliamentary time' to pass legislation.[13] In this forum the Prime Minister's policy proposal will face competition from several different directions. As it will probably fall within a particular policy area, the proposal is likely to be viewed as a competitive challenge by the Minister responsible for that area of government and policy. One or more other Ministers are likely to view it as a competitive challenge to their departments' interests; any seller of policy proposals 'is always likely to have to defend his proposals against damaging amendments proposed by cabinet colleagues' seeking to protect their departments' interests.[14] And in addition to competition from particular Ministers over the content of proposals, there is that general and underlying competition among Ministers for (1) funding from the government's limited budgetary resources and (2) time on the government's crowded legislative agenda.[15]

Of course these various competitive pressures also provide an important selection process for the preservation or elimination of a policy proposal that has not been subjected to the competitive pressures of an election campaign. But they make it difficult for a Prime Minister to sell a policy proposal without becoming involved in a competitive struggle, and the struggle is likely to be both more intense and more widespread if the proposal is a pioneering one. For pioneering policies risk being electorally unpopular and raise the threat of voters' retribution at the next election. This endangers every Minister's career prospects and is therefore likely to stimulate general and strong opposition to the proposal. Indeed the most likely reason for a Prime Minister losing favour with party colleagues 'is the fear that the government will lose the next election under the existing leadership'.[16]

On the other hand, the position of Prime Minister has some inherent strengths that can assist the selling of a pioneering policy proposal. Schumpeter's belief that a Prime Minister can achieve an above-parties leadership of public opinion (as was described in Chapter 1) suggests the Prime Minister might well succeed in selling the public a pioneering policy proposal. In other words, there might be a prime-ministerial version of US Presidents' use of the 'bully pulpit' for what Neustadt described as 'presidential teaching' of the public.[17] The Prime Minister could thereby ease other Ministers' fear of electoral retribution by pointing to public opinion polls favouring the innovation. However, they might take a more jaundiced view of the situation and compare it to US Presidents' tactic of 'going public', of unilaterally shifting the arena of debate away from private negotiations with Congress by making a public appeal to the people to support the President's legislative proposals.[18]

Similarly, Prime Ministers can actually impose a pioneering policy on Cabinet by exploiting their role as the government's principal spokesperson. A Prime Minister can commit the government to particular policies by 'impromptu public comments' and use that public promise to push in private for the government to carry out that commitment.[19] A prime-ministerial committal of the government is particularly likely in foreign affairs, partly because of the number of international gatherings and summit meetings in which heads of state or government are expected to speak for their government and nation.[20] But a Prime Minister will not be able to impose a major foreign policy innovation in this way. Joining the EEC/EU required much more of Prime Minister Heath than some impromptu public comments, and in fact since then Britain has seen no major prime-ministerial foreign policy innovations – certainly nothing comparable to Canadian Prime Minister Mulroney's instigating and negotiating of a Free Trade Agreement with the US.[21]

The spokesperson role also strengthens a prime-ministerial bargaining chip – the right to veto other Ministers' policy proposals. As leader of party and government the Prime Minister has an informal right to veto policy proposals that conflict with the party's election-manifesto commitments or would politically damage the government in some other way.[22] And this is strengthened by a principal spokesperson's right to raise objections to policy proposals that will be difficult for a spokesperson to present and defend. A Prime Minister's veto over government policy making is therefore comparable to the US President's over congressional law making (though the prime-ministerial veto, like the presidential, can be overridden when it goes against a strong current of opinion).[23] The fact that the prime-ministerial vetoing differs from the presidential in being informal, private and within the government probably increases its effectiveness as a bargaining chip that deters negative responses to the Prime Minister's own policy proposals and may secure a quid pro quo acceptance of them.

Prime Ministers' role of government chairperson, too, provides them with policy-selling opportunities. The chairperson's responsibility for preparing the meeting's agenda ensures that a Prime Minister has some formal opportunity to sell a policy proposal to Cabinet. But Schumpeter pointed out that the government's agenda is dominated by 'the incessant stream of current problems', including the 'legacy of open questions' inherited from the preceding government as well as those matters that are 'taken up as a matter of routine politics'.[24] The need to make adaptive responses to these past and present events leaves little time on the agenda (or indeed on the prime-ministerial schedule) for the Prime Minister's personal policy proposals.

As for the chairperson's responsibility for summing up the discussion, this seems to provide an opportunity for ensuring that there will be a favourable collective decision about any prime-ministerial policy proposal. The Prime Minister is responsible for summing up Cabinet discussion into a coherent decision that can be entered in the minutes as official government policy and a directive to civil servants.[25] This gives Prime Ministers an opportunity to push through their own views, as a summing up is a weighing of opinions rather than a counting of heads and is expected to give special weight to the opinions of senior Ministers.[26] But in practice only occasionally will a Prime Minister – when feeling strongly about a matter – feel entitled and be allowed to make a summing-up decision that goes against the consensus of the meeting.[27] Moreover, Prime Ministers cannot get away with introducing and approving policy proposals in the summing up; it can be used only as a last reserve that is thrown in to rescue a proposal from defeat.

Prime Ministers are presumably less likely to be in that desperate situation if they normally tend to dominate Cabinet's discussions. The extent to which they dominate discussion depends not only on their leadership capacities (as was described in Chapter 1) but also on their leadership style, particularly their willingness to give a lead in discussions outside their areas of policy interest and expertise. For example, Prime Minister Wilson was 'content to let colleagues provide a lead' in areas outside his policy interests in foreign affairs and economic matters, but Thatcher gave a lead much more frequently – and in a more aggressive and up-front style.[28] Yet even she normally waited until after the Minister responsible for the area of policy under discussion had been given an opportunity to 'lead off' the discussion.[29] For often the relevant Minister has brought the item or proposal to Cabinet for discussion, and usually has much more expertise than the Prime Minister does in this area of policy – if only because of the staff resources available to the Minister as head of the relevant department of the civil service. Prime Minister Thatcher's total staff numbered fewer than a hundred and included only a handful of policy experts, the Policy Unit, which was concerned with monitoring policies and assessing Ministers' policy proposals.[30] (The nearest British equivalent of a US President's huge Office of Management and Budget is the Treasury department, headed by the Chancellor rather than the Prime Minister.) In fact pre-Thatcher Prime Ministers had tended to intervene in Cabinet discussions only when the topic was within the policy area of a department that they had headed earlier in their ministerial career: 'in those circumstances the Prime Minister knew the arguments; otherwise he could not be expected to intervene'.[31]

The lack of staff resources is also a major limitation on a Prime Minister's ability to develop personal policy proposals, especially if it is an innovative proposal blazing a new trail in a highly technical area of public policy. Proposing innovations in foreign policy may be within the grasp of a gifted amateur but proposing innovations in such policy areas as defence, taxation, health, education and welfare requires assistance from professionally expert and administratively knowledgeable staff. Without their assistance, prime-ministerial brainwaves cannot be converted into credible proposals for government policy.

However, a pioneering Prime Minister can overcome the problem of staff resources – and remove a source of ministerial competition – by having the proposal developed and sold under the auspices of the Minister specialising in that area of government and policy. It has long been recognised that a Prime Minister may provide the initial impulse for another Minister's policy proposal and 'may be every bit as responsible for some policies as the Ministers who nominally sponsor them'.[32] These situations may be confused with or mistaken for instances of the Prime Minister *buying into* a Minister's proposal and helping to sell it to other members of the government.[33] But they can readily be distinguished from prime-ministerial 'buy ins' by identifying who did the initial selling to whom.

By exploiting the wide range of means and opportunities available to them Prime Ministers have the potential to sell – successfully – at least an occasional pioneering policy proposal. Even such an apparently weak Prime Minister as John Major was able to do some successful prime-ministerial pioneering. He has been accused of not projecting 'a strong sense of policy direction' and not providing 'a firm personal lead from the top', but it is also acknowledged that this lack of firm leadership was at least partly because he presided over a Cabinet containing several party-heavyweight Ministers and over a party that was fiercely divided by the question of Britain's integration within the European Union.[34] The Prime Minister's weak position was perhaps epitomised by the fact that he was blocked by Chancellor Clarke and a majority of the Cabinet when he planned to increase spending on education but was himself unable to block Chancellor Clarke's politically unpopular increases in fuel taxes.[35] Yet Major was able to impose on his apathetic colleagues (and a sceptical civil service) his pioneering Citizen's Charter for improving the quality, efficiency and user-friendliness of public services.[36] And although he has been described as an only 'incremental' constitutional reformer, he pushed through significant reforms of the idiosyncratic secretiveness of British governmental and administrative institutions.[37] His example therefore suggests that entrepreneurial-style, pioneering leadership is indeed a matter of what Prime Ministers choose and are able to do.

The next section will confirm this impression by examining an example of an exceptionally strong Prime Minister, Margaret Thatcher, who also led the most innovative government of the 1960s–90s era.[38] She was apparently able to be an entrepreneurial-style, pioneering leader but chose instead to be a *chooser* of policy proposals developed by her Ministers, who provided her with some pioneering proposals to choose from – and by no means all of which she accepted. Her role as leader was therefore to choose whether to reject, buy or buy into policy proposals being sold by the specialised Ministers. When she chose to buy or buy into a pioneering proposal, it would usually be bought by Cabinet and become government policy. But this was not so much a case of prime-ministerial pioneering as of a form of collective pioneering in which the leadership shifted from one specialist Minister to another.

Looking for pioneering PMs: Margaret Thatcher

The obvious place to go looking for examples of prime-ministerial pioneering is Margaret Thatcher's eleven-year tenure of the office. Not only did these years see a marked change in the direction of economic and social policy but also the Prime Minister appeared to play such a pivotal role in this change that observers often used the term 'Thatcherism' to describe the new policy direction. Although Thatcherism covered a wide range of policies, three innovative economic policies seem to exemplify the radical nature of Thatcherist government: (1) the monetarist public-spending cuts in the early, struggling years of government factionalism and unpopularity, (2) the privatisation drive in the middle, politically successful years and (3) the poll tax in the middle and then final, declining years. But on closer examination it appears that none of these three policies was actually the product of personal pioneering by the Prime Minister. She appears to be less the pioneering leader of a dominant government and more the dominant leader of a pioneering government.

As Chapter 5 described, the Thatcher-led Conservative party had raised the innovative monetarist economic issue in the 1979 election campaign. The party's election manifesto had committed a Conservative government to 'publicly stated targets for the rate of growth of the money supply' as well as a 'gradual reduction in the size of the Government's borrowing requirement'.[39] Even if the newly elected Prime Minister had not been a convinced monetarist, she would have had to make some move towards carrying out her party's electoral commitment to a monetarist economic approach – and certainly this would not have been a case of governmental pioneering leadership. But the 1980 budget's introduction of a Medium-Term Financial Strategy (MTFS) focused on M3 money supply *was* a case of governmental pioneering. (Many would also argue that it was a classic case of the risks that governmental pioneering can pose to the community.) The MTFS was actually a global policy innovation, even if only in the strategy for applying monetarist theory to macroeconomic policy.

However, the MTFS was the Chancellor's policy innovation, not the Prime Minister's, and her support for it was a case of buying into his policy proposal, not of selling her own proposal to Cabinet.[40] It is true, though, that her buying into the MTFS was a crucial aspect of its acceptance as government policy. The majority of her Cabinet Ministers, including the party heavyweights, were sceptical about the monetarist approach to economic policy.[41] As monetarism was an electorally manifestoed and mandated policy, the Prime Minister could readily justify her determination to override any opposition from these sceptical Ministers, the so-called 'wets', to the introduction of a monetarist economic approach.[42] But she had also taken care when forming her new government to appoint fellow-believers in monetarism to the key economic posts in Cabinet: Chancellor of the Exchequer (Howe), Chief Secretary to the Treasury (Biffen), and the Ministries of Industry (Joseph), Trade (Nott), and Energy (Howell).[43] Such a phalanx of monetarists in the economically specialised Cabinet posts 'constituted a formidable force driving policy forward', and was made more effective by the Prime Minister's strategy of keeping economic policy off the Cabinet agenda – leaving discussion and decisions on economic policy to be made in the Cabinet committee on Future Economic Policy and in less formal meetings of the economic Ministers.[44] Consequently, there was no prospect of monetarism being only a secondary or electorally cosmetic aspect of economic policy. It made itself felt in the 1979 budget, became very evident in the 1980 budget with the emergence of the MTFS and triumphed in the 1981 budget, which brought the MTFS back on course by making a substantial reduction in the Public Sector Borrowing Requirement (PSBR) – despite the country's deepening recession and very high levels of unemployment.[45]

The strength of the Prime Minister's support for Howe's Medium-Term Financial Strategy, and the limits of her prime-ministerial potential for pioneering, were illustrated later in 1981 when his Strategy's PSBR targets demanded a new round of public spending cuts. The Prime Minister had to seek the full Cabinet's approval for these cutbacks in the spending Ministers' budgets, and the 23 July 1981 Cabinet meeting has been described as 'a time when outright disagreement, amounting to almost open rebellion, reached a climax never attained before or after'.[46] When Chancellor Howe demanded five billion pounds in public-spending cuts, he unleashed such a storm of anti-monetarist protest from the 'wets' that the Prime Minister, after initially supporting the Chancellor, summed up in a more neutral fashion that implicitly acknowledged defeat.[47] This was one of the three occasions when she was overruled 'on issues so crucial to the government's policies that they could easily have broken her administration'.[48] (The other two occasions were her 1982 attempt to have the government radically rethink public expenditure and her later-1980s vetoing of ERM-membership.) However, she was being overruled not as an entrepreneurial-style, pioneering leader but as a Prime Minister who had bought into her Chancellor's pioneering strategy for carrying out an electoral commitment.

Perhaps the closest she ever came to personal pioneering was when she backed a September 1982 Central Policy Review Staff paper proposing radical reductions in public spending, such as replacing the public health system with private health insurance. Although this CPRS paper had been sponsored by the Treasury, it was circulated to Cabinet Ministers on the Prime Minister's authority and only a few months after her personal standing in the opinion polls had almost doubled to 44 per cent with the successful completion of the Falklands war.[49] In addition to enjoying much increased personal prestige, she was leading a Cabinet that she had culled of several 'wets' after her July 1981 defeat.[50] Yet a majority of the Cabinet were strongly enough opposed to the CPRS paper to 'persuade' her to shelve it. If she had successfully sold these politically extreme proposals to her Cabinet colleagues, it would have been an example of truly brilliant entrepreneurial-style, pioneering leadership by a Prime Minister – and would almost certainly have led to defeat in the 1983 election.

By 1983 Prime Minister Thatcher appeared a strong but not personally innovative leader. At the time Burch's analysis of her leadership described the Prime Minister's purpose as 'to maintain and manage policy, not to initiate or recreate it'.[51] Several years later Young would argue that she lacked any conceptual plan, let alone ideological blueprint, for achieving her vision of a better Britain and that in her second term of office (1983–87) Thatcherism became increasingly pragmatic.[52] The monetarist MTFS focus on growth of M3 money supply was abandoned and so, too, was the old goal of reducing the level of public spending in real terms. The new goal of reducing or at least not increasing the public sector's share of GDP meant that the extra tax revenues, the fiscal dividend, produced by a now growing economy could be used for billions of pounds of increased public spending. However, as Young acknowledged, the government was not pragmatically thinking in terms of how to spend the new revenue but instead was giving highest priority to the 1979 electoral promise of steady reductions in the rate of income tax – the standard rate had been reduced from 33 per cent to 27 per cent by 1987.[53] So the Prime Minister still felt the same determination to curb public spending, as she expressed in her new term of abuse for unsatisfactory Ministers: 'He's a spender'.[54] She became 'notoriously impatient with proposals for new policy', which usually were also proposing some increase in public spending, and it has been argued that her prime-ministerial veto helped to prevent the degree of increased spending on new and old policy programmes that would have occurred under any previous post-1945 British government.[55]

But she had another, more active and much more innovative way of securing the funds for tax cuts – a massive privatisation of state-owned industries. The process had begun almost inadvertently in her first term with a series of ad hoc privatisations but became a self-conscious privatisation drive in her second term. Seven more state-owned companies were sold off and there was a steady increase in the proceeds from 1.4 billion pounds in 1983/84 to 4.7 billion in 1986/87 – equivalent to 2.6 per cent of annual government expenditure.[56] Such an extensive privatisation was globally unique, and by the time she left office in 1990 it had led to almost half of the public sector being transferred to the private sector.[57] The *method* of privatisation was also globally innovative. There was a successful effort to spread the privatised shareholding as widely as possible and thus markedly increase the number of people in society who owned shares: the shareowning 'class' increased from only 7 per cent of society to some 20 per cent during the Thatcher years.[58] And it could be argued that a third innovative aspect of privatisation was its use as a 'partisan social engineering' means of shaping voter preferences. For Dunleavy mentioned Thatcherism's huge expansion of the shareowning section of society in his description of the ways that a government can shape voter preferences through social engineering (and another example he pointed to was the Thatcher government's massive sell-off of council houses to their tenants, in over-fulfilment of a 1979 electoral commitment).[59] Finally, privatisation also brought an innovation in political *message*, with such language as 'taking capitalism to the people' being used to justify the aim of increasing the number of first-time shareholders.[60] In 1986 the Prime Minister declared publicly that 'popular capitalism' had 'only just got started' and would be broadened through more privatisations.[61]

But the privatisation drive's innovative aspects were a creative response rather than a product of pioneering initiative. And they were an only partly pioneering, creative response to *several* past, present and future events: (1) the ad hoc privatisations in the government's first term that were motivated largely by the monetarist concern with reducing the PSBR; (2) the need to sell shares to the masses to help sell off the massive four-billion-pound British Telecom share issue that had been initiated in the first term; (3) the post-monetarist problem of how to finance the promised tax cuts while also easing restraints on public spending; (4) the need for a distinctive new policy to fill a post-monetarist 'ideas vacuum' in the government's second term, when it often seemed to lack direction, and (5) the looming problem of finding a vote-winning policy that would ensure electoral success when the government sought a third term.[62] Obviously the privatisation drive did not take the normal shape of a creative response, and was not 'proposed' within government by a particular individual as a particular policy proposal. It seems to have developed almost incrementally and inadvertently until reaching the stage where it could be almost collectively recognised and further developed as a creative response to the government's present and future problems.

Certainly the Prime Minister does not appear to have provided the initial impulse in the development of the privatisation drive. Although in the late 1970s she had been receptive to the idea of privatisation, she had also displayed some political nervousness about it – publicly disowning an inner-party report on privatisation and presenting an election manifesto that promised merely less government control, not privatisation, of state-owned industries.[63] Nor did she play a prominent role in instigating the early privatisations. In Zahariadis's case study of the first-term privatisation of Britoil, the only Minister mentioned is Energy Minister Howell, who seems to have played an important role in instigating and pushing through privatisation.[64] Similarly, in his case study of the pivotal British Telecom privatisation (which carried over from the government's first term into the second and whose size led to the first mass-marketing of shares), it is not the Prime Minister but the Cabinet and the Ministers of Industry who play noteworthy roles. The only mention of the Prime Minister is her *failed* attempt to have British Telecom privatised in the more liberalised, but less lucrative, form of several regional companies rather than a massive nationwide company.[65] Although in 1983 she did present an election manifesto that contained promises to privatise several state-owned industries, this was by no means a bugle call for 'popular capitalism' – the whole manifesto was quite deliberately kept bland and matter of fact.[66] When the privatisation drive got under way in her second term, she was indeed its most important publicist.[67] But this is only what would be expected of a Prime Minister enthusiastically fulfilling her role as the government's principal spokesperson. Her contribution to the development of the privatisation drive seems to have been one of buying into it as a creative response, most likely some time early in her second term, and then enthusiastically selling it to the public.

A similar pattern of prime-ministerial behaviour can be seen, much more clearly, in the case of the innovative 'community charge': the poll tax.[68] The problem that the poll tax was intended to solve had arisen from the Thatcher government's early determination and inability to control *local* governments' public expenditure, which was partly financed by the local property-tax system of 'rates'. In the government's second term the Cabinet Minister responsible for local government instigated a wideranging search for solutions by a study team of civil servants and two junior Ministers, Baker and Waldegrave. They eventually came to the conclusion that introducing a local poll tax was the best way of replacing the rates with a system that ensured all voters would contribute directly to financing their elected local government and would feel the full marginal effect of increases in its spending.[69] Back in the real world, a political crisis over the Scottish rating system was forcing the government to search for an appropriately remedial response, and it has been suggested that such 'external shocks' from the local-government sector were pushing the Prime Minister towards embracing the notion of replacing the rates with a poll tax.[70] Her buying into the proposal for a poll tax seems therefore to be more a matter of a creative response to a minor political crisis than of buying into a spontaneous use of initiative that aimed to solve a longstanding problem.

The poll tax was said by the Prime Minister to have been born at a 31 March 1985 meeting, attended by her and many Cabinet Ministers, in which she bought into the proposal to introduce a 'community charge'.[71] The meeting occurred at the Prime Minister's country residence, Chequers, and was held for the sole purpose of listening to and considering Baker and Waldegrave's proposal for a poll tax. This was typical of the Prime Minister's preference for semi-formal, ad hoc meetings rather than the formal and systematic procedures of Cabinet meetings.[72] And the less formal setting may have helped the two junior Ministers make such an effective sales pitch that the Prime Minister was won over and enthusiastically bought into the proposal. She has been described as being 'converted' by the Chequers meeting and as thereafter showing 'the zeal of a convert'.[73] More prosaically, in September she promoted Baker to the Cabinet post, Minister of the Environment, that would be responsible for having the poll-tax proposal formally accepted by Cabinet and then piloting a poll-tax bill through parliament's legislative process.[74] Not surprisingly, his poll-tax proposal had a smooth passage through the process of formal endorsement by a Cabinet committee and then by the full Cabinet – on 9 January 1986, the policy's official date of birth. It was apparently accepted by the voters in the 1987 election, though the Labour party had decided not to make an election issue of the poll tax's flaws, and after the election the Prime Minister described the poll tax as 'the flagship of the Thatcher fleet'.[75]

But in fact she had merely bought into a pioneering policy proposal that had been sold to her by two junior Ministers who had apparently acquired a lot of expertise in that policy area. As in earlier cases of policy innovation, the pioneering had really been done by the specialised Ministers rather than the Prime Minister. Whereas in earlier cases it was such senior Ministers as Chancellor Howe, in this case it was a pair of highly committed junior Ministers, Baker and Waldegrave.[76] It has been suggested that their commitment to finding a solution to the rates problem had been motivated by a desire to show the Prime Minister that they were reliable Thatcherites.[77] However, the solution that they eventually proposed was not the one that a rational careerist would have put forward – it was too innovative and politically risky to be likely to meet with prime-ministerial approval. It would have to overcome not only her 'pragmatic cynicism about the impossibility of abolishing the rates' but also her usual cautiousness and expert assessment of what the voters would buy.[78] If on this occasion she had correctly assessed the long-term electoral dangers of the poll tax, she would probably have rejected the proposal and its promoters as politically naive and dangerous. Their ministerial careers may well have been permanently blighted and their fate would have been pointed to as an example of the risks involved in pioneering. Instead the poll tax debacle would become a striking example of how buying into a creative response can blight and endanger the career of a Prime Minister. While the privatisation drive had shown the potential political payoffs of creative responses, the poll tax would very clearly display the downside risks of opting for a creative rather than adaptive response. The fervent public opposition to the implementation of the poll tax would cast a shadow over the government's third term and, according to conventional wisdom, was an important factor in the Prime Minister's failure to win the 1990 party leadership election on the first ballot.

But during her long tenure of office this most radical of British Prime Ministers had normally been quite wary of pioneering – and certainly showed little inclination to indulge in it personally by selling pioneering policy proposals to her Cabinet. Although Weller pointed to her as an example of the 'initiator' type of Prime Minister, she is better described as an example of his other category: the 'arbiter' type of Prime Minister.[79] Perhaps the best description of her role is that of a *chooser*, and she herself once claimed to have a constitutional responsibility to choose policy.[80] This quite well describes:

> the hold she personally exerted over a quite unusually high proportion of the policies her Government pursued. What she supported tended to happen. What she neglected or opposed tended not to

happen. What she permitted but did not support, might happen, but only in a context where she had openly distanced herself from the consequences and therefore assisted in the enfeeblement of what she allowed others to do.[81]

In other words, (1) if the Prime Minister bought into a Minister's policy proposal, the government collectively would very likely buy it as an official government policy, (2) if she opposed or even merely overlooked a proposal, the government collectively was very unlikely to buy it, and (3) if she bought a proposal but without enthusiasm, the government collectively might buy it but she would openly decline to sell this new government policy to the public.

However, the fact that this dominating Prime Minister was not selling her *own* policy proposals meant that the specialised Ministers were at least not facing competition from her. To that extent the Prime Minister was encouraging other Ministers to pursue their careerist self-interest or pioneering inclinations by trying to sell new or truly innovative policy proposals to her and the other members of the government. There was still the usual form of inter-ministerial competition in selling policy proposals, whether involving actual policy matters or just the under-lying general competition for budget resources and for Cabinet and legislative agenda time. This form of competition was normally moti-vated by the Ministers' careerist competition for advancement within the government (as by successfully selling policy proposals Ministers helped to establish personal as well as formal leadership of their special-ised areas of government and thus enhanced their prospects of career advancement). But not all the competing policy proposals were career-ist; there were also some pioneering initiatives or creative responses that had arisen from ministerial brainwaves or from ministerial buying and on-selling of administrators' pioneering proposals.

By selling some non-careerist, pioneering proposals to their col-leagues, members of the Thatcher Cabinet enabled their government to develop and maintain some pioneering momentum. A series of differ-ent Ministers successfully selling a pioneering proposal to their leader and colleagues can produce a series of innovative laws and government policies that is comparable to the programme of a personally pioneering Prime Minister. It is true that a collectively pioneering government's series of innovations is likely to be less coherent and systematic than a Prime Minister's personal programme of innovations. But it is also likely to be less prone to the burn-out problem seen in the presidential, one-person form of government. The American experience suggests that new Presidents tend to lose their innovative inclinations after their early, honeymoon months in power and thereafter are interested in making only incremental changes.[82] In contrast, the British experience with the long-lived Thatcher government suggests that a quite rapid turnover of Ministers, as members of Cabinet and as Ministers of particular departments, can enable a collective government to maintain its pioneering momentum for a decade or more – and can explain the 'puzzle' of 'the capacity of Thatcherism to renew itself and regain its radical momentum'.[83] But in the next section the focus will be on a Prime Minister who has carried out a structural centralisation that seems to favour pioneering by the Prime Minister personally rather than by a collectively pioneering government.

Looking for pioneering PMs: Tony Blair

As Margaret Thatcher chose to be a policy-choosing rather than policy-pioneering leader, it is hard to judge what she might have been able to do in the way of personal pioneering if she had been willing to make the effort and take the risks. But the other dominant Prime Minister of the 1960s–90s era, Tony Blair, established in his first term a more centralised structure of government that gave the Prime Minister a greater ability to engage in personal pioneering. It is too early to judge whether Blair made a permanent structural change in British government. The pendulum could swing back quite dramatically towards a more collegial form of leadership, as occurred when the dominant Thatcher was replaced as party leader and Prime Minister by John Major. 'A Prime Minister who leaves because of electoral defeat will be immediately discredited and create a reaction against him, and this is also true of a Prime Minister who leaves when colleagues reckon he or she has passed a "sell by" date'.[84] Nonetheless, Blair's changes were a significant development that strengthened the prime-ministerial leadership role and gave the Prime Minister a greater potential to engage in a centralised programme of pioneering.

Blair quickly established a new structure as well as style of government after his 1997 election victory ended nearly 20 years of Conservative governments. The most obvious feature was his downplaying of the traditional parliamentary and Cabinet aspects of British democracy. Thanks to the Labour party's huge (179-seat) and obedient majority in parliament, he was able to reduce his physical presence in and around parliament to a new low for British Prime Ministers.[85] More importantly, his apparent disdain for the collegial processes of Cabinet and its committees led to the demise of a system of collective govern-ment that had been operated, in varying ways, by all previous Prime Ministers; the Cabinet and its committees would now be used merely 'for purposes of laying down an "audit trail" in the manner of com-pany boards'.[86] Blair preferred a system of (1) informal ad hoc meetings with some chosen Ministers and (2) bilateral dealings with individual Ministers, which included meeting with each of them individually to develop their personal 'work programmes' and to monitor their progress in achieving these agreed targets.[87] He was fortunate to have what has been described as an 'extraordinarily pliant Cabinet' that, unlike pre-vious Labour governments, did not contain 'a large number of heavy-weight ministers, who commanded followings among MPs, and whose resignations would have rocked the government'.[88] The only exception was the Chancellor, Gordon Brown, who was the heir-apparent to Blair and had his own parliamentary following – which may explain why they shared power to a greater degree than any previous combination of Prime Minister and Chancellor.[89]

Indeed a crucial feature of Blair's centralisation is that collective government was replaced by not one-person but *two*-person government. Hennessy has pointed out that the Blair structure involved a command Chancellor operating alongside a command Prime Minister in a 'cen-tralised duopoly'; the diminishing of other Ministers and suppressing of Cabinet collegiality was epitomised by not only 'Tony wants' but also 'Gordon requires'.[90] Brown's leadership in the area of economic policy was acknowledged by Blair in such institutional ways as allow-ing the Chancellor to chair the Cabinet's main economic committee, which traditionally was chaired by the Prime Minister.[91] Brown was also given a stronger system of Treasury control over public spending than any previous Chancellor. Under the new system, the Treasury was to release each periodic instalment of public funds to the spend-ing Ministries only after they had achieved targets or outcomes agreed in advance with Treasury officials.[92] In addition to strengthening the Chancellor's traditional role in economic policy and control of public spending, Blair allowed him to extend his reach into social policy, as when Brown took a leading role in designing the new form of welfare-to-work programme.[93] Prime Minister Blair's share of domestic policy covered those areas in which he had some policy interests – health, education, transport and crime – but he would be so absorbed in the standard prime-ministerial concerns with foreign policy and Northern Ireland that he had much less time than the Chancellor for taking an interest in domestic policy.[94]

The sharing of power between Blair and Brown led to comparisons with the dual executive of the French semi-presidential system.[95] But the Blair structure should be compared to only those semi-presidential situations in which the Prime Minister is more than merely the instrument or loyal lieutenant of the President. For Brown was the 'second biggest beast' in the party as well as government, with a rival 'court' to Blair's, and it has been confirmed by a neutral party figure that 'Tony will not take Gordon on'.[96] Perhaps the best comparison is with the late 1990s sharing of power in China between the Communist party's top-ranking leader, General Secretary Jiang Zemin, and its second-ranking leader, state Premier Zhu Rongji. While Zhu was in charge of the economy, Jiang was in charge of the 'overall situation' but with particular emphasis on party affairs, foreign policy and the military.[97]

From Blair's perspective, though, the key to understanding his new structure was not the two-person government but the *centralisation* of control in an organisational rather than personal 'centre' that included the Treasury and Cabinet Office as well as the Prime Minister's office.[98] Apparently Blair entered power with a determination to prevent departmentalism and ministerial 'feudal baronies', and several years later he was still expressing his concern that Ministers wanting 'to make a personal mark or who go native in the departments can easily lose sight of their role in contributing to the wider government programme'.[99] Clearly he was not concerned about the possibility that without Ministers' personal or on-sold departmental policy proposals, the government's programme might run out of ideas and be reduced to nothing more than making adaptive responses to events. His concern with central control led him to establish prime-ministerial (office) control over Ministers' presenting new policy ideas to the public, as otherwise: 'An interesting idea injected into the media will be taken as a statement of Government policy.'[100] By such means he restricted the specialised Ministers' ability to compete with the centre in selling policy proposals, and thereby increased his potential to institute a centralised, systematic programme of governmental pioneering.

But although Blair was more structurally able than other Prime Ministers to be a pioneer, he did not choose to be one – he showed little interest in governmental pioneering. He was described by various political analysts as being 'averse to taking personal policy initiatives', as a 'preference-accommodator' rather than a shaper of voter preferences, and as 'a more cautious leader' than might be expected – 'reluctant to take risks'.[101] More than five years after he came to power it was still being politely suggested that the 'cautious populist has so far usually had the upper hand over the visionary leader'.[102]

An institutional indication of his lack of interest in prime-ministerial pioneering was his failure to provide himself with the necessary staff resources. Although he doubled the size of his staff's Policy Unit, its 14 staff members were still far too few for developing a policy programme – and the majority of them were actually involved in some form of political communication rather than policy role.[103] In fact his staff seemed to be focused on the Prime Minister's traditional role of being the government's principal spokesperson. Their main ambition was to be the dominant department in presenting the government's message, not the dominant department in initiating the government's policy innovations.[104] It is true that a Performance and Innovation Unit and a Social Exclusion Unit were set up and housed within the Cabinet Office (another indication of the concern with organisational rather than merely personal centralisation of government) but their research and reports do not appear to have stimulated new policy programmes and legislation.[105] Indeed the Prime Minister's personal political lieutenant eventually declared that the leadership needed to be shown in the policy-delivering Ministries rather than the centre.[106] But Blair's centralised structure of government did not encourage his Ministers to show some leadership in their specialised areas of government, such as by trying to sell pioneering policy proposals.

The lack of pioneering impetus from both the centre and the Ministries would contribute to one of the paradoxes of Blair's Prime Ministership. He focused so much effort on purportedly 'modernising' the Prime Minister's role of government spokesperson that he created a credibility gap between his emphasis on communication and his lack of anything substantive to communicate. Blair put more effort than any other Prime Minister into being 'communicator-in-chief', and established a 'media-driven' style and process of government.[107] His critics would argue that in fact soundbite and spin, focus group and media event characterised his government better than any ideological or policy approach. But eventually the lack of substantive content in the media message led to public disillusionment, with Blair's own political strategist reporting that the public was increasingly viewing the Prime Minister as all spin and presentation, as just saying things to please people rather than because he believed them.[108] Rose has argued that Blair's 'managed populism' was a form of 'politics without policy' that contrasted with Thatcherism's divisive but clear identification of policy choices.[109] He has also pointed to the incongruity of Blair copying

President Clinton's concern with approval ratings, with the need to win a daily mandate, when Blair enjoyed such a secure majority in parliament (unlike President Clinton's need to get his bills accepted by a legislature controlled by the opposing party).[110]

This American influence on Blair may have contributed to his failure to provide innovative policy leadership. Riddell has argued that the American-style 'permanent campaign' view of democratic politics that permeated the operations of the Blair Prime Ministership 'can work against risk-taking and produce excessive caution on policy'.[111] A tendency towards governmental policy caution is not such a problem in the American system because it has leadership redundancy built into the system, with Congress ever ready to provide leadership in particular areas of policy if the President is unwilling to provide a lead. But the British system has always been structurally more vulnerable to leadership failure, and Blair's centralisation made it even more vulnerable by reducing the likelihood of the other Ministers providing an alternative source of leadership in their specialised areas of government.

It is not surprising therefore that the Labour government's second term seemed much less innovative than the second term of Thatcher's Conservative government. Labour was returned to power in 2001 with another huge (167-seat) majority, even if on a reduced turnout and a static share of the vote.[112] Despite this continuing parliamentary and political opportunity for pioneering, innovations were not very evident and arguably were less evident than they were in the Labour government's third term. However, in its third term the innovations were actually and surprisingly being driven by Blair in his truncated, 2005–2007 third term as Prime Minister. In fact Seldon has argued that Blair 'was so late to imbed his personal agenda' that had he left power in 2004 'when the Iraq fallout was at its height, he would have been seen by history in a far less favourable light'.[113] Of course this begs the question of whether Blair's third-term innovations were motivated by a careerist desire to be viewed more favourably by history, just as any second-term US President's policies may well be motivated by his concern for how his career will be viewed in his retirement and in the verdict of history.

But leaving aside the question of motivation, Blair's third term certainly saw some evidence of prime-minsterial innovation. For example, the 2005 Constitutional Reform Bill, with its reduction of the office of Lord Chancellor and its creation of a Supreme Court, finally put Blair's personal stamp on the programme of constitutional reform that Labour had carried out during his ten years as Prime Minister. Norton's assessment of Blair's (lack of) influence on this programme argues that the key role in implementing constitutional reform was played by the Lord Chancellor, Irvine, until in 2003 the Prime Minister made an 'incursion' into this policy area that 'precipitated' Irvine's departure from the government and also eventually resulted in the Constitutional Reform Bill.[114] Under Irvine's leadership of constitutional policy making 'particular proposals for constitutional change went through a rigorous process of consultation and deliberation by Cabinet Committee', but Blair's assumption of leadership in this policy area took the form of a personal decision on constitutional policy 'with no consultation or Cabinet deliberation'.[115]

Blair's assumption of leadership in the area of social policy was another example of both his lateness in implementing a personal agenda and how his style of leadership ignored the Cabinet's collegial processes of collective government. Seldon notes that it was only in Blair's second term that he began to implement his personal agenda in social policy and that only in his third term was he able to extend it fully into welfare, education and health policy areas.[116] The person who established his Office of Public Service Reform in 2001 has praised Blair for introducing new ways of deliverying public services as well as changing the 'discourse' in the area of social policy into one of 'social investment in universal services'.[117] She describes the new ways of delivering these services as (1) a performance, target-based and even project-management approach, with a new emphasis on results, and (2) 'getting around bureaucratic inertia' (a) by devolving power to schools and other front-line services and staff and (b) by introducing the 'principle of contestability' to replace the public-service monopoly with a 'mixed economy of suppliers' that involves a range of sometimes competing providers – voluntary and private-sector as well as public-sector – and is intended to produce greater innovativeness and efficiency as well as improving consumer choice and accessibility.[118] In comparison, Seldon describes Blair's 'choice and diversity' agenda as simply 'extending Mrs Thatcher's liberal reforms into the welfare state'.[119] And there are some obvious signs of continuity with the Thatcher and Major governments' approach to the delivery of public services, not only in the business-model approach to 'modernising' them but also in the Citizens-Charter populist approach of having public-service targets 'expressed in a way that the public can understand', such as in standard waiting times for seeing a doctor or for being attended to by a hospital's emergency ward.[120] Nonetheless, it was an innovative move to use typically Conservative methods to achieve typically Labour social goals, and even if it was more of an adaptive innovation than a pioneering initiative, it was certainly not a case of resorting to the drift-into-crisis strategy.

The most politically interesting feature, however, of Blair's social-policy agenda was his takeover of policy leadership from the relevant Cabinet Ministers and his personal, non-collegial style of leadership. His assumption of a 'leading man' role would have gratified Schumpeter but perhaps not other experts on the British form of parliamentary democracy and Cabinet government:

> Blair's informal style and avoidance of cabinet committees earned him criticism from long-time Whitehall watchers, who argued that the PM had no business involving himself in health and education and other domestic matters best left to secretaries of state. It was also said that maintaining Britain's position in the world should best be left to the Foreign Office. One could wonder what it was the PM was supposed to be doing.[121]

Furthermore, regardless of what Blair achieved in his third term and might have achieved in his second term, his *first* term had already brought the 1960s–90s era of British government to a close in a manner that typified its adaptive rather than pioneering nature. The Prime Minister who preceded this era, Harold Macmillan, 'was reported to have replied when asked what complicated his premiership during the 1950s: "Events, dear boy, events." Events should not be underestimated'.[122] Indeed British governments of the 1960s–90s were often apparently distracted or overwhelmed by the need to make adaptive responses to unexpected events, notably a series of economic crises and the twists and turns of a protracted insurgency in Northern Ireland. Only under Prime Minister Thatcher had Schumpeter's model example of democratic government displayed some pioneering impetus and a significant track record of pioneering policies. Moreover, that record included such policy failures as the monetarist MTFS and the poll tax, which confirmed that pioneering is risky for governments and communities.

However, the Thatcherist record's most important implication for Schumpeter's theory of democracy was what it revealed about the role of leadership in the governmental sector. Instead of a prime-ministerial programme of pioneering policy proposals, it showed a Prime Minister choosing to buy into pioneering proposals coming from various members of the government. This was a form of collective pioneering, not prime-ministerial pioneering, in which the leadership shifted from one specialised Minister to another. While Schumpeter may have been correct to emphasise the need for a collective government to accept leadership, the lead need not come from the Prime Minister – other members of the government may give a lead by selling a policy proposal concerning their specialised area of government.

7
Presidential Pioneering and Foreign Policy

Although Schumpeter's and the LE model of democracy are based on the collective government of parliamentary democracy, this needs to be supplemented by some examination of presidential democracy's one-person government and its record of pioneering. As was described in Chapter 1, the one-person government of presidential democracy seems in some ways more compatible than collective government with Schumpeter's emphasis on the 'leading man'. Presidential government is also in some ways more primeval than collective government and still shows traces of the medieval hereditary monarchies from which it is descended.[1] An analyst of US presidential power acknowledged that a 'President, albeit republican, hence temporary, is our substitute for Britain's monarch' not only in terms of being the head of state and, like a seventeenth-century monarch, the chief of government but also in terms of being 'the nearest thing we have to a human symbol of our nationality and continuity – in short, our form of kingship'.[2] The US case of presidential democracy is also the best example to use to supplement the British case of parliamentary governmental pioneering, for (1) it was mentioned by Schumpeter as an alternative to his British model of democracy, (2) it invented the presidential form of government, (3) it was the model for the many post-colonial presidential republics that emerged in Latin America during the nineteenth century and (4) it has enjoyed a uniquely long life as a democracy undisturbed by undemocratic episodes. (In contrast, most of the Latin American cases of presidential democracy have experienced interludes of military rule during their history and indeed as late as the 1960s–80s.) However, this chapter will be using the US case to provide only a supplementary illustrative example of how governmental (executive) pioneering occurs in a presidential rather than parliamentary democracy; it will not be using the

US case to provide a supplementary assessment of the prevalence of governmental pioneering in the 1960s–90s.

The most basic reason for this change in approach is that the US is not a good representative example of the world's presidential democracies – it is an exceptional and perhaps unique case. In particular, no other presidential democracy has displayed a similar tendency for presidential executive and congressional legislature to compete for policy leadership. Although this inter-institutional competition for leadership contrasts neatly with the *intra*-institutional competition within a *parliamentary* democracy's cabinet executive, it also contrasts with other presidential democracies' tendency towards presidential dominance of policy making and even of the formal law-making procedures. Presidential predominance became a traditional feature of Latin American government in the nineteenth and twentieth centuries and is still discernible. Most Presidents in Latin America 'cannot now rule absolutely', as 'many of their predecessors used to do in the past', but they tend to differ from the US model of presidential democracy in their 'proactive' and agenda-setting relationship with the legislature; often they are equipped with such formal powers as the use of 'urgency' bills or decrees that enable the President 'to force congress to vote on his initiatives within a certain time limit' or 'to legislate without the previous approval of congress'.[3] However, the US case displays a Latin American degree of presidential predominance in the area of foreign policy, which also provides some notable examples of presidential pioneering. The Truman Doctrine mentioned in Chapter 2 is one of several instances of US Presidents' pioneering initiatives or creative responses in foreign policy. Of course such pioneering is not typical of foreign policy in other presidential democracies, largely because they have not given such a high priority to foreign policy and have not had the opportunity for such ambitious foreign-policy innovations as Truman's global campaign to contain the spread of communism. A simple quantitative indicator of this difference in priority and opportunity is the frequency with which US Presidents have since 1895 used their constitutional powers as Commander in Chief to deploy the country's armed forces against or within a foreign country. Another simple quantitative indicator is the destructive power of the nuclear arsenal that US Presidents developed to deter a nuclear attack by the Soviet Union during the decades of Cold War rivalry for global power and influence.

As was noted in Chapter 1, by the beginning of the 1960s Schattschneider was writing of the 'primacy of foreign policy' in US politics. His thesis was confirmed by such events as the 1962 Cuban

Missile Crisis, the 1964 electoral humiliation of Goldwater and the 1968 electoral victory of Nixon at the height of the Vietnam war. In the early 1970s President Nixon's foreign policy of détente and arms-control negotiations with the Soviet Union reduced the dangers and significance of Cold War rivalry, which also seemed to be overshadowed in the later 1970s by the economic problems arising from massive increases in the price of oil. But during the latter half of the decade there was also mounting concern in the US about the Soviet Union's continuing military build-up and about the spread of communism and Soviet influence in the Third World. This expansion culminated at the end of the decade with the Soviet invasion of Afghanistan, which was the catalyst for a revival of Cold War tension between the two superpowers. And there seems to have been a return to the 1960s situation after President Reagan took office in 1981 and introduced his foreign policy of increased US military and non-military competition with the Soviet Union.

Yet President Reagan's second term of office, in 1985–88, saw the winding down of the Cold War, and was followed a few years later by the end of the Soviet Union itself. Thereafter economic policy became at least as important as foreign policy in US politics and was probably more important in the period from 1992 until 2001. As would be expected, foreign-policy pioneering became less prevalent than it had been in the 1960s–80s and therefore this chapter will focus on the Reagan era as the high tide and turning of the tide in presidential pioneering in foreign policy.

The other crucial transitional period in the history of US presidential pioneering is the era in which foreign policy was presidentialised. From then on the US case became a good example of that presidential predominance in policy making which in other presidential democracies is evident in domestic policy as well as foreign policy. So this chapter will also focus on the era of President Franklin Roosevelt, who not only provides examples of pioneering foreign policy but also presided over and contributed to the presidentialisation of this sometimes vitally important area of policy making.

Presidential leadership – Neustadt's model

The institutional structure of presidential democracy differs from that of parliamentary democracy in more ways than having a one-person government rather than a collective government. Instead of the 'power to decide' being shared among elected leaders in a collective government it is shared by the elected one-person government with other elected leaders in an independent legislature. As was described in Chapter 1, the people's elected representatives in the congressional legislature not only provide between-elections acceptance or rejection of leadership by the presidential executive but also may modify these leads or even assume a leadership role and use its legislative powers to set a direction for state and society. The American presidential democracy was described as using competition for leadership between presidential executive and congressional legislature to ensure that the political community receives sufficient leadership as well as to ensure that such leadership is kept under some form of democratic, elected control between elections.

In fact the US case of presidential democracy is exceptional and perhaps unique in the way that it disperses opportunities for leadership as well as control over leadership to such a wide range of state institutions – not only the federal executive and legislature but also state/local government and even the judiciary. The role of the fifty state-level and myriad local-level governments in providing additional sources of leadership to their territories and, by example, to the whole country is one of the features of US political history. In a few instances they have also provided leadership internationally, as when the state of Wisconsin extended the franchise to women or when the city of New York introduced zero-tolerance policing. Furthermore, even the unelected judiciary has been given an opportunity to provide some leadership as well as to exercise some control over the leadership of other state institutions, for the Supreme Court has in some of its judicial-review decisions given authoritative, legally binding 'leads' that in any other democracy would be considered 'political' decisions that should be made by the legislature, such as the court's decisions about women's right to abortion and corporations' right to finance politics. (This distinctive feature of the US case of presidential democracy therefore goes beyond the boundaries of Schumpeter's definition of democracy, which specifies that political decisions are made by individuals who have won a competitive struggle for the people's vote.) However, it is the interactive and reversible leadership relationship between the presidential executive and congressional legislature that produces most of the key decisions in the country's policy making. Thus Neustadt's well-known description of US democracy as 'a government of separated institutions sharing powers' included federalism and judicial review among his examples of the sharing of powers but his institutional leadership model of US politics focused on the President's relationship with

Congress and with the public opinion that exerted so much influence over Congress.[4]

The leadership model that Neustadt included in his 1960 classic *Presidential Power* should be included alongside Downs's and Schattschneider's as the three great and enduring leadership models created by American political scientists in the late 1950s. It is true that Neustadt's leadership model fails to allow (1) for competition between President and Congress for leadership over areas of policy (especially when the President belongs to a different party than the majority party in one or both houses of the legislature) and (2) for Congress to give a lead with or without meeting resistance from the President, as when its legislation is or is not vetoed by the President. But this limitation of the model is not so significant in the area of foreign policy, where a President's policy leadership seldom faces resistance, let alone actual competition, from Congress.

Neustadt's leadership model is more difficult to discern than Downs's and Schattschneider's because he seems to place more emphasis on power than leadership and because he labelled his model's key leadership activity as 'persuasion'. For example, Neustadt famously argued that presidential power 'is the power to persuade' and declared: 'Command is but a method of persuasion, not a substitute, and not a method suitable for everyday employment'.[5] It is only on closer examination that his notion of persuasion is revealed to be a type of leadership that is usually similar to Schumpeter's market-like type or to what would now be described as deliberative leadership.

The influence of presidential democracy's institutional structure on Neustadt's leadership model is evident in his description of the President's role of 'clerk' and the 'great initiator', which requires a President 'to do something about everything' even though it is 'an open question' whether these initiatives will lead to people doing 'what he wants done'.[6] What he is initiating is seldom a pioneering initiative and usually is an adaptive response to a crisis or is merely a routine matter of government, such as the annual budget proposals he sends to Congress. And he is actually initiating fewer things than are initiated by a parliamentary democracy's collective government as well as being less sure that people will do what the government wants done. For example, a President's legislative initiatives – whether routine, programmatic or crisis-driven – are viewed by his fellow elected leaders as merely one aspect of Congress's legislative agenda and process. After all, the presidential share of legislative powers goes no further than the right to veto legislation, not to monopolise or even control it. In contrast, a parliamentary government not only controls the legislative agenda and process but also provides most of the bills, including all those involving public expenditure, as well as being confident that its bills will be passed by parliament.

A President cannot be confident about having his leadership accepted even when he uses his public office's *unshared* powers, notably those he wields over the military as Commander-in-Chief and over the civil service as the head of the executive branch of the state. As Neustadt pointed out, even a formal executive order of the President is not always 'self-executing' in the sense of giving a command that appears automatically to produce compliance; this is likely to happen only when five factors are present: (1) the President is unambiguously involved, (2) his words are unambiguous, (3) his order is widely publicised, (4) the recipients have no doubts about his authority to issue the order to them and (5) the recipients have 'control of everything needed to carry it out' – if any one of these factors is not present, 'the chances are that mere command will not produce compliance'.[7] Considering how rarely all five factors will be present, it is clear why Neustadt declared command to be an unsuitable method for 'everyday' use. But it is harder to understand why he also declared command to be a method of *persuasion*, and he may have been referring to the fact that so often an executive order or other command must be accompanied by persuasion if the President wishes to ensure the command will be executed. Indeed Neustadt argued that when orders are not self-executing, the administrative departments and agencies of the executive branch require from the President the same kind of persuasiveness, and sometimes the same degree of persuasiveness, as when he is persuading Congress to accept his lead.[8] Not surprisingly, Neustadt contrasted leadership in *form* with leadership in *fact* and certainly the US President seems a striking and strange case of a monarch-like formal leader being expected to give a lead over a huge range of policy but without being allowed anything like an authoritative type of leadership – so that in fact many of his policy proposals are not accepted or are accepted only in part and/or only after some persuasive selling.[9]

The explanation for this strange situation is that the US President is a formal leader without sufficient powers to exercise authoritative leadership and having to rely on the market-like, deliberative type of leadership that Neustadt terms 'persuasion'. Under this heading he is describing the President's selling of leads to recipients who may or may not buy the lead – it is an open question. And the President's persuasive selling of leads is the same type of market-like leadership that

Schumpeter described Prime Ministers using within their Cabinets. Schumpeter himself suggested a possible 'analogy' between the functions of a Cabinet Minister and those of the President's key allies in Congress: 'the managers of the administration's forces in Congress'.[10] Neustadt took this analogy further in a 1966 article that depicted the President as 'a sort of super-Prime Minister' who presides over the functional equivalent of the British Cabinet, composed of influential 'Secretaries, Senators, White House staffers, Congressmen, or others' who are linked together through the person of the President:

> Anyone who has an independent power-base is likelier than not to get 'ministerial' treatment from a President. Even his own appointees are to be wooed, not spurred, in the degree that they have their own attributes of power: expertise or prestige, or a statute under foot.[11]

A President having to 'woo' even his own appointees if they have attributes of power is comparable to a Prime Minister wooing heavyweight Ministers with a power base in parliament or with such other attributes of power as prestige or expertise. Despite being a monarch-like one-person government, the President is reduced to using the same 'soft sell' leadership as a Prime Minister uses with senior fellow-leaders in his collective government. And the President may have to use soft-sell leadership with junior as well as senior members of the congressional legislature if his intermediaries in Congress or the White House cannot ensure that his policy proposals will be bought by these rank-and-file legislators.

Another crucial but more obvious similarity between the prime-ministerial and presidential situations is that careerist self-interest is the standard motivation of the Prime Minister's and President's fellow-leaders. In *Presidential Power* Neustadt pointed out that congressional legislators 'frequently appear to be in business by themselves. So, in a real though not entire sense, they are and have to be', and so the President has to convince these legislators 'that what the White House wants of them is what they ought to do for their sake and on their authority'.[12] In other words, they have to be convinced that it is in their careerist self-interest to do what he wants them to do. And as Neustadt argued, this involves more than the use of 'charm' or 'reasoned argument'; it also involves bargaining, and indeed the 'power to persuade is the power to bargain'.[13]

His emphasis on the role of bargaining in fact seems too extreme. It is true that bargaining is typical of the market-like selling of leads amongst formal leaders, which was depicted by the LE model in Chapter 4 as analogous to inter-firm selling of producer goods not only because the selling is aimed at relatively few buyers but also because it may involve some complex and even secret sales *negotiations* about altering the proposal/product to make it more appealing *or* about *side deals* relating to other proposals/products. However, Neustadt's concept of political bargaining is focused on side deals and does not discuss bargaining about altering the proposal/product, as when a President alters his policy proposal – even before he has made it public – to make the proposal more appealing to legislators. Instead the President uses his 'bargaining advantages' and a supply of 'trading stock' that comprises his authority, in the sense of his shared and unshared powers, and his extraordinary status as the country's pre-eminent formal leader and holder of a monarch-like public office.[14] Those he is bargaining with 'need or fear' this authority and status because 'at some time, in some degree, the doing of *their* jobs, the furthering of *their* ambitions may depend upon the President' – depend upon his use of presidential powers and/or status to assist or to hamper the furthering of their careerist ambitions.[15]

In effect Neustadt was presenting an early example of an exchange theory of politics, in which the congressional legislator is buying the presidential policy proposal in exchange for assistance or neutrality at some time in the future when the legislator will need or fear presidential intervention. This exchange relationship seems to be the core of his leadership model and of his concept of presidential power, as is evident by his formulae that (1) power is the power to persuade, (2) the power to persuade is the power to bargain and (3) bargaining involves an exchange of assistance/neutrality in return for accepting the presidential lead on a policy.

Furthermore, two aspects of presidential power that Neustadt identified – professional reputation and popular prestige – are related to presidential bargaining. The President's professional reputation in Washington DC is an important aspect of his power because the political leaders whom he is trying to persuade 'must be convinced that he has skill and will enough to use his advantages' and, in particular, they must anticipate – in accordance with the 'law of anticipated reactions' – how he will use his bargaining advantages in response to their doing or not doing what he wants.[16] In other words, the President's ability to sell a policy proposal to them depends upon his reputation for having the skill and the will to deliver needed assistance or neutrality in exchange for buying the proposal – and also to deliver feared sanctions as retribution for refusing to buy the proposal. The second aspect of presidential power, popular prestige, involves anticipated reactions, too, but an anticipation by political leaders of how the *public* will react – in terms of the effect on these leaders' careers – to their doing or not doing what the President wants: 'the prevalent impression of a President's public standing tends to set a tone and to define the limits of what Washingtonians do for him', if only because 'public disapproval heartens Washington's resistance' but public approval 'counts in power by establishing some checks upon resistance'.[17]

By increasing these aspects of his power, professional reputation and popular prestige, a President obviously would improve his bargaining position with other leaders. But Neustadt was surprisingly pessimistic about the possibility of increasing the President's popular prestige, and focused on the defensive goal of bolstering rather than boosting prestige. He claimed that 'merchandising' a President's personality and programme cannot protect against the threat to his popular prestige that arises when the public's hopes and fears are frustrated; all a President can do in such circumstances is teach the public, through events as well as words, to bear with these frustrations and at least not hold him to blame.[18] This merchandising and teaching are similar to what Chapter 4's LE model described as politicians competing in the electoral/party sector by selling opinion leads to the public in an analogous manner to firms selling consumer products to a mass market. And some analysts of presidential power have indicated that such between-elections leadership of public opinion can go beyond merely defensive goals and achieve something more positive for a President.

Presidential prestige and foreign policy

These achievements may well be in areas not directly concerned with his personal prestige but with the prestige of the Presidency as an *institution* or with the prestige of a presidential *policy* – which he is proposing or is already implementing. In the case of institutional prestige Campbell and Jamieson's recent *Presidents Creating the Presidency: Deeds Done in Words* contends that eloquent rhetoric can expand 'presidential capital', thereby increasing a President's 'capacity to lead' and thus the likelihood that he will claim more of 'the power that lies at the intersection' of separated institutions sharing powers.[19] This presidential capital is an institutional version of the merely personal prestige that constitutes the ordinary form of political capital. It not only boosts the popular prestige of the President ex officio but also boosts his status as the country's pre-eminent formal leader and thereby increases the trading stock of status and authority that he uses when bargaining with other leaders – a double-whammy increase in his capacity to lead in fact as well as form by having fellow-leaders do what he wants done.

In the case of boosting the prestige of a proposed or actual policy Presidents have long resorted to selling these policy leads directly to the public. If the selling is successful, the policy acquires sufficient popular prestige to make careerist political leaders think about the anticipated reaction of the public to those who oppose the policy. Presidents' foreign policy is perhaps the best example of how policy can become part of the prestige aspect of presidential power. Graebner's analysis of Presidents' role as Commander-in-Chief argued that historically a President's 'real power to advance his foreign policy agenda' has been based on his capacity, 'through qualities of leadership', to build and sustain popular support for this policy agenda, for 'assured of strong public support in his clash with congressional critics, a president faced almost no limits to his control of external policy'.[20] In addition to whatever leadership qualities they might have, Presidents have a 'special access to the public mind' through such advantages as access to prime-time television, their controlled press conferences and their employment of eloquent speech writers.[21] Their communication advantages increased dramatically in the middle of the twentieth century with the introduction of radio and then television. Campbell and Jamieson's historical study of presidential rhetoric includes inaugural addresses, eulogies for heroes or victims, 'war rhetoric', State of the Union addresses and even veto messages, but they acknowledge that modern technology has provided occasions for rhetoric, such as the fireside chat on radio or the televised press conference, that were not available to Presidents of Lincoln's and Washington's time.[22] On the other hand, Presidents have always exploited the inherent advantages that some occasions for rhetoric have provided, notably the use of war rhetoric. Presidential war rhetoric has always tended to

> simplify and dramatize events in ways that capitalize on the executive's privileged access to information while stifling dissent and enlisting the strongest possible support. Strategic misrepresentations permeate past and present presidential war rhetoric.[23]

And the misrepresentations that occur in the selling of war and of other facets of foreign policy are not subjected to the same degree of public criticism by opponents or the media as are the misrepresentations that occur in presidential selling of opinion leads about domestic policy.

The relatively sacrosanct nature of presidential pronouncements on foreign policy and the relatively bipartisan attitude of Congress towards presidential foreign policy are indicative of a 'presidentialisation' that is no less significant than the 'primacy' of foreign policy noted by Schattschneider.

The presidentialisation of foreign policy was noted by Neustadt in his article on the President as a super-Prime-Minister. He pointed out that the 'diplomatic and defense spheres yield our man authority for binding judgements' and explained that a President's 'personal choices are authoritative, for he himself is heir to royal prerogatives' in these spheres – which originated in a medieval monarch's role as war leader and responsibility for the defence of the realm.[24] These authoritative personal choices and authority for binding judgements are epitomised by his constitutionally recognised and unshared powers as Commander-in-Chief. Two of the three examples of 'self-executing' orders that Neustadt provided in *Presidential Power* were cases of orders being given to the military. In the MacArthur case President Truman signed an order as Commander-in-Chief that relieved General MacArthur of command and in the other case President Eisenhower signed an executive order that 'authorised and directed' the Secretary of Defense to use such armed forces as were necessary to enforce the court's decision to desegregate a school in Little Rock.[25]

Yet the presidentialisation of foreign policy is more a matter, in Neustadt's terms, of status than of authority. Congress has sufficient constitutional powers of its own to challenge the President's control of foreign policy. As Graebner pointed out, the key congressional powers in the area of foreign policy are not the Senate's special powers of declaring war and ratifying treaties but rather the general budgetary and appropriations power of the purse. He pointed to the use of the appropriations power to end US involvement in Vietnam as evidence that Congress possesses 'the ultimate power over foreign affairs' if it is willing to use that power; the 'congressional Democrats, in 1973, were determined to terminate the war by exercising Congress's power of the purse'.[26] As he argued, the President is usually protected from such challenges by his status as the elected leader who is primarily responsible for the country's foreign relations and therefore is entitled to be given the power – through congressional acceptance of his leadership – that he requires to carry out this responsibility:

> Members of Congress, no less than the American people generally, have recognized the responsibility that the chief executive, as official

spokesman of the nation, carries for the defense of the country's interests abroad.…They have hesitated from the beginning to *risk their political lives* by challenging the notion of presidential *primacy in matters of external policy*, especially when the country was in a crisis mood.[27]

In Neustadt's leadership model this is another situation where careerist leaders do what the President wants them to do because they anticipate that the public reaction to them rejecting his lead would endanger 'their political lives'. It is therefore a fourth variant of the popular-prestige aspect of presidential power; in addition to (1) a President's purely personal prestige, (2) the institutional prestige of the Presidency and (3) the prestige of his personal policies, there is also (4) the ex officio prestige of presidential initiatives in foreign policy. Like his purely personal prestige, it is probably not capable of being boosted by selling opinion leads to the public, no matter how eloquent the rhetoric, but it is a further explanation of the presidentialisation of foreign policy and of why a President is more likely to be a leader in fact as well as form in this area of policy.

Roosevelt's pioneering foreign policy

Franklin Roosevelt is rightly regarded as one of the greatest Presidents, who created the modern Presidency and led his country through the domestic crisis of the Great Depression and to victory in the Second World War. However, Dallek points out in his magisterial history of Roosevelt's foreign policy that he was also one of the most visionary Presidents:

> One of FDR's principal attributes was his capacity to define and enunciate a vision of where he wished to lead the nation.…Roosevelt, borrowing from the Bible, said it best in his first Inaugural: 'Where there is no vision, the people perish.' No twentieth-century presidency has been richer in broad statements of America's role in world affairs than Roosevelt's.[28]

It was in this 1933 inaugural address, too, that Roosevelt presented his pioneering vision of the US role in world affairs: 'I dedicate this nation to the policy of the Good Neighbour – the neighbour who respects his obligations and respects the sanctity of his agreements in and with a world of neighbours'.[29]

Although this vision is usually labelled the Good Neighbour policy, it might be better described as the Good Neighbour in a *World of Neighbours* policy. After all, it was the *international* dimension or application of neighbourliness that distinguished Roosevelt's vision as an innovation in foreign policy; the ideal or concept of the Good Neighbour had long been used to describe international relations among the countries of North and South America and, more recently, had been used by President Hoover to describe a central theme of his foreign policy – improved US relations with Latin America.[30] The US had for decades been prepared to intervene politically and militarily in the affairs of Latin American countries, especially its near neighbours in Central America and the Caribbean, and even Woodrow Wilson's idealistic attitude to international relations had developed an interventionist tinge when applied to his own neighbourhood. President Wilson's approach in Latin America has recently been summed up as 'political intervention and democratic proselytization'; his Pan-Americanism 'was a brand of idealism that evolved into a kind of moral meddling' and 'led him to undertake more armed interventions in Latin America than any of his predecessors'.[31] In contrast, President Hoover had emphasised non-intervention and had backed up his Good Neighbour words with the deeds of withdrawing US forces from Nicaragua and from Haiti.[32] 'Roosevelt appropriated the same concept and gave it world-wide application', making it applicable 'to the foreign relations of the United States throughout the world'.[33]

His extension of the concept was an innovative and politically risky change in foreign policy. The most significant political risk was that 'this formulation directly challenged isolationist sentiments'.[34] Isolationists were not too concerned about the role that the US played in its own backyard or hemisphere – whether the role was interventionist, neighbourly or simply one of benign neglect – but they were opposed to any policy of US engagement of any kind in the rest of the world. In shifting from a hemispheric to a global application of the Good Neighbour policy Roosevelt was therefore likely to alienate isolationists, and so it is not surprising that his new vision of US foreign policy was not presented to the public during his election campaign against Hoover.[35] In a typical case of governmental rather than electoral pioneering he had waited until after being elected to present this innovation to the people – waiting until a suitably symbolic and ceremonial occasion gave him the opportunity to use the rhetoric of national commitment.

But 1933 was also the year that Adolf Hitler came to power in *Germany*. It would become impossible to envision international relations in neighbourly terms, except in the defensive sense of helping one another deal with the criminal threat posed by the fascist-militarist regimes in Germany, Italy and Japan. In fact Roosevelt's Good Neighbour vision seems to have returned to the traditional hemispheric rather than global perspective. The concept of the Good Neighbour 'came to mean the policy pursued by the United States government in its dealings with the twenty other republics of the Western Hemisphere' or at least acquired 'its most specific meaning' in relation to Latin America – where it proved to be an effective policy: 'its practical consequence was the achievement of nearly unanimous support for the United States throughout World War II'.[36]

During the war, however, the Good Neighbour vision still influenced Roosevelt's approach and goal in the true Clausewitzian sense of war being 'other means' of pursuing foreign-policy ends. Kimball's assessment of Roosevelt's wartime leadership as Commander-in-Chief noted that his 'good neighbour' approach 'began long before 1944' but was clearly still influencing his grand strategy and his vision of how he wanted the post-war world to be: 'He had a postwar vision that, vague as it was, he pursued with remarkable consistency'.[37] Both Kimball and Larrabee emphasise the consistency of Roosevelt's strategies and his rejection of any military proposal that conflicted with them, and indeed Larrabee's massive volume on Roosevelt and his military lieutenants concludes that he was

> almost rigidly consistent in his overall geopolitical strategies for waging the war: in his support of Britain, Russia and China; in his insistence on crushing Germany first; in his resolve on unconditional surrender by all his enemies; in his intent to establish a postwar 'united nations' directed by a firm (which is to say, U.S.-controlled) union of the major victors. Nothing was allowed to get in the way of these aims, and military objectives were subordinated to – or fortunately coincided with – their attainment.[38]

The goal of establishing a United Nations directed by a US-controlled union of the major victors hardly seems compatible with the Good Neighbour vision of the country's global role. Instead of neighbourly engagement the US seems intent on a paternalist hegemony or even a disguised form of great-power domination. However, the United Nations embodies the often-overlooked World of Neighbours aspect of Roosevelt's vision; events may have overtaken the more limited global role he had originally envisioned for the US but these same events had re-emphasised the need for all the nations of the world to adopt a neighbourly attitude to one another.

Roosevelt's pioneering included innovative secondary policies, too, that helped to implement his foreign-policy and strategic goals. Perhaps the most important was his creative response to the problem of maintaining the flow of military supplies to Britain, which by the end of 1940 could no longer pay for them on a cash-and-carry basis. The President responded by inventing the concept of Lend-Lease and also the brilliant metaphor – lending a *neighbour* a hose to put out a fire – that he used to sell the policy to Congress and the public.[39]

His use of the metaphor in a radio-broadcast fireside chat to the public is an example of Roosevelt's pioneering of something larger than a particular policy, issue or institution – the actual presidentialisation of foreign policy. Like his Good Neighbour vision, it would be a case of only partially successful pioneering. Roosevelt is a transitional figure who took the Presidency a long way from Wilson's historic debacle of failing to sell US membership of the League of Nations to Congress and the public but by 1941 had not taken it as far as Truman's post-war capacity to commit the US to the Marshall Plan, the Truman Doctrine and the massive military intervention in the Korean war.

In fact Roosevelt was a quite circumspect pioneer in 1940–41 and was especially cautious in leading Congress and the public into confrontation with Nazi Germany. As Casey points out in *Cautious Crusade*, the 1930s 'were the high-water mark of American isolationism. Preoccupied with day-to-day economic issues, disillusioned with America's involvement in the Great War, and concerned lest U.S. participation in another foreign conflict irrevocably destroy the nation's constitutional and social fabric, until 1940 much of the population shared a number of core convictions' that included: (1) US strategic invulnerability behind the maritime barriers of the Atlantic and Pacific oceans, (2) an 'overwhelming desire' to remain at peace, virtually at any price, and (3) a wariness of foreign entanglements, political as well as military, because these might lead to war – indeed there was a preference for 'impartial neutrality' even in a war between democracies and non-democracies.[40] In mid-1940 there was a shift in public opinion in response to Nazi Germany's military defeat of France, which left Britain to fight on alone against the expanding fascist tide and led American public opinion to favour aiding Britain and expanding the US military to ensure the country's invulnerability.

But there still remained an overwhelming desire to remain at peace, and Roosevelt continued to be very cautious about attempting to lead public opinion by words or deeds. He believed that the way to achieve a 'broad, stable consensus for fighting' was *not* through 'educational talks to the public or strong Executive action, but through developments abroad that aroused the country to fight'.[41] Nonetheless, he continued with his attempts to lead public opinion in an interventionist direction. For example, his 14 May 1941 Pan-American Day speech, which was broadcast by radio and filmed for the newsreels, warned that the war in Europe was encroaching on the Atlantic and coming 'very close to home', referred several times to a Nazi plan for world domination, and announced the declaration of an unlimited national emergency.[42] Yet despite the favourable response in newspaper editorials and telegrams to the White House, there was no follow-up to the speech in terms of shifts in policy or of new policy proposals for Congress to consider. Roosevelt believed that he had gone 'further than I had thought possible even two weeks ago' in leading public opinion towards intervention, but he was very sensitive about 'what the public was and was not ready for' and clearly believed it was not ready for him to go further in deeds as well as words.[43]

Without this shift in public opinion, Congress would be unlikely to accept presidential leadership about intervening militarily against Nazi Germany. In 1941 'any attempt to secure congressional support for an openly interventionist measure was potentially calamitous to the administration. If it failed, ... then the President's leadership would have been repudiated, undoing all that had been done before' in achieving congressional acceptance of his policy of providing aid to Britain (and to the Soviet Union after it was invaded by Germany in the middle of the year).[44] Late in the year his revision of the Neutrality Act to allow Lend-Lease aid to be sent to Britain in US ships produced such close votes in Congress that it 'reinforced Roosevelt's conviction that winning a declaration of war from Congress would require a substantial provocation from abroad'.[45] And the President was receiving reports on public opinion that indicated a fear of the expected economic costs of war and of the heavy casualties expected from sending an army to Europe to defeat Germany; there was stronger support for war with Japan but not if war was sparked by Japanese aggression against non-American territories.[46] In the event the Japanese attack on Pearl Harbor on 7 December solved these problems for the President and also gave him the opportunity to realise some of his vision of the US's global role in a more neighbourly world.[47]

Roosevelt's pioneering also included institutional innovations that were a creative response to the domestic and foreign crises that he was facing. In 1939 he shifted into his Executive Office not only the Treasury's Bureau of the Budget but also the Joint Army-Navy Board (the forerunner of what three years later became the Joint Chiefs of Staff), which had previously been located in the armed services departments but would now be 'joined by a special link to the President alone'.[48] The timing of these institutional innovations suggests that they were as much pioneering initiatives as creative responses, for 1939 was too late to be a response to the economic crisis of the Depression and too early to be a response to the national-security crisis that arose in mid-1940 with the fall of France.

What is more, Roosevelt pioneered a restructuring of presidential buying of policy proposals that matched any improvement in the selling of policy leads that accompanied his presidentialisation of foreign policy. He has long been known for his encouragement of competition among his subordinates and advisors. Some fifty years ago Neustadt identified this feature as Roosevelt's technique or method for information-gathering, but it was also increasing his ability to *choose*:

> Not only did he keep his organizations overlapping and divide authority among them, but he also tended to put men of clashing temperaments, outlooks, ideas, in charge of them. Competitive personalities mixed with competing jurisdictions was Roosevelt's formula for putting pressure on himself, for making his subordinates push up to him the *choices* they could not take for themselves. It also made them advertise their punches, their quarrels provided him not only heat but information. Administrative competition gave him two rewards. He got the choices and due notice of them.[49]

A third reward was that his choices were being improved by having a larger *range* of possible choices to choose from when he had to decide on a policy to implement or on a policy proposal to sell to Congress and perhaps also to the public. Presumably this is why Roosevelt is also known for preferring an 'inventive' set of subordinates and advisors 'even at a cost in the time and energy he had to spend in what he called the "hand-holding" of his "prima donnas" '.[50] Encouraging competition was a structural method of producing a similar effect with perhaps less cost in time and energy and certainly with less dependence upon finding exceptional personnel – inventive individuals may be almost as rare as pioneers.

In combination or singly the two methods increased the diversity of the policy proposals being sold to the President by his subordinates and advisors. Increasing the diversity of variations by encouraging competition seems rather anomalous from a political-evolutionary perspective of 'selection of variations for preservation', which normally emphasises the role of competition at the selection stage rather than at the variation stage. However, encouraging competition at the variation stage does seem a good example of how competitiveness prevents rigidity, such as the effects of vested interests or unconscious bias, and therefore increases the likelihood that the appropriate adaptive response will be made. Finally, in terms of the economic analogy with the market this is a case of market-like selling of leads amongst formal leaders, analogous to inter-firm selling of producer goods, in which a discerning buyer is stimulating competition among sellers so as to increase the range of modifications – and perhaps even new products – that are available for him to buy.

The encouragement of competition among the sellers of policy proposals was very evident in Roosevelt's approach to foreign policy. Dallek pointed out that 'he divided responsibility for foreign affairs among a variety of agencies and men...pitting Welles against Hull, political envoys against career diplomats, Treasury against State, Stimson against Morgenthau, and a host of other official and personal representatives against each other for influence over foreign policy'.[51] In fact Roosevelt could be duplicitous as well as manipulative in his efforts to encourage competition. Allison's crisis analysis of the making of foreign policy, *Essence of Decision*, described Roosevelt's operating style as including a willingness 'to encourage the principal members of his government to get involved in an issue on the assumption that he agreed with their substantive recommendation'.[52]

On the other hand, Allison's analysis of decision making during the 1962 Cuban Missile Crisis also showed how a lack of competition can produce a dangerous reduction in the range of policy options presented to Presidents. What he labelled *reticence* occurs when a President's subordinates or advisors refrain from selling – or selling 'loudly' – to him because of such careerist concerns as not wanting to alienate their presidential buyer with an unwanted sales pitch.[53] Furthermore, there seems to have been some cartelisation of the foreign-policy sector, for when Richard Nixon became President he expressed his determination not 'to be confronted with a bureaucratic consensus that leaves me no options but acceptance or rejection, and that gives me no way of knowing what alternatives exist'.[54] His problem and countermeasures were discussed in George's classic 1972 article on competition or 'multiple advocacy' among a President's foreign policy advisors. He described the problem as one of 'bureaucratic politics' restricting competition among subunits of the executive branch:

> Left to their own devices, those subunits which share responsibility for a particular policy area often adapt by restricting competition with each other. As a result, policy issues may not rise to the presidential level, or when they do, they often take the form of concealed compromises that reflect the special interest of actors at lower levels.[55]

The sub-units' restriction of competition with each other was a typical case of cartelisation in a policy sector but the new President did not deal with the problem in the Roosevelt-like fashion of encouraging competition; instead Nixon applied the old bureaucratic remedy of throwing a new or newly empowered organisation at the problem. He gave the National Security Council more staff and the responsibility for developing what George describes as an 'advocate-free' centralised search and evaluation process that looked for policy issues and options at their pre-bureaucratised stage.[56]

George's own preference was for a different form of central intervention that sought in Roosevelt-like fashion 'to maintain and make use of internal competitive processes' to remedy what he described as the 'imperfect competition' produced by bureaucratic politics and other factors.[57] He was particularly concerned about the possibility that the objectively best policy option might lose out to another option that not only might be more persuasively argued (marketed) but also might be presented by an advocate with more (market) power and more bargaining skills (in making modifications or side deals).[58] This concern would also be expressed by later analysts of presidential policy making. For example, Lambright's study of policy making in the area of science and technology depicted such bureaucracies as NASA and the Defense Department as 'sellers' of policy proposals to the President but claimed that he may become 'the victim' of sellers that are good at marketing or are bureaucratically powerful.[59] A President therefore has to know when to say 'No' to such sellers and also has to be prepared 'to reach down into the agencies to help pull a laggard technology that is not getting the administrative push it needs' because of the ineptitude or weakness of its bureaucratic seller.[60]

Similarly, a 1981 textbook's analysis of the making of foreign policy emphasised the role of marketing in the selling of policy proposals – and also raised the problem of what it termed *overselling*. Groups competing for influence in the making of foreign policy might oversell a policy proposal not only by 'insisting that it will definitely solve the buyer's problems' but also by exaggerating these problems 'in order to enhance the buyer's feeling that he or she absolutely needs the policy "product" being offered'.[61] What is more, this competitive selling of policy proposals was now a textbook-recognised aspect of the presidentialisation of foreign policy.

> All proponents of specific policy preferences especially seek to sell their 'products' to their potentially best customer – the president. His approval and support are obviously decisive. The competition is therefore intense.[62]

If indeed there was 'intense' competition to sell to the President, then there had been some return to the situation that Roosevelt had created and maintained in the 1930s–40s. In this aspect of the presidentialisation of foreign policy he was clearly a trailblazing rather than transitional figure. And he had proved himself to be a pioneer in the practical mechanisms of government as well as being one of the most visionary Presidents. However, in 1981 another visionary pioneer was inaugurated as President and he would eventually present the people with a policy that seemed as idealistic – and unattainable – as being a good neighbour in a world of neighbours.

Reagan's foreign-policy pioneering

Ronald Reagan's operating style as President was unflatteringly labelled by Neustadt in 1990 as 'ignorance and insistence'.[63] The 'ignorance' aspect was his lack of interest in detail combined with a willingness to delegate, while the 'insistence' aspect was his initial and sustained policy commitments that were based upon convictions he held prior to taking office. Neustadt provided an extended analysis of how this operating style led to disaster in the case of the Iran-Contra affair. But he also acknowledged that the President's sustained commitments based on prior convictions 'enabled him to act, to differentiate, to choose, not as the puppet of his aides but on his own, despite his equally unusual disdain for detail'.[64]

These prior convictions might also take the form of visionary beliefs, such as that communism would eventually collapse and that the world should be free of the threat of nuclear war. And the sustained commitments based on these visionary convictions would be very evident in

Reagan's two famous instances of foreign-policy pioneering: the Reagan Doctrine and his policy of seeking to eliminate nuclear weapons. They are now less well remembered than other aspects of his foreign policy, notably the disastrous overture to Iran that became the Iran-Contra affair and, more importantly, the receptiveness to Gorbachev's overtures that contributed so much to ending the Cold War and laying the foundations for the collapse of communism in 1989–91. In fact it is possible that none of Reagan's foreign policy is as well remembered as his electoral pioneering, mentioned in Chapter 5, and his presiding over the personal-computer/IT economic boom of the 1980s that was probably the US's last Schumpeterian economic revolution and laid foundations for the prosperity (and short-lived budget surpluses) of the Clinton era. However, Reagan should also be remembered for his visionary attempt to eliminate nuclear weapons and also for what became known as the Reagan Doctrine, which emphasised that insurgency was not criminality but a form of warfare that could be used by good guys as well as bad guys.

Yet the Reagan Doctrine is difficult to categorise as a case of presidential pioneering because it appears to have been virtually foisted on the President by the columnist Charles Krauthammer. In April 1985 he depicted this new foreign-policy doctrine as committing the US to support armed resistance to communism or, more specifically, to support insurgents fighting to overthrow a communist regime and/or fighting to expel the Soviet Union's forces from their country.[65] He based this interpretation on remarks that the President had made in his 6 February State of the Union message and in a radio address that he gave ten days later. In the latter the President had described US support for the Contra insurgents fighting against the Sandinista regime in Nicaragua as being the continuation of a US tradition of supporting freedom fighters, which extended from Simon Bolivar's fight against Spanish colonialism to the French Resistance's fight against Nazi occupation; in the State of the Union message he had remarked that 'we must not break faith with those who are risking their lives – on every continent from Afghanistan to Nicaragua – to defy Soviet-supported aggression and secure rights which have been ours since birth' and that US support for such 'freedom fighters' was a matter of 'self-defense'.[66] On both occasions the President seems to have been intending not to present a new foreign-policy doctrine but to sell to Congress and the public his proposal that the US resume giving aid to the Contras – aid that had been ended when Congress had passed legislation prohibiting military aid to the Contras.[67]

On the other hand, the Reagan administration's aid to the Contras had been part of a wider approach or strategy that had been operating for several years and had included aid to insurgents in Afghanistan and Cambodia as well Nicaragua. Scott's (1996) *Deciding to Intervene: The Reagan Doctrine and American Foreign Policy* argued that this constituted an at least implicit or tacit 'doctrine' and that it had been applied in varying degrees to not only Nicaragua, Afghanistan and Cambodia but also to Angola and Mozambique. The doctrine was first formally codified in National Security Decision Directive 75, 'drafted in 1982 and signed on 17 January 1983', as merely one aspect of a multi-pronged strategy aimed at weakening the Soviet Union's domestic as well as global position.[68] But the doctrine was apparently first formally proposed – and as a stand-alone, single-pronged policy – in a March 1981 meeting of the National Security Planning Group, where CIA Director 'Casey proposed a CIA-directed program to provide covert aid to resistance movements in Afghanistan, Angola, Cambodia, Cuba, Grenada, Iran, Laos, Libya and Nicaragua ... President Reagan reportedly responded by asking Casey to develop the idea'.[69] As Casey had been Reagan's campaign manager in 1980, the President was buying into a policy proposal from a subordinate who was also one of his closest political advisors.[70] And this advisor would have been selling the proposal not as an innovation in doctrine but a means of implementing one of the President's prior convictions and indeed visionary beliefs.

Reagan had for decades espoused a vision of the US helping to bring about what he considered to be the inevitable collapse of communism – through internal political change – in the Soviet Union as well as its Eastern European satellite states.[71] In the 1970s his anti-communism had been focused on the military build-up by the Soviet Union and by the expansion of its influence and assertiveness in the Third World, but the wider or longer-term vision was still evident. Thus he could (1) warn about the Soviet military build-up and international assertiveness by claiming 'the Russians feel that they are more virile' and that 'we are the Carthage of our time' while (2) also claiming that communism 'is a form of insanity – a temporary aberration which will one day disappear from the earth because it is contrary to human nature'.[72] Compared to this visionary prior conviction, the pioneering Reagan Doctrine was a relatively low-level policy that the President did not have to be dogmatic about.

In fact the President seems to have viewed it is a matter of 'detail' that he could afford to be flexible about and – in terms of Neustadt's ignorance-and-insistence description of his presidential operating style – about which he could afford to be 'ignorant' rather than 'insistent'. Scott pointed out that:

> In truth, President Reagan's involvement in the doctrine that bears his name was episodic at best. Most of the time, President Reagan was a spectator to disputes between advisers, bureaucratic agencies, the executive and legislative branches, and complicated groupings of all three. In fact President Reagan was active and assertive only in the cases of Nicaragua and Afghanistan.[73]

One result of this operating style was that the Reagan Doctrine was applied to no more than five cases and was applied with varying degrees of strength or commitment – depending partly upon the different compromises among the individuals who influenced policy making and had differing interpretations of the 'doctrine'.[74] Only in the case of Afghanistan was the doctrine consistently applied, with substantial military assistance being supplied to the insurgents fighting against the occupying Soviet forces and their local puppet regime. And even this case was affected by the President's operating style in relation to matters of detail. One of the 'several critical instances' when he avoided using his authority to resolve policy disputes among his subordinates was the dispute over supplying the Afghan insurgents with technologically advanced Stinger missiles:

> Reagan refused to resolve the disagreement. Only when the State Department sided with those in favour of supplying the missiles was the logjam broken. When presented with a consensus, Reagan agreed and 'decided' to send the missiles.[75]

Such an operating style clearly has wider implications for the presidential role in foreign policy and for leadership in that policy area. Scott suggested that operating style, policy interests and other personal factors may result in policy leadership shifting, even 'by default', from the President to the foreign-policy bureaucracy; he also pointed to examples of how policy leadership about the details of applying 'the Reagan Doctrine' shifted to *Congress* by default as well as through opposition to the Nicaraguan case: 'congressional involvement was not limited to cases in which the president failed to lead, as the Nicaragua case clearly indicates', but 'the president's disinterest and inaction prompted individual members and the institution as a whole to act'.[76] So evidently US democracy's capacity to use Congress as an alternative source of leadership, as was described in Chapter 1, could be applied to foreign policy, too, even several decades after Roosevelt's presidentialisation of foreign policy.

The contrast between Reagan's and Roosevelt's operating style is also very evident and was pointed out by Neustadt. 'For curiosity and interest in detail, they evidently were at opposite poles', and Reagan's 'lack of detail often left him without the wherewithal for resolution' of disputes among his staff.[77] Furthermore, Roosevelt's actual encouragement of differences among his staff as a means of strengthening his control seems at the opposite pole to Reagan's emotional dislike of such disputes – he apparently grew distraught when his staff argued in his presence.[78] But Reagan had inherited a foreign-policy sector in 1981 that was a textbook case of intensely competitive selling of policy proposals, and without the appropriate form of leadership – by a buyer of policy proposals who was decisive as well as discerning – there was always likely to be problems. When there was no policy leadership coming from either the President or Congress, this 'multivoice' sector experienced 'disagreement and conflict between advisers, agencies, and departments' that could produce compromises, stalemate, contradictory actions and parallel policies in the application of the President's own 'Reagan Doctrine'.[79]

On the other hand, the President's operating style had important advantages as well as disadvantages. As noted earlier, Neustadt acknowledged that the *insistence* component of the ignorance-and-insistence style involves sustained policy commitments, based on prior convictions, that enable a President to make his own choices and to act with a sustained sense of purpose and determination in pursuing these 'conviction' policies. Even the ignorance component of the operating style can be viewed in the more positive light of prioritisation and efficiency – of not wasting time, effort and political capital on matters of detail but instead allocating these scarce resources to matters of substance. In Reagan's case this sense of purpose and priority is evident in his most important pioneering initiative, which occurred in what was then the most important area of government policy – protecting the people from nuclear war – and involved a dramatically innovative change in policy.

In his televised speech of 23 March 1983 he presented to the public his vision of eliminating the threat of nuclear war by developing the technology to shoot down nuclear ballistic missiles – labelled the Strategic Defense Initiative (SDI) by its supporters and 'Star Wars' by its opponents:

> Let me share with you *a vision of the future which offers hope*. It is that we embark upon a program to counter the awesome Soviet missile

threat with measures that are defensive. ... It will take many years, probably decades of effort on many fronts. There will be failures and setbacks, just as there will be successes and breakthroughs. And, as we proceed, we must remain constant in preserving the nuclear deterrent and maintaining a solid capability for flexible response. But isn't it worth every investment necessary *to free the world from the threat of nuclear war?* We know it is.[80]

The vision implicitly replaced the long-standing MAD (mutual assured destruction) deterrent policy with a new policy of relying on defence but its more innovative aspect was what the President saw (idealistically) as the implicit consequences of this shift in policy, namely the eventual elimination of nuclear weapons by mutual agreement among the nuclear powers.

The President had not presented this very innovative and some would say utopian vision to the electorate in 1980 but it was a long-held conviction and produced a sustained policy commitment from the President. Lettow's research has confirmed that since as far back as the 1960s Reagan had abhorred nuclear weapons and also believed (1) that there was an imminent but avoidable prospect of a nuclear war that (as he believed the biblical story of Armageddon had foretold) would end civilisation, (2) that the MAD policy was militarily as well as morally deficient, (3) that the solution to the threat of nuclear war lay in some form of missile defence, and (4) that achieving such a defence would lead to a reduction in nuclear weapons and eventually to their elimination.[81] Furthermore, Lettow shows that this long-held conviction produced a sustained policy commitment by a President who was undeterred by opposition within his administration or the public to his SDI policy and who 'determinedly and skilfully used his power to establish and pursue his ideas as official U.S. policy' – even though these ideas were 'visionary, even utopian'.[82]

However, Reagan's greatest success in freeing the world from the threat of nuclear war would come through the working relationship that he established with the new Soviet leader, Mikhail Gorbachev. This new leader came to power in the Soviet Union some two years after Reagan's SDI speech and would show a liberalising, even democratising tendency that Reagan recognised as offering a great opportunity to end the Cold War. Perhaps because of his long-standing conviction that communism would be ended by internal political change, the President made what seems an almost 'creative' response to this change in the Soviet Union – when other anti-communists and even such pragmatic conservatives as

Nixon were wary about Gorbachev.[83] Mann argues in his recent account of the ending of the Cold War that Reagan's 'decision to do business with Gorbachev' actually 'set the course for the end of the Cold War. If Reagan had not been responsive, then events might have taken a different course during the crucial period from 1985 to 1989'.[84] But perhaps the judgement that Reagan himself would have most appreciated was made by one of his critics, who recently acknowledged that during the late 1980s 'Reagan may have worked harder than any president before or since in trying to convert his imaginative vision that he could personally save the world from a nuclear Armageddon into a reality'.[85]

8
Legislative Pioneering

A congress of individuals

This chapter aims to assess the prevalence of top-down pioneering leadership in the legislative rather than governmental sector – the selling of innovative legislative bills rather than innovative proposals for government policy. As with the chapter on governmental pioneering, the assessment is based upon just one country and institution, in this case the US and its congressional legislature rather than Britain and its Cabinet government. But the US Congress has been chosen not because of its significance to Schumpeter's theory of democracy – which ignored it – but because this legislature is the most likely to have seen many examples of entrepreneurial-style, pioneering leadership. For although the notion of entrepreneurship within the legislature has long been recognised by political scientists, it seems to be solely or very largely associated with the US Congress's Senate and House of Representatives. The independence and power of Congress is one of the distinctive features of the US political system and exemplifies what Kingdon described as the founding fathers' success in designing a constitutionally fragmented system that dispersed power.[1] Thanks to Congress's independence from the executive and to the independence that the individual legislators enjoy within Congress, this legislature offers its members a unique opportunity to sell one another innovative bills, whether as spontaneous initiatives or creative responses to changes occurring outside the legislative sector.

The US Congress is not only a very independent legislature but also very much a congress of individuals. More than 40 years ago Neustadt pointed out that the American constitutional structure of separated institutions sharing powers means that the individuals 'who share in governing this country frequently appear to act as though they were in business for themselves. So, in a real though not entire sense, they are and have to be'.[2] Legislators provide a striking example of this self-employed, businesslike approach when they operate in the electoral/party sector. Although the US has the appearance of a two-party duopoly, the two major parties are more analogous to rival franchising operations than to competing business associations or firms. Their election candidates are individually analogous to a businessman who has successfully bid for the local franchise of one of these nationally known brandnames and must rely largely on his own efforts and strategies in his local competition with the rival brandname's franchise-holder. As Mayhew noted more than 30 years ago, a member of Congress has to mobilise his or her own resources 'to win a nomination and then to win election and reelection. He builds his own election coalition and sustains it'.[3] But once elected he acquires publicly funded staff, administrative and advertising resources that help him sustain this election coalition. In particular, US legislators have been provided with an increasingly abundant supply of personal staff that can be deployed not only in legislative activities but also in servicing constituents and working on the election campaign.[4]

By the mid-1960s members of Congress were energetically working to enhance their individual electoral security by building a personal image and providing services for constituents – in fact displaying such enterprise that they would later be described as 'electoral entrepreneurs'.[5] However, these electoral entrepreneurial activities did not necessarily involve *issue* entrepreneurship. On the contrary, Mayhew pointed out that innovative issue behaviour ran the risk of electoral disaster and that it would be sensible for a reelection-seeking legislator to adopt conservative strategies aimed at keeping an existing electoral coalition together.[6] But he also noted that if the legislator was in great danger of electoral defeat, it might be rational to gamble on ostentatious issue innovation; electorally endangered legislators may indeed function as 'issue pioneers' who 'test out new issues and thereby show other politicians which ones are usable'.[7] This argument is similar to later theories of issue selection/evolution and of heresthetically changing the dimension of alignment by introducing a new issue. Like Riker's theorising about heresthetical issues, though, it is describing an adaptive response that is forced upon the issue innovator by strong electoral competition. For example, when Mayhew pointed to Senator Joseph McCarthy as one of the most successful 'issue entrepreneurs', he also explained how the Senator's innovative anti-Communism issue arose from a desperate search in 1950 for a new issue that would save him from an electoral defeat in two years' time.[8] And as the Cold War was already well under way, McCarthy's anti-Communist witchhunt was a merely adaptive innovation rather than a creative, unpredictable and risky response (which it would have been if he had raised the issue a few years earlier).

By the mid-1960s Congress's legislative activities, too, were becoming individualised after an era that had 'nurtured the development of legislative expertise and individualized policy creativity' and had seen 'the development of members as policy entrepreneurs'.[9] In both houses of Congress power had been dispersed from party leaders to more than a dozen legislative standing committees, each specialising in a particular area of legislation. The committees could now provide their members with power as well as the expertise acquired from carrying out the committee's role of culling and revising the legislative bills introduced by committee members, other legislators or the executive and then reporting back acceptable bills for deliberation and voting on the floor of the house. The individual legislator's power, expertise and policy creativity would be expressed in the 1967–68 Congress's legislative record: over 70 per cent of the bills enacted into law had been introduced by an individual legislator rather than by an executive communication from the President, a Cabinet Secretary or an agency head.[10] The 1970s saw a further tendency towards individualism and the dispersal of power, most notably from House committees to subcommittees, and by the 1980s many Representatives as well as Senators apparently saw themselves 'in policy entrepreneur terms'.[11]

In more recent times political scientists have also depicted them as being political entrepreneurs, bill entrepreneurs or legislative entrepreneurs. But although these various conceptions of congressional entrepreneurship were referring to legislative activism by individual legislators, none referred to the use of initiative and the selling of *innovative* bills – the distinctive features of *pioneering* entrepreneurial-like leadership in the making of laws.[12] Instead, Schiller's, Hall's and Wawro's 1990s research on entrepreneurship was focused on the basic, common features of selling bills within the legislature: introducing and promoting the bill.

Selling bills: introducing/promoting legislation

Schiller's notion of Senators' political entrepreneurship was focused on their introduction (primary sponsorship) of new bills. By the mid-1980s

Senators were introducing nearly 2700 public bills in a two-year period.[13] Although only 236 of these bills eventually became law, the Senators were clearly providing one another with a huge quantity of legislative-bill leads to accept, reject or revise. Moreover, this bill-selling often involved more than simply offering the product for sale; Schiller described Senators as 'promoting' as well as introducing their bills and as 'pushing' bills that they had introduced.[14] She also discovered that some Senators introduced many more than the average 27 bills per two-year period, with the most prolific Senator actually introducing over a hundred bills.[15] In terms of her bill-introduction approach to entrepreneurship, such extraordinarily energetic bill-sellers would have every reason to be considered true entrepreneurs.

Hall's study of Representatives' participation in House legislative activities used a broader notion of entrepreneurship than the introduction-oriented approach. He described entrepreneurship in terms of authoring a bill *or* working behind the scenes to build support for a bill.[16] For example, a Representative privately negotiating with members of his subcommittee about a bill that he had not authored was described by Hall as a 'bill entrepreneur'.[17] Such promotional entrepreneurship took the form of private sales negotiations about modifying the product to suit individual buyers, as it involved negotiating revisions of the bill that would make it more acceptable to his colleagues before their subcommittee began its public markup (revision) of the bill. Another example of promotional entrepreneurship, in this case by several entrepreneurs, can be found in Hall's description of how a bill aimed at reducing unemployment had stimulated what he called 'political entrepreneurship' by African-American and Hispanic members of the House.[18] This included not only one of them being the principal author of the bill but also three others helping with negotiating and redrafting the bill during its committee stages. At any stage of the legislative process such a multi-pronged selling effort may be needed to ensure that the bill is bought by enough colleagues – a large enough coalition of legislators – to move it through to the next stage in the process. Hall noted that although typically only a few legislators will become involved in 'entrepreneurial efforts' on behalf of any particular bill, their efforts are 'crucial to successful coalition building in Congress'.[19]

Wawro's book on legislative entrepreneurship in the House focused on the promotional efforts of its introducer (primary sponsor). He acknowledged that 'some cosponsors help draft and push the legislation and hence deserve some of the credit for "entrepreneuring" it'.[20] But he preferred to concentrate solely on the primary sponsor's entrepreneurial activities, as they are much more readily identified and measured and were probably more substantial than those of the bill's cosponsors. For when Representatives introduce (primary sponsor) a public bill, they are typically taking on responsibility for not only its contents but also such promotional duties as spreading information about the bill and building a coalition in support of it.[21] Wawro also focused on the *quality* of the bills being introduced, and he included measurements of bill-drafting skills among the several quantitative indicators that he used to measure each Representative's degree of entrepreneurship. Bill-drafting skills, specifically the quantity and range of issues addressed, were measured by the number of titles and index items in a Representative's bills, policy knowledge was measured by the number of times a Representative testified before House committees about bills that concerned him or her, and coalition-building skills were measured by the number of other Representatives who cosponsored his or her bills and by the number of times a committee or party leader was one of the cosponsors.[22] With these indicators Wawro computed 'entrepreneurship scale scores' for Representatives during the 1975–94 era, and then performed a multivariate statistical analysis whose results supported his hypothesis that: 'The probability of advancing to a prestigious position within the House increases the more a member engages in legislative entrepreneurship'.[23]

Indeed he argued that 'career concerns' about advancing to these prestigious party and committee leadership positions are a strong *motivating* force that encourages members to engage in legislative entrepreneurship.[24] It is quite understandable that a Representative would have careerist aspirations to acquire such positions, as they are the nearest thing to formal leadership positions within the House. (Much the same could be said of Senators and the equivalent party and committee leadership positions in the Senate, even though these positions are less prestigious and powerful than their House counterparts.) So it appears that extraordinary bill-selling leadership may well be motivated by a careerist aspiration for the leadership positions that provide this individualised legislature with some degree of direction-setting coordination.

Careerist leadership in Congress

Before the 1970s 'Congress was a place where most members sought a lengthy, somewhat leisurely career that would progress in measured and predictable stages' – there was a 'regular ladder of career progress'.[25] Through long service on a legislative standing committee they would develop some degree of expertise about its particular, specialised area of legislation and policy. Seniority alone would guarantee them promotion to chairmanship of this committee, or at least their subcommittee, and open up the prospect of being elected by their party colleagues to a party leadership position, such as Majority/Minority Leader or Whip.

But in the early and mid-1970s new career opportunities were opened up within Congress. This was due to the increased availability of sub-committee leadership positions, the decline of seniority as a criterion for promotion, the inclination of newly elected legislators to seek advancement outside the set career paths, and the fact that many legislators were becoming 'adept at melding policy initiatives into their own career development'.[26] The melding of policy initiatives into career development was a new, bill-selling version of a traditional feature of successful congressional careers: acquiring a reputation for expertise in a particular policy area. Thus a 1985 article on how congressional careers had changed not only emphasised legislators' new attraction to the role of policy entrepreneur but also pointed out that one of the remaining old verities was the importance of developing 'expertise in a subject area' – as in the case of a Representative who rose to the position of Deputy Whip in only his third term after having been 'active in shaping policy alternatives on an array of economic issues'.[27] Instead of congressional career paths being comparable to those of a staid bureaucracy, by the 1980s they were better compared to those of a collective government in which a Minister's prospects for advancement are enhanced by establishing informal, personal leadership of his or her specialised area of government. In the ministerial case this leadership of a policy area was attained through the successful selling of policy proposals, but in the case of congressional careerists such informal leadership – and enhanced prospects for career advancement – was attained through selling legislative bills.

In fact Wawro contended that Representatives operated an 'incentive system' that provided 'incentives for each other to engage in legislative entrepreneurship by making appointment to these positions contingent on a member's entrepreneurial activity'.[28] As he acknowledged, this argument is similar to Mayhew's theory that members of Congress use selective incentives to motivate their colleagues to take on leadership positions that involve gruelling and electorally unrewarding legislative work.[29] Although Mayhew had based his economic model of congressional behaviour on the abstract assumption that legislators are motivated by a singleminded seeking of reelection, he had also theorised that a system of Olson-style selective incentives – offering rewards of personal prestige and power within the legislature – is used to motivate some members to take on party and committee leadership positions that provide all members with the collective good of protecting Congress's institutional prestige and keeping its legislative business moving.[30] Wawro's argument went a step further by suggesting that the prestige and power rewards attached to leadership positions are also used to motivate members to engage in *entrepreneurial* activities, which might be said to provide the collective good of pushing high-quality bills through Congress's fragmented legislative process. Moreover, he pointed out that the prestige and power attached to leadership positions are rewarding because they help to satisfy the three goals that Fenno had identified in the early 1970s as US legislators' basic goals: reelection, influence within the House/Senate and making good public policy (though the order of priority varies according to individual legislators and their circumstances).[31]

Another difference from Mayhew's theory is that Wawro applied his argument to a more extensive range of leadership positions.[32] He referred to extensive committee and party 'hierarchies' that extended down to respectively the subcommittee level and the lowest level of the extensive Whip system.[33] He also argued that the elective nature of these positions was a genuine case of being chosen by one's party colleagues rather than being some form of self-selection, such as the use of seniority as a criterion for choosing subcommittee leaders.[34] And he could have pointed out that the elective nature of these positions means that party and committee leaders who had satisfied their career aspirations could not simply rest on their laurels; they had to live up to their colleagues' expectations or else be replaced at the next party-caucus elections for these positions. Ever since the Democratic party caucus replaced three committee chairmen in 1975, all committee and subcommittee chairs have realised that they do not have secure tenure of their position.[35]

So it would seem that US legislators' bill-selling is basically a careerist, adaptive leadership that introduces and promotes legislative bills in adaptive response to external change. For example, the rapidly promoted Deputy Whip known for his expertise in economic matters was described as having a problem-solving approach to policy, as when he sought some solution to the problem of rising medical costs.[36] Such problems often come to legislators' attention as public issues that are in turn often the product of economic and social changes. Loomis has argued that 'few serious issues escape congressional scrutiny and action' and that Congress is 'especially responsive to changes in the society at large'.[37] However, often it is responding to changes in the political rather than social environment, such as a new President's legislative programme. Thus President Clinton's health-care plan stimulated an openly ambitious Representative to author his own, competing health-care plan.[38]

Furthermore, the adaptive legislative response may be stimulated by a change in the electoral/party sector, in turn often produced by social change, that threatens to bring a legislative career to an abrupt and untimely end. As Mayhew pointed out, continual reelection is the prerequisite for pursuing a career in Congress; reelection is 'the goal that must be achieved over and over if other goals are to be entertained'.[39] And one of his examples of electoral issue pioneering, Senator Magnuson's championing of the consumer, was actually a reelectoral adaptive response that involved bill-selling as well as raising a new issue.[40] This case had already been identified by Price in his widerang-ing studies of the Senate as a legislative institution. He had identified Magnuson as one of the Senators who had been entrepreneurially active in the area of consumer-protection legislation: they were 'acting as policy entrepreneurs, stimulating more than responding to fledgling consumer groups'.[41] In 1965–66 the Magnuson-chaired Senate Commerce Committee had displayed an unusual amount of initiative in reporting bills on consumer affairs, and he had been especially prominent in promoting such consumer-protection bills as the Traffic Safety Act and Cigarette Labelling Act.[42] But his use of bill-selling to create a new political image of himself as the champion of the consumer seems to have been motivated by electoral career concerns, for he had nearly been defeated in the previous senatorial election and was having to deal with changes in the political complexion of his constituency.[43] His bill-selling creation of a new image therefore seems to have been an adaptive response to a constituency-level change in the electoral/party sector. Even if the bills and image were quite innovative, consumer protection was becoming too politically fashionable in the mid-1960s (as will be seen in a later chapter) for them to be classed as a creative response rather than an adaptive innovation.

A very different type of electorally careerist bill-selling occurs when a legislator's careerist aspiration is to be elected to a higher public office – as when a Senator has presidential ambitions or a Representative aims to become a Senator. The presence and implications of this form of careerism have long been recognised by observers of congressional behaviour. Fenno noted that some legislators' goal is a political career beyond the House or beyond the Senate, Mayhew suggested that these ambitious legislators have to develop a new political image in preparation for their appeal to a new constituency, and Loomis pointed out that Representatives with senatorial career ambitions need to attract some statewide rather than merely districtwide media coverage and publicity.[44] An obvious way of pursuing these aims is to introduce and promote bills that are likely to create a new image or attract statewide media attention. And even if these bills are carefully tailored to fit the new image or audience, they may well have innovative qualities. In his study of political innovation Polsby noted that some politicians saw policy innovation as a means of nurturing their ambitions for higher office.[45] He pointed to two presidentially ambitious Senators who were 'notably active and entrepreneurial', and suggested that often a Representative who has been incubating an innovation will soon after be found running for higher office.[46]

However, if this and other forms of congressional careerism are often the motivation for innovative legislation, it begs the question of whether there is much innovating left to be done by *pioneering* legislators. If careerist adaptive responses can account for such a large amount of innovative legislation, does this mean that there are only a few cases of pioneering, *non*-careerist innovation – or at least too few to be worth looking for and presenting as evidence of pioneering leadership in this sector of a democratic political system?

Pioneering leadership in Congress

Despite the seemingly dominant role of careerism as a motivator of innovative legislation, there is still room for a significant amount of pioneering, non-careerist innovation. For example, the statistical relationship between Wawro's entrepreneurial scale scores and promotion to leadership positions does not imply that legislative innovation is always motivated by careerist aspirations for these positions. As has been noted in earlier chapters, every careerist can be expected to indulge in pioneering at least once in his or her career. What is more, non-careerists may well have leadership positions thrust upon them and have good non-careerist reason to accept them. Wawro acknowledged that House members should favour promoting 'individuals with superior entrepreneurial ability because these individuals are best qualified to use the resources associated with prestigious positions to make the machinery of the legislative process work'.[47] If non-careerist legislators had displayed this superior entrepreneurial ability when selling their bills, they would therefore be favoured for promotion to leadership positions. And they have good non-careerist reason to accept a leadership position. For as Wawro had earlier pointed out, acquiring a leadership position can help to satisfy all three of the congressional goals that Fenno identified: the non-careerist goal of *making good public policy* as well as the careerist goals of reelection and influence in the House or Senate.

The fact that making good public policy was identified by Wawro as one of the legislators' goals is also circumstantial evidence that some pioneering bill-selling does occur in Congress. For it is reasonable to expect that the desire to enact good public policy would occasionally motivate legislators to use their initiative and spontaneously introduce/promote innovative bills. Less circumstantial, more direct evidence of pioneering bill-selling can be found in Hall's testimony that there are numerous case studies of 'the activism of some legislative entrepreneur' being motivated 'by personal or ideological commitments, beliefs about justice and fairness, or some general concern that the public interest is being sacrificed for political gain'.[48] Furthermore, Parker has put forward an economic interpretation of congressional behaviour that assumes members of Congress are discretion-maximisers rather than merely reelection-seekers. According to his model, their election campaigning and creation of barriers to entry (such as government-subsidised advertising) are aimed at not merely reelection but the creation of large vote surpluses that would give them the electoral safety to exercise discretion – to follow their personal predilections rather than those of constituents and interest groups.[49] His examples of discretionary activity include ideological legislative behaviour, altruistic voting, passing public-interest legislation and operating as policy entrepreneurs.[50]

It is true that legislators' opportunities for pioneering legislative initiatives are limited by the competition among bill-sellers for space on the crowded legislative agenda. Walker pointed out in the 1970s that the agenda has to give priority (1) to annually recurring legal necessities and government housekeeping requirements, such as the budget and appropriations, (2) to more sporadically recurring items that are also virtually forced upon the agenda, and (3) to national crises or pressing problems, where the media and public are expecting some immediate action by Congress.[51] There is, of course, usually some space left on the annual agenda for several legislative items that are not merely responding to crises or to recurring requirements. But Walker pointed out that there is intense competition for this space, which he termed the 'discretionary' part of the agenda, and that therefore any discretionary bill can expect only a short-lived span of legislative attention before the competitive pressures for agenda space become too strong.[52] Clearly there is little opportunity to introduce a pioneering bill and push it through the crowded as well as fragmented legislative process.

On the other hand, the crisis part of the legislative agenda offers opportunities to introduce and promote at least *partly* pioneering bills – as creative responses to external crises. An interesting example can be found in Schuck's account of the creative bill-selling leadership provided by Senator Simpson and Representative Mazzoli in the 1982–85 reform of immigration law. He described these two legislators as policy entrepreneurs who were 'under few constituent pressures on immigration' and were 'not thought to harbor higher political ambitions'.[53] But nor were they spontaneously introducing/promoting their bill on immigration. Each was chairman of an immigration subcommittee and therefore was expected to respond to the apparent immigration crisis of the early 1980s by introducing or promoting a bill that would address the crisis. What *was* unexpected was the creativity of their legislative response. They put together a bill that was so ambitious that although it initially failed to pass the House, the Representatives gave Mazzoli a standing ovation in recognition of what was seen as a 'heroic effort'.[54] He and his Senate counterpart had taken the risk of trying to sell their colleagues an ambitious reform of immigration law rather than offering them merely a marginal change or minimal innovation that would have been readily accepted.

But what makes this case particularly interesting is that it included a reframing of the external change to make it appear dramatic enough to justify an ambitious response. The two pioneers and other reform-seeking legislators magnified 'an already acute fear of change into a deep sense of crisis' and, by 'defining the crisis in ways that invited certain policy solutions', created a political opportunity to sell a sweeping reform of immigration law.[55] The reframing of the external change into an appropriate crisis was an important part of a creative response that transformed these recognised policy entrepreneurs into pioneering legislative leaders.

Yet despite the various evidence of legislative pioneering's existence and potential, there is no reliable way of assessing its extent and its historical tendency to increase or decrease in the 1960s–90s period. While there has been substantial research on entrepreneurship in Congress, including some quantitative research, it has not been looking for the *pioneering* entrepreneurship of innovative initiative or creative response. Although the background conditions of the 1960s–90s would seem to favour an increase in pioneering, they also appear to favour a career-ist form of innovation that is difficult to distinguish from pioneering without closer examination – on a seemingly case by case basis. Until such research is forthcoming from students of congressional behaviour, all that can be said is that the available evidence seems to suggest that legislative pioneering is less prevalent than might at first appear and showed no obvious tendency towards an overall, long-term increase or decrease during the 1960s–90s period.

9
Administrative Pioneering

The entrepreneurial-like administrative leader

Senior-level public administrators provide a very unpublic, anonymous form of political leadership within their sector of the political system. They privately give one another (and often politicians in the governmental or legislative sectors) a lead by selling proposals for administrative policies, government policies or legislative bills. Although administrators' proposals are normally motivated by careerism and are merely adaptive responses, on some occasions they are entrepreneurial-style, pioneering proposals.

But a distinctive feature of administrative pioneering is how often it involves the creation of innovative institutions rather than policies, laws or issues. These innovative institutions are organisations that have been created as administrative tools and gone on to be institutionalised. The new administrative tool may have been created from scratch, as with Pinchot's Forest Rangers, or may have been created through modifying an existing organisation, as in the case of Hoover's FBI. Similarly, the administrative pioneer may have openly and even formally proposed establishing the new tool or may have almost surreptitiously used a series of more minor policy proposals and shrewd administrative measures to bring the new tool into existence. In fact the creation of an innovative administrative tool is quite commonly attributed to a pioneering administrator rather than to the pioneering leader(s) in the governmental or legislative sector who on-sold the administrator's proposal. This suggests that the administrator not only has played the most important part in bringing about the innovation but also has become a well-recognised and even *publicly* recognised leader in his or her specialised area of administration and policy.

As in the case of legislative pioneering leadership, the American political system is where examples of administrative pioneering are likely to be found in some numbers and therefore will be used to assess the prevalence of administrative pioneering in the 1960s–90s period. The US federal administrative sector has produced some historically famous examples of administrative pioneer, and the notion of 'entrepreneurship' has been applied quite often to its administrators.

But, as in the case of the US legislature, the various notions of entrepreneurship that have been applied to the administrative sector have not included the Schumpeterian, pioneering kind of entrepreneurship. For example, in the early 1980s a comparative study of the role of politicians and public-sector bureaucrats in western democracies argued that the 'institutional disaggregation' of the American system leads to institutional incentives that 'generate entrepreneurial instincts in American bureaucrats'.[1] This institutional disaggregation included not only the independence of the legislature from the government but also the role of powerful interest groups. Their influence over Congress and, in turn, its readiness to reject the executive's bills meant that American bureaucrats had to have closer or more active relations with interest groups and legislators than did their equivalents in other western democracies.[2] However, this conception of entrepreneurial activities seems to involve no more than having to spend a lot of time and effort in selling proposals to several different buyers – interest groups and Congress as well as the presidential government. There is nothing to distinguish the selling of *pioneering* proposals from the selling of proposals for adaptive responses. Like the many cases of applying the notion of entrepreneurship to the US legislature, there is no concern with the Schumpeterian, pioneering kind of entrepreneurship.

Several years later, Doig and Hargrove's book on innovative administrative leadership went a step further and emphasised the innovative element involved in administrative entrepreneurship. Because of 'the fragmented nature of the American political system, [administrative] leaders bent on *innovation* must gather support from private interest groups, other government agencies, the media, and elected officials'.[3] As the political system's fragmentation and decentralisation obstructs orderly innovation, there is a need for leaders who 'can define new goals, build coalitions that knit together public and private interests, and carry out other entrepreneurial tasks'.[4] However, as will be seen later in the chapter, they did not espouse a Schumpeterian notion of administrative entrepreneurial leadership.

Similarly, Lewis's landmark theory of 'public entrepreneurship' within the US administrative sector is not based on Schumpeter's concept of entrepreneurship. Nonetheless, Lewis's work showed that the giants among the entrepreneurial-style, pioneering administrative leaders (1) can become public figures who obviously provide some form of political leadership within their specialised policy area, (2) can be driven by a pioneering mission in life and (3) can achieve a degree of political autonomy that might well be viewed as a misappropriation not only of their administrative powers but also indirectly of the governmental or legislative powers enjoyed by the country's formal leaders.

Very public and autonomous pioneering administrators

In his (1980) *Public Entrepreneurship: Toward a Theory of Bureaucratic Political Power* Lewis defined a public entrepreneur as 'a person who creates or profoundly elaborates a public organization so as to alter greatly the existing pattern of allocation of scarce public resources'.[5] (What he termed 'elaborating' an organisation means acquiring new policies for it to implement and/or making important changes to the organisation as an administrative tool.) Obviously this is not a very Schumpeterian conception of administrative entrepreneurship. There is no mention of initiative or innovation and instead the focus is on the allocation of public resources. This was probably due to Lewis's concern with public entrepreneurs' constitutionally paradoxical amount of autonomy and power. He argued that since the 1930s the typical public organisation had become less responsive to its constitutional masters, the elected public officials.[6] And some public organisations had become 'unusually potent political forces' under the leadership of public entrepreneurs who 'attempt to expand the goals, mandates, functions and power of their organizations' in ways that had not been foreseen by their constitutional masters.[7]

Of course it had long been known that the organisational needs of public-sector bureaucracies played a major role in the making of public policy. Moreover, Polsby was already describing such needs as a routine source of the stimulus for bureaucracies' invention of innovative public policies (even if only such forced adaptive innovations as the saving of a research laboratory from closure).[8] He also pointed to the role of individual policy entrepreneurs within the federal bureaucracies. Such entrepreneurial individuals had 'ideas of their own and opportunities to write these ideas into the law of the land'.[9] But he suggested that there was a 'symbiosis' between these policy entrepreneurs and political leaders, with the politicians enacting the entrepreneurs' preferred policy alternatives (buying and on-selling their policy proposals) and the entrepreneurs letting the politicians take the public credit for these policies.[10]

In contrast, Lewis argued that public entrepreneurs had become public figures and political leaders *in their own right*, though only as specialists in a particular area of expertise:

> Somewhere between the man on the white horse and the organization-as-machine metaphor lies the public entrepreneur. He resembles that strong man and embodies much of the leviathan, but only in his corner of the social universe. He tells us what to do about many things, but not about all things.[11]

However, a recent study of bureaucratic autonomy in the US between the Civil War and the New Deal indicates that Lewis may have been wrong in thinking that such policy-expert political leaders have become more evident since the 1930s. Carpenter describes how the early 'administrative entrepreneurs' exploited their own and their agencies' reputations for 'expertise, efficiency or moral protection' to win autonomy and new policies for the Department of Agriculture and the Post Office.[12] (Perhaps the earliest example is the Comstock anti-pornography law of 1873 that transformed Comstock's Post Office into a guardian of the nation's morals.) He presents 'a narrative of organisational evolution and bureaucratic entrepreneurship' that is dominated by such publicly well-known administrators as Pinchot of the Forest Rangers and Dr Wiley of the 1906 Pure Food and Drug Act.[13] As chief chemist for the Department of Agriculture, Wiley was the country's leading crusader for legislation to protect consumers from impure food and drugs, and his effectiveness as a pioneering administrator was largely due to 'the publicity and even sensationalism he was able to mobilize for his cause'.[14] The tendency for some pioneering administrators to become publicly recognised policy-expert political leaders has clearly been a distinctive feature of the American political system for a century or more.

Their status as *pioneering* as well as publicly recognised leaders arises from the innovativeness of their policy or organisational proposals and the non-careerist motivation that lay behind these proposals – as a creative response or spontaneous initiative. In the case of Lewis's examples of public entrepreneurship, it is clear from his description of them that they are not careerists and indeed seem to have a pioneering mission in life. He pointed out that their goals cannot be described as 'making it to the top',[15] and that their lives were focused on a particular policy or organisational goal, such as the public entrepreneur 'who lived his life only to build the nuclear submarine' or the one who 'prowled the urban scenes and rural pastures in search of something to build or change according to his desire and his perception of what the public wanted (or should want, if it thought about it)'.[16] Although the three examples that Lewis chose as his prime illustrations of the public entrepreneur were very much 'driven men', he emphasised that they did not start out as careerists and never would derive their life's satisfaction from careerist rewards but from the accomplishment of their own ends, which they claimed were the ends that society dictated (or should dictate, if it thought about it).[17]

These three prime illustrations of public entrepreneurship were J. Edgar Hoover, Admiral Rickover and Robert Moses. The most famous of the three is Hoover, who needs no further introduction as the man who transformed the FBI into an internationally renowned and almost mythic institution. His surreptitious elaboration of the FBI organisation into a de facto national police force was an incremental, step-by-step form of elaboration that was accompanied by his repeated denunciations of the very idea of a national police force as unconstitutional and unrealistic.[18] Some ten years after he became Director of the Justice Department's Bureau of Investigation, Hoover put together the key group of incremental steps that took the Bureau and him to a nationally prominent position from which he never looked back. For during 1932–35 he created such national organs or influences as the FBI Crime Laboratory, the FBI Law Enforcement Bulletin, the FBI Police Training School, and an unprecedented media blitz that produced a mythology or holy trinity of the G-Man, the Bureau, and the Director.[19] Hoover is therefore an example of how a pioneering administrator's well-directed series of minor proposals and administrative measures can culminate quite quickly in the surreptitious elaboration of his organisation into something quite innovative – in this case the foundations of a de facto national police force. He is also a perhaps unique example of the pioneering administrator viewing his innovative tool as the main goal of his pioneering mission, not as merely a means for achieving a policy goal; Hoover actually avoided new law-enforcement roles, such as tackling organised crime and drug trafficking, that might endanger the FBI's image of omniscience and incorruptibility.[20]

Rickover is best known for his brilliant leadership of an innovative and technically difficult engineering project: the development of nuclear propulsion for submarines and of a nuclear-powered submarine fleet. His instigation of this nuclear-propulsion project was a 'triumph of entrepreneurship' that required him to sell an innovative proposal not only to his superiors in the Navy but also to the civilian Atomic Energy Commission and in a sense even to private-sector contractors.[21] Moreover, to carry out his innovative policy goal he created a complex and loosely knit military/civilian organisation centred upon his personal position as the de facto head of a division of the Westinghouse corporation as well as the formal head of branches of the Navy's Bureau of Ships and the civilian Atomic Energy Commission.[22] His unique military/civilian organisation also went on to win the AEC's contest to develop the world's first commercial electricity-generating reactor, and in successfully completing this project he set the country's nuclear power industry firmly on the road to the light-water type of reactor.[23] But unlike Hoover, Rickover did not view his organisation as anything more than a tool for achieving policy goals, especially his pioneering mission of building a nuclear-powered submarine fleet.

Robert Moses is not as well known as Hoover or Rickover but carried out a massive construction programme of new parks, bridges, highways and other public works in New York city and state in the 1920s–60s. His pioneering mission was apparently to improve and modernise (particularly automobilise) the urban environment of New York through this long-term series of public works. But unlike Hoover and Rickover, Moses did not focus upon any particular administrative tool; he created various new organisations and viewed them as merely 'tools to get things done'.[24] This approach has led to unfavourable comparisons being made with Austin Tobin's elaboration and institutionalisation of the New York Port Authority as a lasting administrative legacy that has long outlived him.[25] But Moses could be said to have brought about a significant administrative innovation and legacy by elaborating the actual *concept* of a public authority. For his Triborough Bridge Authority attained an unprecedented degree of autonomy by entering into a contractual agreement with its bond holders that indirectly removed most of the controls which public officials might have exerted over this supposedly 'public' administrative tool.[26]

In fact Lewis pointed out that Moses himself, like Hoover and Rickover, achieved a degree of autonomy that most people would believe to be impossible within a public-sector bureaucracy.[27] He memorably described Moses as an example of a newly evolved, better-adapted form of capitalist entrepreneur that had insulated itself from both the economic and political marketplaces.[28] Similarly, Hoover established a legendary autonomy from Presidents as well as from Congress, and Rickover's autonomy from the Navy and Defense Department was dramatically displayed when his military superiors tried to retire him but were blocked by his supporters in Congress.[29] It is not surprising that Lewis viewed autonomy, in the sense of freedom from accountability, as a defining characteristic of the public entrepreneur.[30]

But autonomy can involve much more than just freedom from accountability. For example, it can also involve freedom from interference in decisions about what, how and when to do things. Hoover, Rickover and Moses established what Lewis described as an 'apolitical shield' against political (and administrative) interference by creating a public image of professional, politically neutral concern for the public interest.[31] Moreover, this public image could be used as a sword as well as shield: it was a 'power-generating element of incalculable value, and our three entrepreneurs employed it to the utmost to obtain and secure mandates and resources'.[32] Thus the autonomy of these three administrators included the power to obtain new things, including the acceptance of new policy proposals, from their administrative and political superiors.

Such a high degree of autonomy also seems to be implied by Lewis's definition of the public entrepreneur as the creator or elaborator of an organisation. By attributing these organisational innovations to an administrator, not to the politicians who formally create or elaborate the organisations, Lewis seems to be implying that some administrators have achieved such a high degree of autonomy that in practice they have indirectly wielded some of the governmental and legislative powers of the country's formal leaders. These highly autonomous administrators still need to have their proposals bought and on-sold by the country's formal leaders but can confidently expect quick and easy sales to happy customers – or indeed subtlely *coerced* customers. As Carpenter has pointed out, politicians may suffer electoral or other costs if they refuse to buy the proposals of such autonomous administrators.[33] A classic example described by Lewis is how Hoover's highly effective selling of his Bureau and himself to the public over the heads of Presidents and legislators would have enabled him to inflict some electoral costs on politicians if they were not happy to be his loyal customers for policy proposals and budget requests.[34] Even the non-coercive influence that forestry administrator Pinchot exerted over President Theodore Roosevelt, as a friend and policy ally, has in fact been described as a 'usurpation'.[35] Pinchot, Hoover and other highly autonomous administrators might well be viewed as having misappropriated not only their public administrative powers but also some of their political superiors' governmental or legislative powers.

However, autonomy is not the only reason why the creation or elaboration of an innovative organisation might be attributed to an administrator rather than to a politician. Another reason is that the administrator brought about the new organisation by putting together a package of measures (Rickover) or incremental steps (Hoover) whose on-sellers and buyers were not fully aware of the organisational implications of what they were doing. In these cases the achieving of a high degree of autonomy is a result rather than a means of creating or elaborating the organisation.[36] As the head of the new organisation the pioneering administrator is in a position to achieve a degree of autonomy that will ensure he or she is able to carry out a pioneering mission and perhaps move on to a second-stage mission, such as Rickover's goal of creating a nuclear-powered surface fleet.

Many politicians would envy these autonomous administrators their career security, power to do things and freedom from accountability for their actions. (It is true that an autonomous administrator's leadership does not extend beyond the area of his or her policy expertise but most elected politicians, too, never become anything more than policy-specialised leaders in a collective government or congressional legislature.) On the other hand, even the most autonomous administrators are still dependent upon the elected politician's willingness to buy their proposals and to refrain from interfering in their areas of administration and policy. Any misappropriation of powers cannot be formally legitimated and is always vulnerable to elected politicians reasserting their formal right to exercise the power to decide. Doig and Hargrove argued that an administrative entrepreneur's eventual failure is often linked to a loss of support from politicians, whether because of a shift in the tide of politics or because the entrepreneur has fallen out of favour with a political patron or the patron's successor.[37] Many examples of this political vulnerability can be found in the (1987) collection of biographical studies of prominent US administrators, *Leadership and Innovation*, that Doig and Hargrove edited and introduced.[38] Thus the collection's two Defense Secretaries, Forrestal and McNamara, were marginalised when they lost the confidence of the President. And in Pinchot's case, his unusually influential position as a friend and policy ally of the President was ended by Theodore Roosevelt's retirement, and he was further weakened when he fell out with Roosevelt's successor, President Taft. Similarly, Hanks's position as head of the National Endowment for the Arts (NEA) was weakened when her strong links to the Nixon administration were ended by the President's resignation. The retirement of a sympathetic congressional chairman (of the House's Interior Appropriations Subcommittee) also weakened her position and highlights her dependence upon congressional as well as presidential support. Webb was very conscious of the need for NASA to maintain broad political support, congressional as well as presidential, and his worries about political vulnerability were confirmed by the budget cuts of 1967–68 that preceded his retirement. At the subnational level, Lilienthal was at least able to use his Tennessee Valley Authority (TVA)'s grassroots-democracy ideal and myth as protection against interference from Washington. But Tobin resigned from the New York Port Authority partly because he could no longer expect the Governors of New York and New Jersey to back his proposals for new programmes and projects.

These cases of political vulnerability seem in striking contrast to the degree of autonomy achieved by Hoover, Rickover and Moses. Yet Hoover was the only one of the three to retain his political invulnerability until the end of his career. Rickover was forced by lack of presidential support to give up his second-stage mission of creating a nuclear-propelled surface fleet; Moses was politically out-manoeuvred and consigned to a consultancy after nearly half a century of pursuing his pioneering mission.[39] There were limits to how far or for how long even their autonomy could extend.

Nonetheless, these three individuals stand out as quite extraordinary even when compared to other administrative pioneers. The more regular cases of administrative pioneering are much less powerful and prominent and are much less likely to have their innovation attributed to them rather than to politicians. Later in the chapter there will be a 'tip of the iceberg' assessment (using fluctuations in the number of the more prominent examples as an indicator of fluctuations in the prevalence of the comparatively anonymous or hidden examples) that will estimate how prevalent the regular form of administrative pioneering was during the 1960s–90s. But first the iceberg-tip sample will have to be expanded to include more than just the three giants described by Lewis. Some other suitably prominent administrative leaders are likely to be found in Doig and Hargrove's earlier-mentioned collection of biographical studies, but their credentials as *pioneering* administrative leaders will have to be examined and approved before they can be included in this select sample.

Checking out pioneering credentials

The collection contained a broad and well-balanced range of prominent administrative leaders. The technologically famous cases of Rickover and Webb (with their nuclear-propulsion and moon-landing projects) were balanced by the natural-resource and historically early case of Pinchot, the innovative head of the Forestry Division of the Department of Agriculture. Similarly, the studies of two famous Defense Secretaries, Forrestal and McNamara, were balanced by studies of Ball and Cohen's contribution to social security and of Hanks's development of the National Endowment for the Arts. The subnational level was represented by studies of Lilienthal and the famous Tennessee Valley Authority and of Tobin and the New York Port Authority. In addition to Rickover, the list included two cases that Lewis had mentioned as possible examples of public entrepreneur, Lilienthal and Webb, but did not include his other two possible examples: General Groves of the Manhattan Project and Admiral Raborn of the Polaris missile system.[40]

The book's title and subtitle, *Leadership and Innovation: A Biographical Perspective on Entrepreneurs in Government*, implied that it would be using an innovation-centred notion of administrative entrepreneurship. Its editors confirmed that impression by describing the biographies as studies of public-sector managers whose careers were 'linked to innovative ideas and to efforts to carry these ideas into effect' – and by noting that the term 'entrepreneur' was often used to describe innovative activity in the business world.[41] However, there was no definition of innovative activities by public-sector managers, nor was there any mention of innovation in the suggested checklist of entrepreneurial leaders' activities. The only indication of what was meant by innovation was the comment that these entrepreneurs are personally involved in devising and implementing new programmes 'or *other* significant innovations'.[42]

The individual biographical studies by various contributors were just as reticent about specifying what was innovative activity. The nearest thing to an actual definition of innovation was Shapley's description of public-sector entrepreneurs as organising 'institutions and programs to run along new, often *original*, lines'.[43] Her study of Defense Secretary McNamara described his introduction of an original managerial system, the Planning Programming Budgeting System (PPBS), that was soon copied by other departments and even spread to the private sector.[44] But PPBS was not an innovative organisation or public policy or even a revolutionary managerial innovation that had a major effect on the administrative sector.

In contrast, Cooper's study of Pinchot contained a textbook example of an innovative administrative organisation being created from scratch. Pinchot's uniformed force of Forest Rangers was a unique administrative tool whose nearest equivalent was the military or the Texas Rangers.[45] Another example of a globally unique administrative innovation can be found in Hargroves's study of Lilienthal and the TVA. Lilienthal's introduction of grassroots democratic participation in the TVA was publicised nationally and even internationally as embodying 'altogether new precepts of democratic public administration'.[46] He was actually espousing a new philosophy of decentralised and democratic public administration, with a multipurpose regional administration operating through grass-roots democratic participation.[47]

However, the question of what constitutes a significant innovation arose again in Wyszomirski's study of Hanks's leadership of the NEA. Although Hanks energetically developed the fledgling NEA by adding many new programmes for assisting the arts, she tended to introduce innovative programmes that had already been instituted by another organisation and had shown that they could achieve results. Wyszomirski described this tendency as adopting 'pretested program initiatives' or 'adapting ideas that had already been piloted elsewhere'.[48] But Hanks appears much more innovative in her mobilisation of the arts constituency to lobby Congress in support of her new programmes and funding requests. She continually mobilised new segments of the arts constituency (even promoting the establishment of such new organisations as the National Opera Institute) and rewarded them with NEA benefits for their lobbying efforts. Eventually she began to run out of arts interests to incorporate into her 'political support coalition', but by then she had mobilised and organised the once politically weak arts community into 'a potent political interest group' that arguably constituted an innovative auxiliary, political arm of the NEA.[49]

There is no doubt that her leadership of the NEA became Hanks's pioneering mission in life. In 1977 her commitment to the mission led her to make the ultimate sacrifice of retiring early, after only eight years at the helm, so that the NEA could benefit from a different type of leader.[50] A similarly strong non-careerist motivation, though of a different nature, is evident in the case of Tobin's long and innovative 1942–71 leadership of the New York Port Authority. Doig's study of Tobin actually quoted from Schumpeter's *Theory of Economic Development* account of entrepreneurship, with its emphasis on the unusual motivation of entrepreneurs.[51] Doig argued that Tobin maintained his entrepreneurial motivation and energy throughout his many years at the Port

Authority, and resigned when political changes meant that 'the job was more a burden than a range of new and stimulating challenges'.[52] In Tobin's case therefore the pioneer seems driven more by a love of the job's challenges than by commitment to a pioneering mission that is carried out through the job. Nonetheless, there is no question about Tobin's pioneering credentials as a non-careerist user of initiative and maker of creative responses.

But in other cases administrators' pioneering credentials *are* questionable as regards their use of initiative or making of a creative rather than adaptive response. For example, Marmor's study of Ball and Cohen's influence on social-insurance policy innovation indicated that 'in the disability and medicare cases, it was less that new ideas were introduced than that older visions were reintroduced in more amenable times'.[53] Furthermore, he suggested that if other social-insurance experts had filled Ball's and Cohen's positions, there would have been little difference in the final outcome, which hardly suggests that they were showing unusual initiative or making an imaginative and unpredictable, creative response.[54] Although he referred to them as social-security entrepreneurs, public entrepreneurs and programme entrepreneurs, there is little evidence of their also being pioneering entrepreneurs.[55]

Doubts can also be raised about the pioneering credentials presented by Lambright's study of Webb's entrepreneurial leadership of NASA and its Apollo moon-landing project. Webb had displayed some administrative entrepreneurship when director of the Bureau of the Budget in 1946–49, but after a less successful stint as a State Department undersecretary, he returned to the private sector and continued with his business career until asked by Kennedy to become head of the fledgling NASA.[56] He introduced several new features that arguably elaborated it into an innovative administrative tool. In particular, he introduced a new form of partnership with private-sector industry, which carried out most of NASA's work through some 20,000 different companies.[57] Webb sought to establish a close and trusting public/private-sector relationship that differed markedly from the traditional legalistic relationship between a government agency and private-sector contractors. Instead of relying on the traditional threat of inflicting punitive legal sanctions for performance/cost failures, he preferred an interdependent and problem-solving partnership that saw NASA deeply involved in supervising private-sector companies' handling of NASA-related technical projects. Later he went so far as borrowing experts from Boeing to assist NASA's monitoring of its North American Aviation contractor. However, it was Rickover who had been the first to institute public-sector managerial control of work carried out by a private-sector contractor, even if he had shown a more authoritarian and hard-nosed attitude towards his contractors.[58]

There must be doubts, too, about how much entrepreneurial initiative or creativity Webb used in proposing the Apollo project.[59] Soon after its creation NASA had devised a manned moon-landing programme called Apollo but the moon-landing goal had not been proposed to President Eisenhower or to Kennedy as the incoming President. Webb did not know whether the new President would support such a major project and 'was himself somewhat ambivalent initially', as he 'feared that there might not be the long-term political support necessary to support such a project'.[60] This makes a striking contrast with Rickover's determined sales effort aimed at getting a nuclear-propulsion project up and running. Furthermore, Webb initially described Apollo to President Kennedy as a vehicle for trips to the vicinity of the moon, not for a moon landing, because he did not want to propose a goal that 'went beyond what I thought Kennedy was willing to approve'.[61] Again, this does not seem very entrepreneurial-like behaviour, especially in the administrator's dream situation of being able to sell proposals directly to the President.

In April 1961 there was a marked change in the political environment, with Kennedy now asking for recommendations about how to develop a space programme that would make the US number one in space. For in that month the Soviet Union had put the first man in space, and American morale had been further damaged by the Bay of Pigs fiasco. 'Now the opportunity was there, and Webb made the most of it.'[62] But in proposing the Apollo project in response to the President's prompting, he seems to be making more of an adaptive than a creative response. After all, would a rationally self-interested careerist administrator have responded any differently from Webb in this situation?

A question mark also hangs over his failure to sell President Johnson and Congress any major post-Apollo project. But Lambright argued that it is doubtful whether anyone could have done so in such an unfavourable political environment, and certainly NASA was suffering budget cuts even before Webb's 1968 resignation and the completion of the moon-landing project in 1969.[63] He also seems to have had the rug pulled out from under him by the President's unilateral decision to bring forward Webb's intended resignation.[64] If he had been given more time to prepare his departure, he might have been able to live up to his reputation for turning a problem into an opportunity and have produced 'a lemon into lemonade' creative response to the post-Apollo problem.

But it is unlikely that he would have matched the brilliant example described in Cornell and Leffler's study of Forrestal. As Secretary of the Navy Department he turned the unwanted pressure for creating a unified Department of Defense into an opportunity to create an innovative administrative tool – the National Security Council. At an early stage in the debate over defence-unification he began selling an imaginative, unpredictable and patriotically motivated proposal to create a council that would coordinate national-security decision making among military and civilian departments.[65] The establishing of a National Security Council was thus a truly creative response that was combined with the adaptive innovations Forrestal used to defend the Navy's interests against the threat posed by pressure to replace the service Departments with a unified Defense Department. Indeed, 'more than any other single individual he shaped the National Security Act of 1947' that established the NSC and a unified but tripartite and confederal Department of Defense – which he headed for two unsuccessful and personally disastrous years.[66] As so often happens with creative responses, Forrestal's NSC innovation has proved to be controversial but it also has had a greater effect than the innovations of most other prominent pioneering administrators.

Assessing the prevalence of administrative pioneering

With this larger sample of prominent examples, a proper 'tip of the iceberg' assessment can be made of the prevalence of administrative pioneering in the 1960s–90s. The iceberg method of assessment assumes that fluctuations in the number of highly prominent examples of a phenomenon will provide a rough and ready indicator of fluctuations in the prevalence of less prominent, more regular examples.

In the case of administrative pioneering, the fluctuations indicate that the 1960s–90s was not as good a period as the 1920s–50s had been – the period when Hoover, Moses, Lilienthal, Tobin, Rickover and Forrestal rose to prominence. In fact the 1960s–90s period was not much better than the early era of administrative pioneering, which had seen not only Pinchot but also Wiley and such nineteenth-century examples as Comstock.

The 1960s–90s period also seems to have peaked quite early – in its first decade. Hoover, Moses and Tobin were still operating and a new group, Webb, McNamara and Hanks, were making or beginning to make their pioneering mark. But the 1970s saw no new figures emerge and witnessed the demise of all the remaining examples from earlier decades. It is not surprising that Carpenter's recent study of the early era of bureaucratic autonomy (the 1870s–1920s) suggested that such autonomy is less likely to occur in contemporary American politics.[67]

In contrast, at the beginning of the 1980s Lewis had believed that public entrepreneurs, the most autonomous and prominent of administrative pioneers, were by no means a thing of the past.

> [For] public entrepreneurs of the future live embryonically in one organization or another. They plan, scheme, wait and watch for that moment when the entrepreneurial leap is possible. Most won't make it or will be only partially successful. But they are there, and the structural conditions for their creation and for the production of thousands of their successors appear to be excellent.[68]

It is hard to see why he believed there were 'excellent' structural conditions for the emergence of a new generation of Hoovers and Rickovers. He acknowledged that his book was more concerned with the entrepreneurs themselves than with the 'general historical conditions of a structural variety which are conducive to their entrepreneurship'.[69] But the book had noted that Rickover had taken advantage of the Cold War situation, that Hoover had been assisted by the rise of the gangster desperado and by the Bureau's wartime counter-intelligence role, and that Moses had capitalised on the Depression and New Deal.[70] If historical circumstances of similar drama and magnitude were unlikely to arise in the post-1980 world, what other sorts of helpful or opportune structural conditions might there be? The answer seems to lie in Lewis's description of the public entrepreneur as a new kind of political leader 'successfully adapted' to great and immediate transformations that the 'traditional political system itself could not (or would not) respond to'; the public entrepreneurs gave the impression that they 'possessed a knowledgeability and a capacity to carry out monumental tasks that no other element of the political system seemed able to accomplish'.[71] These great transformations and tasks clearly have a strong technological aspect, which the public entrepreneur exploits through explicit or implicit claims to knowledgeability and technical capacity. Technology was at the heart of Rickover's development of nuclear power, was central to Moses's public works, and was prominent in Hoover's highly professionalised FBI.

Moreover, in a later (1988) analysis of public entrepreneurs and technological change Lewis confirmed that the constant development of technology has created historical conditions that are conducive to the rise of public entrepreneurs. In this article he acknowledged that innovative change was the hallmark of public entrepreneurs, and focused on their management of technological innovation.[72] Introducing fundamental, not merely incremental, technological innovations also means 'creating or designing organizations *to create* technological change'.[73] His three historical examples of this combination of technological and organisational innovation were the Manhattan Project to invent an atomic bomb, Nazi Germany's development of the V2 rocket, and the Soviet Union's rocket and space programme. In each case the technological and organisational innovations were fathered by a scientist-engineer (Oppenheimer, von Braun and Korolev) who displayed political-administrative as well as technological virtuosity. Indeed Lewis argued that each of these geniuses possessed a new, 'technoauthority' form of charismatic legitimacy based on our modern era's 'secular religion' of technology.[74]

But he also went on to argue that such giants have passed from the scene and that their mediocre successors have exploited the legacy of that heroic era for much less innovative ends. For there is now a 'technological teleology' that is evident in the strong tendency to 'elaborate' the new defence/space technology, with its accompanying computer technology.[75] And the continual elaboration of these new technical systems and situations has presented an opportunity for some individuals to become 'techno-entrepreneurial' leaders of not only their organisations but also 'the public-policy processes that are supposed to direct them'.[76] However, Lewis pointed out that these techno-entrepreneurial leaders were concerned with elaborating *existing* technology rather than introducing such fundamental innovations as the atomic bomb.[77] Techno-entrepreneurship therefore involves a much humbler form of organisational and policy innovation than did the public entrepreneurship of the heroic, technologically innovative era.

It seems that the extinction of the giants of public entrepreneurship was due to the changing technological conditions of the 1970s–80s as well as to the lack of dramatic historical circumstances. The IT revolution that was occurring in the private sector of the economy – and was being promoted by business entrepreneurs, such as Gates and Jobs, who would become as famous as Hoover or Rickover – was not having a similar effect on public policy and administration. Instead a new recognition and prominence was given to a debased notion of public entrepreneurship under the title of 'policy entrepreneurship'. The concept of policy entrepreneurship was not always used in this manner, as is evident in Mintrom's argument for viewing policy entrepreneurship as an exceptional and extraordinary case of policy making.

> In the world of quiet, business-as-usual politics, where incremental policy change is the rule, we should not expect to find individuals acting in the capacity of policy entrepreneurs....So, we might call the notion of policy entrepreneur a concept for extraordinary politics. To say this, of course, is to tightly circumscribe our expectations of the concept's applicability. This, I think, is a good thing.[78]

But clearly the concept was being applied in a loose manner and not being confined to cases of 'extraordinary politics'. Landy's mid-1990s criticism of policy entrepreneurship in federal administrative agencies suggested that it had actually become a career *norm* rather than something extraordinary. Senior-level and even middle-level bureaucrats had come to believe that 'they are expected to be policy entrepreneurs', while students of public policy and administration were being taught to celebrate the fact that 'bureaucrats often function as policy entrepreneurs' and these students were therefore entering 'government service under the impression that their job is to know their line of policy and sell it'.[79] It seems that the notion of policy entrepreneurship was being applied to merely the standard form of administrative policy-selling that had always gone on behind closed doors but was now being given more recognition and respectability. As Page and Jenkins have recently pointed out, the American policy bureaucrat's role has 'a much greater emphasis on lobbying and advocating than civil servants doing policy work in the UK, or probably Europe more generally, where the emphasis is on designing'.[80]

Landy argued that the American public would benefit from these bureaucrats trading 'the job of salesperson' for a role that allowed them to be more sceptical about policy proposals.[81] But policy proposals often do in fact take the sceptical form of defending the status quo, whether against 'inappropriate' proposals for an adaptive response or 'dangerous' proposals for a pioneering initiative or creative response. A sceptical, status quo proposal is likely to involve not only pointing out the flaws and costs of the proposals for change but also describing the benefits of sticking with the existing policy. The seller of such a proposal is arguably giving a lead, setting a direction, to no lesser extent than the seller of a proposal for change. And it is true that defending the status quo is often not a matter of resisting adaptation or preventing pioneering but of protecting the public from careerist change for change's sake.

Nonetheless, there may be advantages for a democracy in having its civil servants' competitive careerism fixated on selling policy proposals. This may well stimulate them to produce a more diverse range of proposed adaptive responses to an external change (and is perhaps particularly likely to encourage the international transfer of policy ideas). It is then up to the competitive pressures within not only the administrative sector but also the overall democratic political system to ensure that the optimal or most useful response is selected and transformed into law or public policy.

The importance of the overall democratic selection process is starkly illustrated by the most notorious historical example of a *non*-democratic political system: Nazi Germany. As was mentioned in Chapter 1, the Nazi regime sought to transform its civil servants into administration leaders. What it succeeded in doing through this leader-principle ideology and through Hitler's personal method of administration was to create a highly competitive administrative sector that encouraged the most energetic or frenetic proposal-selling ever seen in any country's administrative sector. And a famous analysis of the 'bureaucracy of murder' showed how this competitiveness made the regime's anti-semitism more effective than it would have been under a standard form of bureaucracy.[82] After Hitler had created in effect a market for anti-semitic policies, an increasing number of various party/state offices responded to the new market demand, but SS bureaucrat Eichmann 'accumulated more power into his hands in the same way that a competitive firm accumulates more customers: by being better than his competitors'.[83] For example, in 1938 he introduced an adaptive innovation that sped up the bureaucratic processing of the huge number of Jews who had been forced into emigrating. When the outbreak of war put an end to the Nazis' forced-emigration policy, Eichmann sought to protect his career prospects by proposing various Jewish-resettlement schemes, but these were superseded by Hitler's 1941 order to carry out the genocidal Final Solution 'in which Eichmann was to act only as a transportation man' – and 'was never to rise as high in the hierarchy as he felt he deserved'.[84] Although Breton and Wintrobe's analysis depicted Eichmann and other energetic proposal-sellers as bureaucratic entrepreneurs, it also described these administrators' initiatives as being motivated by incentives, rewards and other *careerist* motivations.[85]

Careerism's motivating power was displayed even at the lowest administrative level of the Holocaust. Browning's *Ordinary Men* investigation of Reserve Police Battalion 101's massacre of some 1500 Jews in the Polish town of Jozefow pointed out that careerism was one of the reasons why most of the battalion were willing to take part in the massacre. 'The two men who explained their refusal to take part in the greatest detail both emphasized the fact that they were freer to act as they did because they had no careerist ambitions.'[86] One of the pair compared his position and motives to those of fellow officers in this police battalion: 'I was somewhat older and moreover a reserve officer, so it was not particularly important to me to be promoted or otherwise to advance'; his fellow officers 'on the other hand were young men and career policemen who wanted to become something'.[87]

10
Policy Advocates' Pioneering

Policy advocates are similar to senior public administrators in being normally anonymous political leaders who lack the governing and legislative 'power to decide' that is bestowed on the democracy's formal leaders. Like the senior administrators, they are policy-expert leaders who give a lead by selling specialised policy proposals to one another and to other political leaders, but they do most of their proposal-selling within the many specialised policy-based sectors. Sometimes they will be selling pioneering rather than adaptive proposals, and on rare occasions innovative policies have been actually attributed to a pioneering policy advocate rather than to the politicians that formally enacted them into law or government policy.

Another similarity with administrators is that on rare occasions a policy advocate has become a public figure. The most notable example of a publicly prominent policy advocate, Ralph Nader, was widely considered in his heyday to be one of America's most influential political leaders. Such cases do not involve the sort of autonomy and possible misappropriation of powers that occur in the case of prominent administrators. But they do pose similarly important constitutional and theoretical questions, especially when a policy advocate enjoys more influence over legislation and policy making than many politicians achieve and is accountable, if at all, only to an interest group or some other employer. It is not surprising that Schumpeter was a strong opponent of policy advocates exerting between-elections influence on a democracy's elected leaders. However, he might have taken a more favourable view of policy advocates if he had considered that they, too, provide a democracy with a form of political leadership that it can accept or reject.

A final similarity with administrators is that the US political system is where examples of pioneering policy advocacy are likely to be found in some numbers and therefore will be used to assess the prevalence of pioneering in the 1960s–90s period. Entrepreneurial-style, pioneering leadership by policy advocates has been more prevalent and prominent in the US than in any other democracy, and was well represented in the impressive list of policy innovations that Wilson presented more than thirty years ago to illustrate the role of policy entrepreneurship in American history.[1] Of course, this is partly because policy advocates are much more numerous in the US than in any other democracy. By the 1980s there were more than 7000 lobbying organisations registered in Washington, and in 1994 it was estimated that some 91,000 people earned their living 'from Washington-based attempts to influence policies'.[2] But the sheer number of policy advocates is also presumably an indication of their successes and opportunities, as is their 'population explosion' in the 1960s–90s when, for example, the number of registered lobbyists increased from only about 1000 in the 1960s to some 23,000 by the beginning of the 1990s.[3]

Policy (advocate) entrepreneurs in action

The pioneering activities of policy advocates were implicitly included in Kingdon's analysis of 'policy entrepreneurs' in his (1984) classic *Agendas, Alternatives and Public Policies*. He applied the notion of policy entrepreneurship to all sectors of the political system but it best fits the policy advocates, whom he depicted as a residual grouping that included lobbyists, Washington lawyers, academics, journalists, consumer advocate Ralph Nader, and even a Seattle doctor who persuaded his local Senator of the virtues of several new health policies.[4] But applying Kingdon's notion and analysis of policy entrepreneurs to the policy advocates does not mean that a policy-entrepreneurial policy advocate is necessarily engaged in Schumpeterian, *pioneering* entrepreneurial-like activity.

Kingdon defined a policy entrepreneur as anyone who advocates a policy proposal and invests resources (time, energy, reputation and sometimes money) in this advocacy in the hope of a future return.[5] Such a notion of policy-advocate entrepreneurship could be applied just as well to an ambitious careerist as to an altruistic crusader. Kingdon acknowledged as much when he noted that the future return on investment in advocacy 'might come to them in the form of policies of which they approve, satisfaction from participation, or even personal aggrandizement in the form of job security or career promotion'.[6] The future returns in job security and career promotion would motivate only standard, careerist examples of policy advocacy, and on occasions

Kingdon seems to be describing only careerists, as when he referred to policy entrepreneurs' characteristic 'restless search for something to propose. If they cannot propose large ticket items, they will search for proposals that are less expensive.'[7] This seems to be a restless search to find something to sell, to be in the business of selling, rather than searching for something innovative to sell.

However, Kingdon's analysis of policy advocates' selling of proposals is certainly applicable to pioneering as well as careerist policy advocacy. He noted that introducing new policy proposals in a policy-based sector, which he called a 'policy community', can be quite informal and free-wheeling.[8] It is often a matter of trying out ideas on others in the policy community rather than presenting them with written-up and detailed proposals for new policy. (If bought by an administrator or legislator, the proposed policy idea would be developed into a much more formal and detailed proposal, such as a legislative bill, before being on-sold in the legislative or administrative sector.) He noted, too, that a surprisingly wide range of policy ideas are proposed in a relatively open and loosely knit policy community but that the more closed and tightly knit policy communities have a common language and ways of thought.[9] In other words, policy advocates' market freedom for selling proposals can vary dramatically from one policy-based sector to the next, and some sectors are cartels in thought as well as deed.

He also made a distinction between what he termed the 'softening up' and 'coupling' stages of advocacy in and outside the policy community. Both stages involve policy advocates promoting the proposals they have put up for sale, just as congressional legislators have to promote as well as introduce bills. The first stage is the softening up of not only the policy community but also public opinion by publicising, educating, and simply keeping the new proposal alive until more favourable circumstances arise.[10] The second stage is the coupling of the 'policy' stream to the other streams involved in agenda setting and policy making: (1) the 'problems' stream and (2) the 'politics' stream of election results, changes in the national mood and other major political events. In this stage the advocate lies in wait for a window of opportunity to open and then attempts to couple '[policy] proposals to political momentum' and 'solutions [proposals] to problems'.[11]

Kingdon's concept of coupling was derived from the 'garbage can' model of organisational choice, which he had creatively applied to agenda setting by US federal political institutions.[12] He added the notion and role of policy entrepreneur to the garbage-can model's emphasis on not only the coupling of streams but also how this processing of the particular mix of garbage in the can at a particular time will often involve a solution searching for a problem rather than vice versa. The solution in search of a problem was very evident in Kingdon's example of how mass transit was coupled to a succession of newly prominent problems. Urban mass transit was at first sold as a traffic-management tool and as a solution to the traffic-management problem, then was marketed in terms of environmental concerns and as a solution to the pollution problem, and finally was repackaged as a way of reducing car usage and as a solution to the energy problem.[13] None of these three couplings to problems was very successful; their main benefit seems to have been in keeping the mass-transit proposal alive in case more favourable circumstances arrived. (Nor were any of these repackagings an imaginative and risky, unpredictable reframing that would have constituted a creative rather than merely adaptive proposed response.) In more successful cases of coupling the advocate may go further and actually perform a brokering and negotiating role that produces the 'critical couplings' among people involved in agenda setting and policy making.[14] In other words, the policy advocate is now selling a more detailed, formal proposal to administrators or legislators and helping them sell it to one another – even brokering deals between them – in their private sales negotiations.

But before the policy advocates can get this far in the coupling stage, they must first succeed in coupling their policy proposals to the problems and politics streams. Kingdon's description of the coupler as lying in wait for a window of opportunity is more reminiscent of an adaptive response than a pioneering initiative, but elsewhere he describes policy entrepreneurs' coupling as more continuous: 'They push for their proposals *all the time; long before a window opens*, they try coupling after coupling that fails; and by *dumb luck* they happen to come along when a window is open'.[15] In fact he rated persistence or sheer tenacity as probably the most important quality for a successful policy entrepreneur.[16] For even highly skilled and knowledgeable policy advocates can make mistakes about whether or not an opportunity has arrived.[17] A persistent, continuous selling effort therefore seems the most important way in which policy advocates, whether adaptive careerists or pioneering users of initiative, can maximise their chances of eventually making a sale. But in one case a crusader who had the dumb luck to come along at the right time achieved a rapid series of brilliant successes that made him more famous than any policy advocate before or since.

Nader and others

Among pioneering policy advocates Ralph Nader is in a class of his own. He came to personify the 1960s–70s drive for consumer-protection policies, was held in higher regard by the media than any other public figure, and by 1974 was rated the fourth most influential person in the country.[18] Nader was also Wilson's most important example of his concept of a policy entrepreneur, who 'serves as the vicarious representative of groups not directly part of the legislative process' and proposes policies that 'will confer general (though perhaps small) benefits at a cost to be borne chiefly by a small segment of society', such as business firms.[19]

But Nader is an important example, too, of what Kingdon described as the dumb luck of coming along when a window of opportunity opens. The 'temper of the times' was probably the fundamental reason for the emergence of consumer protection in the latter half of the 1960s – making it 'good politics and politically feasible'.[20] In fact it was Senator Ribicoff's announcement in early 1965 that his subcommittee would hold hearings on highway safety that led to the still unknown Nader attaching himself to the subcommittee staff as an unpaid researcher, who went on to dominate the hearings from behind the scenes as well as through his public testimony.[21] The congressional window of opportunity remained wide open when the resulting traffic-safety bill was sent on to Senator Magnuson's Commerce Committee. For here it was supported by a committee chairman who was looking for a new image as protector of the consumer (as was described in Chapter 8) and therefore allowed the bill to be marked up and final-drafted in constant consultation with Nader as well as with the lobbyist representing the automobile manufacturers.[22] As Walker later argued, a crucial ingredient in passing the traffic-safety legislation was the support provided by 'a group of political entrepreneurs' within the Senate, notably Ribicoff, Magnuson and Nelson.[23] Like other pioneering policy advocates, Nader had to sell his policy proposal to Senators or Representatives who were willing and perhaps wanting to act as entrepreneurial-style, pioneering legislators. Nonetheless, the resulting 1966 National Traffic and Motor Vehicle Safety Act will always be 'Nader's bill'.

In this and subsequent examples of his policy advocacy he seems to have combined the softening-up and coupling stages of sales promotion. Similarly, in his coupling of streams he supplied the political momentum as well as the policy proposal and always linked his exposure of a problem with a call for particular remedial action – a proposed solution.[24] He could readily supply political momentum to his policy proposals through his reputation as a publicist as much as by his brilliant use of the press, and indeed Nader's involvement virtually guaranteed that a proposal would receive high priority from Congress.[25] Within Congress he worked with legislators' staff and committee staff in drafting bills and mobilising legislators to introduce strengthening amendments and support stronger bills.[26] Through these various combinations and strategies he was able to initiate successful campaigns for legislation raising hygiene standards in the meat industry and raising safety standards for natural-gas pipelines, coal mining, and the use of radiation.[27]

However, 1970 was 'the last year in which he took a strong hand in the shaping of a law', as he had become disillusioned with legislative methods of pursuing his pioneering mission.[28] His disillusionment with operating in or through Congress stemmed from his frustration with its weak, tame legislation on consumer protection and with the failure to implement even these weak laws – the bills that he had fought for had become 'spoiled victories'.[29] He had become the most successful and celebrated policy advocate in history, but he exemplified the pioneer's fixation on 'getting the thing done' rather than doing what was required to have a successful career.

Nader's only near-rival in the history of policy advocacy is Louis Brandeis. He had operated more than half a century earlier, during America's previous era of consumerism and government regulation of big business – the Progressive era. Brandeis was one of McCraw's four *Prophets of Regulation* and was actually 'regarded as the patron saint of the whole regulatory tradition'.[30] Unlike Nader, he came to national fame through winning a series of sensational courtroom battles, such as his 1910 case against the railroads. But he was similar to Nader in being a master of using media publicity to present his cause as a crusade for good and against evil, especially against what Brandeis referred to as the 'curse of bigness'. For example, when he took up the cause of the currency-reform movement's opposition to big banking and the securities industry, he launched a classic muckraking campaign that helped mobilise public support for the 1913 Federal Reserve Act.

On closer examination, though, Brandeis appears a much less effective consumer advocate than Nader. In particular, McCraw's study of Brandeis emphasised that usually his opposition to big business arose from a desire to protect small business rather than the consumer.[31] His concern for the survival of small business led him to support protective price-fixing by small-business associations, especially retailers, and to depict price competition as unfair competition by big businesses that were seeking to replace the small independent retailer with huge vertically integrated corporations. Moreover, Brandeis failed in his attempt to sell Congress a protective price-fixing bill, despite drafting the bill himself and testifying on its behalf to a House committee – which refused to buy it. Nor did he play any significant part in the legislative coupling that helped pass the apparently Brandeisian 1914 Federal Trade Commission Act, which created a watchdog against 'unfair methods of competition in commerce'. Too busy in the courtroom to help sell the bill within Congress, he used one of his friends to carry out the negotiating and brokering form of coupling: 'working night and day with the congressional committees, shuttling back and forth between the White House and Capitol Hill, taking a major part in drafting and redrafting the bills until they were in exactly the right form'.[32] Brandeis declined President Wilson's offer of a seat on the Federal Trade Commission but accepted nomination to the Supreme Court, bringing to an end the policy-advocate stage of his mission in life.

But entering the ranks of the judiciary is not always incompatible with engaging in well-publicised and pioneering policy advocacy. An interesting example that emerged in the 1980s was Judge Jack Love's invention and advocacy of the electronically monitored form of house arrest or 'home confinement'.[33] His invention was inspired by a Spiderman comic's description of the electronic monitoring of Spiderman's movements around the city. With the help of an electronics engineer, Love developed this idea into a new way of incarcerating offenders in their own homes – through an electronic monitoring device attached to the offender's person. The judge promoted the use of the device as a means of delaying the point at which young offenders had to be incarcerated in prison, but this has been only one of the ways in which electronically monitored home confinement has been put to use.

Another 'moonlighting' source of well-publicised policy advocacy is the tendency of very public and autonomous administrators to indulge in a pontificating form of policy advocacy that is not linked to administrative policy proposals. For example, Hoover's status as a publicly recognised leader in his specialised area of policy expertise, public safety, encouraged him to make public pronouncements about the dangers to America of moral decadence, the New Left and the lenient handling of criminals.[34] Rickover, too, exploited his publicly recognised expertise by indulging in some purportedly expert policy advice to Congress on a wide range of defence-related matters. When the Defense Department and the President refused to accept his second-stage pioneering mission of creating a nuclear-propelled surface fleet, he found a new role for himself as 'an elderly curmudgeon' who was allowed by Congress to 'berate the Navy, the Defense Department, systems analysts, the Naval Academy and current procurement practices'.[35]

In fact many years earlier Pinchot had shown how easy it is for such a well-known pioneering administrator to find a new niche as a crusading policy advocate.[36] During his time as a pioneering forestry administrator Pinchot had been converted to the cause of conservation by what seems to have been an almost religious experience in 1907 during a ride in Rock Creek Park. 'Thus, according to Pinchot, the "world movement" for conservation was born. It had come to him as a prophetic revelation.'[37] After his dismissal by President Taft, he went on to become a crusader for conservation, organising the Conservation League of America and the National Conservation Association as well as becoming the country's most influential policy advocate in the areas of forestry, rangeland and water-use.[38]

Late in the twentieth century, though, it seemed more appropriate for a pioneering policy advocate to come from a business background rather than public administration. A striking example was insurance-company boss J. Patrick Rooney, who played an important role in bringing about the innovative 1996 legislation giving tax-favoured status to Medical Savings Accounts (MSAs) created by small employers.[39] The idea of MSAs had been invented in the 1980s by economists at the National Centre for Policy Analysis, but Rooney's selling of it as a policy proposal led to his being called the 'father' of MSAs. Even if his insurance company stood 'to gain handsomely from the expansion of MSAs',[40] this does not affect his status as a policy-advocate version of the 1990s tendency for political pioneers to come from a business background, as in the earlier-mentioned examples of Berlusconi and Perot.

Assessing their fate: punctuated equilibrium

There are too few examples of prominent pioneering policy advocate to apply the 'tip of the iceberg' method that was used to assess the prevalence of pioneering administrators. However, the overall impression is that US policy-advocate pioneering experienced its golden age in the later 1960s and early 1970s before declining to a level in the 1980s and 1990s that was not as high as its Progressive-era silver age. The post-peak decline of the 1970s–80s was not as severe as the decline that administrative pioneering seemed to suffer in these decades but it is more difficult to explain, as the overall number of policy advocates was continuing to increase quite markedly. This continuing expansion could be expected to have produced a marked increase in the supply of pioneering policy advocates, considering that even careerists are likely to indulge in pioneering at least once in their careers and these pioneering inclinations would have been unusually prevalent among the policy advocates of the flourishing public-interest groups, such as those associated with the environmental movement.[41] But for some reason the likely increase in the supply of pioneering policy advocates did not result in an increase in pioneering policy successes. On the contrary, there is an impression that policy-advocate pioneering actually declined quite markedly after the golden age of the later 1960s and early 1970s – when the conditions for pioneering seem to have been unusually favourable.

These unusually favourable conditions can be at least partly explained by Baumgartner and Jones's (1993) theory that American politics is characterised by a pattern of punctuated equilibrium that includes periods of rapid change and 'positive feedback':

> Our primary thesis is that the American political system, built as it is on a conservative constitutional base designed to limit radical action, is nevertheless continually swept by policy change, change that alternates between incremental drift and *rapid alterations* of existing arrangements. During quiet periods of policy making, negative feedback dominates; policy innovations seldom capture the imagination of many individuals, so change is slow or rare. During *periods of rapid change, positive feedback dominates*; each action generates disproportionately large responses, so change accelerates. ... Punctuated equilibrium, rather than stability and immobilism, characterizes the American political system.[42]

It is hardly surprising that pioneering policy advocacy seems to have peaked during one of these periods of rapid change and positive feedback.[43] Proposing innovative policies is likely to be easier and more attractive in a period of rapid change than in one of slow or rare change, and Baumgartner and Jones pointed out that during a period of rapid change pioneering policy advocates or 'policy entrepreneurs' can *contribute* to as well as benefit from the predominating 'positive feedback'. For example, they can assist the 'diffusion' or 'expansion' of issues and policy proposals (that is, help spread them into other areas of the political system) by redefining proposals to mobilise previously uninterested people.[44] Baumgartner and Jones labelled this a 'Schattschneider' mobilisation in honour of his seminal theory of conflict expansion by the losers of a policy debate, who have good reason to appeal to people not currently involved in the debate.[45] The Schattschneider mobilisation was mentioned in Chapter 5, when analysing the life-cycle of issues and when looking at how an innovative election issue can arise from redefining or reframing. But selling redefined proposals to politicians to use as Schattschneider-mobilising election issues is only one of the ways and directions in which pioneering policy advocates can spread issues and policy proposals through the political system. They can also spread them to the public (in the form of a public issue), the legislative sector and various other areas of the political system.

This spreading of issues and proposals throughout the political system is often a byproduct of another contribution that pioneering policy advocates can make to a period of rapid change – their destruction of the 'policy monopolies' that had been established in many policy-based sectors during the preceding period of slow or rare change.[46] A frustrated policy advocate whose pioneering has been blocked by one of these cartel-like policy monopolies may be able to destroy it by redefining the pioneering policy proposal as a public issue and then selling it to the public as part of a Schattschneider mobilisation. Brandeis did this during the Progressive era with proposals to curb the power of big business, and Nader did it in the 1960s–70s with proposals for consumer protection. But there are a number of other venues apart from public opinion to which a monopoly-destroying policy proposal can be shifted.[47] For example, it can be sold to a pioneering politician to use as a Schattschneider-mobilising election issue or to introduce into the legislature as a new bill. Although these politicians often get all the credit if they succeed in on-selling the proposal, it was the policy advocate who made the key marketing decisions of shifting the proposal to a new venue and deciding which venue would be the most suitable. Baumgartner and Jones pointed to such possible new venues as electoral politics, Congress, federal administrative agencies, the courts and the subnational level of politics: 'Many venues with only vague or ambiguous constraints on their jurisdictional boundaries create opportunities for strategically minded policy entrepreneurs to shop for *the most favourable locus* for their policies.'[48]

Searching for the most favourable venue in which to sell a proposal might also be described as *hawking* a policy proposal around the political system. As was noted in Chapter 4, the cartelisation of a policy-based sector can provoke a frustrated policy advocate into hawking a policy proposal around the political system in search of uncommitted buyers.

In the case of Nader's traffic-safety proposals, the hawking policy advocate ended up selling in two different venues at the same time and benefited from an unusual form of interaction or synergy. For at the same time as he was making a marked impact through his role in the Senate hearings on traffic safety, he was also attempting to sell his proposals directly to the public by publishing a book, *Unsafe at Any Speed*, about the problem. The book was published in November 1965 (after Nader's work and testimony for Senator Ribicoff's subcommittee) but had little impact until in March 1966 General Motors admitted that it had been investigating Nader and his private life.[49] The resulting publicity not only made him and his book famous but also helped Nader and his Senate allies to bring about the National Traffic and Motor Vehicle Safety Act.

However, hawking policy advocates also have to learn how to reframe their proposals to make them more marketable in a new venue. They resort to 'changes in the image' of their proposed policies 'in an effort to attract the attention of members of the new venue', such as a congressional committee, subnational government or federal/state court.[50] The hawking policy advocates are therefore well able and well placed to make a very important contribution to the positive feedback that occurs in periods of rapid change – a contribution that might be described as *opening the venues' veto gates*.

It is often noted that the American political system has many positions (veto gates) and personnel (veto players) that can exercise some form of veto over policy making.[51] But the veto gates are often also venues, as in the notable cases of the Presidency and the Supreme Court, and therefore provide hawking policy advocates with another location in which to sell their proposals. If the proposal is accepted in this venue, the opening of its veto gate will be followed by the increasingly rapid and easy opening of the other gates on the proposal's path to becoming law or public policy. For in a period of positive feedback, political efforts produce increasingly large marginal effects – each change is larger than the previous one – in a process that has long been described by political scientists as escalation, bandwagons or slippery slopes.[52] Once the first veto gate has been opened, the others are likely to open in a process that is more like a damburst flood than a line of falling dominoes. The large number of venue/veto positions in the American political system therefore facilitates rapid change by providing a large range of alternative points of access – any one of which can begin a positive feedback process. 'The multiple venues of politics are often seen as inhibitors of change, but this may not be true. Federalism, separation of powers, and jurisdictional overlaps are opportunities for change as much as they are inhibitors of change.'[53]

Whether they are predominantly opportunities or inhibitors will depend largely on an uncontrollable environmental factor – is the period one of positive feedback or of negative feedback? The onset of a period of positive feedback is similar to what Kingdon described as a change in the national mood that provides new opportunities for policy advocates. Changes in the national-mood component of the politics stream was his most important example of how policy entrepreneurs' capacity for 'using the forces beyond their control' enables them to exploit an opportunity and bring about new policies.[54] In fact the national mood seems as uncontrollable and influential as the changes in climate that have had a major impact on the planet's biological affairs.

> The people in and around government sense a national mood. They are comfortable discussing its content, and believe they know when the mood shifts. The idea goes by different names – the national mood, the climate in the country, changes in public opinion, or broad social movements. But common to all these labels is the notion that a rather large number of people out in the country are thinking along certain common lines, that this national mood changes from one time to another in discernible ways, and that these *changes in mood or climate* have important impacts on policy agendas and policy outcomes.[55]

But if the change in the national mood is towards policy conservatism, in the sense of not wanting change of any kind, it would have a negative impact on all policy agendas and advocates except those intent on preserving the status quo. In other words, it would encourage what Baumgartner and Jones described as a period of negative feedback and slow or rare change. Moreover, when they quoted Kingdon's description of the national mood, they pointed out that taking account of public opinion (polls) was only one of the ways in which political leaders sense a national mood; they also base their sense of the national mood on the actions of interest groups, state legislatures, the courts and various other actors.[56] In that case, the actions of policy advocates in the 1980s–90s might well have given their fellow political leaders the sense that the national mood was one of stalemated policy conservatism, in the sense of the various opposing groups cancelling out one another's policy agendas. For the 1960s–70s period of positive feedback had resulted in a 'more crowded, more complicated, and more representative system' of interest groups – and 'criticism and conflicts are more likely when many sides are well organised'.[57]

The increase in the numbers and representativeness of policy advocates may well therefore have reduced the opportunity for successful pioneering at the same time as it was increasing the supply of pioneers. This helps explain why pioneering policy advocacy appears to have passed its peak by the 1980s–90s. The increased number of policy advocates may actually have been providing at least as much entrepreneurial-style, pioneering leadership as in earlier decades but without as much noticeable effect. After all, leadership is by no means always accepted, and pioneering leadership by policy advocates is perhaps the most likely form of pioneering to be rejected by other political leaders when it appears that the times are *not* changing.

Conclusion

In this concluding appraisal of leadership in democracy the emphasis will continue to be on innovation but with more of an eye on the future than the past. However, the past is a useful indicator of future tendencies in this area as in many other areas of politics. Part II's assessment of the prevalence of pioneering innovation in the 1960s–90s was not very encouraging, even though the assessment was focused on the country that has the best claim to being considered a truly entrepreneurial democracy.

Pioneering did not seem to be very prevalent in any sector of the political system and, more importantly, did not seem to have become more prevalent in recent decades. The US electoral/party sector did not show much evidence of innovation or of any tendency toward an increasing prevalence of innovative issues. (The governmental sector in Britain rather than the US was no better in terms of prime-ministerial pioneering, and although it was more impressive when viewed in terms of collective governmental pioneering, even this source of innovation had declined dramatically since its peak in the 1980s.) It is true that the US legislative sector showed evidence of quite frequent attempts at innovation but it was difficult to be sure that this was pioneering rather than a careerist form of innovating. The US administrative sector actually gave a strong impression of decline in pioneering, with the apparent extinction of the prominent and autonomous form of administrative pioneer. And the US policy advocates were facing a distinctly more difficult and discouraging environment for pioneering in the 1980s–90s than in the preceding golden age.

The global prospects for entrepreneurial democracy therefore do not seem to be very favourable. If even US democracy shows no evidence of a rising wave of pioneering, it is hard to be optimistic about the prospects for entrepreneurial democracy in the rest of the world. After all, other democracies not only lack its long experience of multi-sector political pioneering but also lack its opportunities for pioneering innovation – they are in a global position that makes large-scale pioneering more difficult than in America. These other democracies are more prone to what Finley described as the 'paltry politics' that characterised the ancient city-states when they lost their independence.[1] In present times such lack of independence is related as much to economics as to politics. Governments have lost much of their independence in economic policy making and are left with only 'a mediating role between external forces and internal capacities to benefit from those forces'; the state itself has been seen as only 'an adaptive entity and its activities as a politics of adaptation'.[2]

On the other hand, emphasising the importance of opportunity seems rather incongruous when discussing pioneering innovations, as a distinctive feature of this entrepreneurial-style leadership is its 'reliance' on extraordinary or exceptional *individuals* rather than circumstances. The focus should therefore be on the personnel rather than opportunity factor, and on some earlier-quoted remarks by Schumpeter about democracy's need to attract the right sort of political personnel: 'the democratic process may easily create conditions in the political sector that, once established, will repel most of the men who can make a success at anything else'.[3] These remarks seem even more applicable to the men and women who can provide entrepreneurial-style political leadership – they are likely to be repelled by the conditions in the political sector and therefore make their pioneering efforts in other sectors of society.

It might be argued that an entrepreneurial democracy no longer needs to attract pioneering individuals because innovations can now be carried out through organisations rather than exceptional individuals. Schumpeter himself argued in the 1940s that the economic entrepreneurial role could now be performed within organisations. Not only was entrepreneurial 'personality and will power' less significant in environments that had become accustomed to economic change but also with innovation 'being reduced to routine', technological progress was increasingly being turned out by teams of trained specialists.[4] This trend has continued and in fact Drucker's 1980s text on innovation and entrepreneurship was confident that a whole business organisation can be imbued with the entrepreneurial spirit and made 'greedy for new things' – or at least develop 'the habits of entrepreneurship and innovation'.[5]

But it was noted in Chapter 2 that such innovation is merely an adaptive response to change and does not involve entrepreneurial initiative. What Drucker described as 'systematic innovation' is therefore 'purposeful and organized search for changes' and 'systematic analysis of the opportunities such changes might offer for economic or social innovation'.[6] Analysing the opportunities offered by changes also excludes the other version of Schumpeterian entrepreneurship, the creative response to change, because the opportunities are being analysed in cost-benefit terms rather than in economically non-rational terms (as was described in Chapter 2). So if innovation has become an organisational rather than personal activity, it is an innovation that lacks the pioneering and creative dimensions of Schumpeterian entrepreneurship. Whether it has thereby lost some capability for carrying out creative-destructive economic revolutions is a moot point.

In any case, the *political* entrepreneurial role has certainly not yet become organisational rather than personal – and seems unlikely to become so in the future. Even in the case of economic change, Schumpeter warned that although consumers no longer resisted innovation, vested interests would continue to resist some forms of economic innovation.[7] In politics, not only the vested interests but also the consumers continue to resist political innovations – the consumers have certainly not become accustomed to political innovation. Without a supply of pioneering leaders, the entrepreneurial role will not be performed and entrepreneurial democracy is unlikely to spread or even survive.

What is more, it is crucial for a democracy to maintain a supply of leaders who are willing and able to carry out the 'merely' *adaptive* innovations. If adaptive innovation becomes too hard for future generations of political leaders, there will be some costly delays caused by their resort to the drift-into-crisis strategy described in Chapter 2. And a reluctance to make adaptive innovations can become a life-or-death problem for democracy if a large-scale crisis situation occurs and requires a series of immediate innovations. The classic example is how the German democratic political system failed in the early 1930s to make the appropriate adaptive responses to the crisis created by the Depression – without these adaptive innovations the democracy was unable to survive.

In contrast, the US political system of the 1930s responded in a way that enabled its democracy to survive the Depression crisis. During the New Deal era its political leaders produced a series of innovations in policy and institutions that included changes to political as well as economic institutions. For example, Greenstein has credited President

Roosevelt's 'entrepreneurial leadership' during this era as contributing to the emergence of the modern Presidency, in which the President is the main source of policy initiatives.[8] In particular, the Presidency took on such a significant legislative role during the New Deal era that from then on Congress 'looked automatically to the Executive for guidance; it expected the administration to have a "program" to present for consideration'.[9] However, Roosevelt was joined by a host of other innovators. Not only was the civil service reinvigorated with a new spirit of excitement and innovation but also a cohort of young innovators came to Washington to staff the agencies created or expanded by the New Deal.[10] Innovative administrators 'often pushed programs of their own' and together with innovative legislators, such as Senators Wagner and La Follette, contributed to 'a reinvigoration of the whole political system'.[11] Furthermore, the political system also seems to have been transformed into an entrepreneurial democracy, complete with pioneering administrators and legislators as well as a pioneering President.

But the political system was carrying out adaptive innovations, not pioneering the creative responses that an entrepreneurial democracy would have been risking in these circumstances. As was discussed in Chapter 2, an adaptive response enhances the democracy's survival prospects or deals with a problem in a way that no politically significant interest finds unacceptable in the long run. And the often politically cautious nature of the New Deal innovations is typical of the adaptive rather than pioneering innovation. The landmark 1935 Social Security Act epitomises the New Deal's political caution, which led to the Act's pension component taking the form of a contributory insurance scheme, to the unemployment-benefit component being financed by payroll taxes and to the lack of any health-care component – a missed opportunity that was still plaguing US politics in the twenty-first century.[12]

If this caution was due to the effects of rigidity's resistance to adaptation, it was a rigidity that included unconscious biases as well as vested interests. Indeed 'the ultimate constraint' on the New Deal was the 'underlying conservative response of the people themselves to the Depression', specifically 'the pervasive commitment to self-help, individual liberty, localism, and business-oriented individualism'.[13] It is a form of rigidity that probably cannot be overcome by presidential selling of opinion leads, or even by a more competitive political system, and so is very likely to force adaptive innovations into the panda's-thumb, suboptimal type of adaptation described in Chapter 3.

However, rigidity's biggest influence on adaptive leadership was produced by an unconscious bias in the ultimate or key buyer of policy proposals – the President himself. Roosevelt failed to accept proposals that he use Keynesian deficit-spending to strengthen the economy's recovery from the depths of the Depression:

> many in Washington were familiar with the Keynesian doctrine in a general way, if not in specific detail, before 1937, and they pressed their views vigorously on the President.... Under the circumstances, it is understandable, albeit regrettable, that Roosevelt did not take up the new economics. The President's reluctance to abandon the economic beliefs of a lifetime, ideas which most of the country shared, is less remarkable than the resiliency he did show in adapting himself to new ways of thinking.[14]

As a result of this failure to adapt, the President's economic approach fell between two stools in the later 1930s, for in addition to being too conservative to use Keynesian remedies it was too radical to restore business confidence and encourage the business community to invest.[15] The policies and rhetoric that angered or frightened business (and Schumpeter) at least helped prevent the New Deal being outflanked on the left by a surge of populism that might have threatened democracy. But nothing was gained from the President's 1937 attempt to balance the budget by expenditure cuts, which were followed by a dramatic reversal of the economic recovery and a severe recession that was not overcome until the deficit-financed increases in military spending from 1940 onwards.

In fact it has been suggested that the foreign-policy crisis created by the rise of Nazi Germany indirectly solved the economic crisis created by the Depression. 'Without the military boom in response to the German war machine, Roosevelt's presidency would probably have been remembered as compassionate and helpful but ineffective in solving the fundamental problems of the Depression'.[16] A more tactful way of making this point is Badger's description of the New Deal as a 'holding operation', which 'enabled the people to survive the Depression and hold on until the World War II opened up new opportunities'.[17] Similarly, the New Deal's adaptive innovations, whatever their failings or oversights, at least enabled *democracy* to survive until new opportunities were opened up by the world war.

But only an optimist would suggest that a similar holding operation in the future would be followed by new opportunities produced by such an extraordinary external factor as a world war. Any severe domestic crisis will therefore require something more than a 1930s-like holding operation; it will require a more useful set of adaptive responses or some successful pioneering – some successful creative responses. In other words, it will require something even better than what was produced by the legendary host of innovators that Schumpeter saw at work in the US before he began to write about leadership in democracy.

Appendix: Schumpeter on Development (Evolution)

In his early analysis of entrepreneurship *The Theory of Economic Development* (published in German in 1912 and in English in 1934) Schumpeter used the term 'development' to describe what he would later refer to as economic 'evolution'.[1] There was good reason for him to avoid using the term 'evolution' in this theorising about economic change.[2] His focus on innovative, revolutionary change was quite different from the gradualist view of change associated both with the Darwinist conception of biological evolution and with the approach of the most celebrated economist of the time, Alfred Marshall, who believed that the economist's 'Mecca' lay in economic (Darwinist) biology.[3]

The tendency among some English economists to adopt a Darwinian evolutionary approach had culminated in 1890 with Marshall's classic *Principles of Economics*. He has been described as the 'Darwin of economics' because his marginalist form of economic analysis focused on how business firms responded or 'adapted' to (price) changes in their environment.[4]

> Alfred Marshall's marginalism is evolution applied to economics. The businessman and the consumer make *no great leaps, but step by step* they try to improve their situations. Individuals, companies and governments all *adapt* to changing prices. The fittest firms survive. Low profits drive out the weakest.[5]

Schumpeter's theory of economic development, published some 20 years after Marshall's opus, used a similar marginalist/evolutionary terminology but only in the context of distinguishing such routine economic changes from the revolutionary economic changes that he termed economic 'development'.[6] These revolutionary changes are 'discontinuous changes in the traditional way of doing things', and are to be distinguished from the continuous (marginal) changes involved in 'continual *adaptation* through innumerable *small steps*'.[7] In fact he defined economic development as the carrying out of discontinuous – not marginally – new combinations of productive means, such as innovative consumer goods, new methods of production or of organising an industry, and even new markets or sources of supply.[8] Economic development was therefore readily distinguishable from the circular flow of the economy, which involves 'only small variations at the *margins*, such as every individual can accomplish by *adapting himself to changes in the economic environment*, without materially deviating from familiar lines'.[9] Similarly, economic development differed from the 'mere' growth of the economy, which 'calls forth no qualitatively new phenomena, but only processes of *adaptation*'.[10] Schumpeter was therefore using an orthodox marginalist/evolutionary perspective to describe the routine forms of economic change (in the circular flow and mere growth) while arguing that a quite different, developmental perspective was needed when analysing revolutionary economic changes.

But in fact the orthodox 'evolutionary' interpretation of economics involved such important divergences from Darwin's ideas that it could well have included Schumpeter's 'developmental' changes as merely one more anomaly within an already strained or loose analogy with biological evolution. For if Marshall's marginalist perspective was indeed 'evolution applied to economics', it could not be a very close application of Darwinian evolution – the differences between biological and economic processes were too significant. For instance, economic processes involve *directed* variations, not the *un*directed variations produced by random biological mutation, and therefore have been described by a contemporary evolutionary economist as having 'a limited Lamarckian character'.[11] Lamarckism's emphasis on directed variation clearly distinguishes it from Darwinism, which superseded it as a theory of biological evolution and established a two-step process (variation plus direction through selection) as the standard conception of evolutionary processes:

> Lamarckism is, fundamentally, a theory of *directed* variation. If hairy coats are better [because of colder temperatures], animals perceive the need, grow them, and pass the potential to offspring. Thus, variation is directed automatically toward adaptation and no second force like natural selection is needed [for direction].[12]

Business firms are therefore acting in a Lamarckian fashion, making a directed variation, by responding to a change in their environment. But the process has an only limited Lamarckian character because the businesses' responses *vary* – with probably one or more firms even adopting a wait-and-see approach and sticking with the status quo – and therefore the process needs a second force like natural selection.[13] For example, Nelson and Winter's seminal (1982) work on economic evolution claimed to be an 'unabashedly Lamarckian' theory that included 'the timely appearance of variation under the stimulus of adversity',[14] but it described variation in firms' responses and, like Darwinism, required a second force and step – a selection that takes time to eliminate the least satisfactory responses and to make the better responses more prevalent:

> [F]irms have but limited bases for judging what will work best; they may even have difficulty establishing the range of plausible alternatives to be considered. It is an essential feature of such situations that firms do different things, and some of these things turn out more successful than others. Over time the least satisfactory of the responses (from the point of view of the organizations making them) may tend to be eliminated and the better of the responses may tend to be used more widely, but it is another essential feature of such situations that these selection forces take time to work through.[15]

Nelson and Winter acknowledged that these selection forces are the economic equivalent of natural selection. For the firms that correctly judged what (response) would be successful will be rewarded by the market with the profits that will enable them to survive and grow, which in turn means that a growing proportion of an industry will be doing those successful things (the successful responses).[16] It is true that this biologically analogous expansion of profitable firms is not the only way in which the more successful responses become increasingly prevalent in an industry. Nelson and Winter acknowledged that these responses may eventually be adopted by *other* firms in the industry through imitation of a more successful firm or through learning from trial and error (feedback).[17] But the imitation and feedback occur in (and in a sense are motivated by) a biologically analogous context of survival/expansion that is linked to market profitability – and to the competitive pressures of the market.

It is these competitive pressures that force other firms to adopt one of the more successful responses or else suffer the consequences in terms of their profitability and thus their survival and growth prospects. Schumpeter emphasised that the adaptive response is a *forced* response.[18] It is an impersonal and indirect form of coercion exerted by the pressures of market competition upon firms: they either make/adopt a successful response or suffer the consequences. Thus in a competitive economy there is 'competitive elimination' of the old means of production by new combinations of productive means.[19] Schumpeter was being quite orthodox in pointing to the selection pressures exerted by market competition:

> The perception that market competition in a sector constitutes a particular sort of selection environment was explicit in the writings of many of the great nineteenth- and early twentieth-century economic theorists. Schumpeter was well within this classical tradition.[20]

However, Nelson and Winter also pointed out that as 'selection works on what exists, not on the full set of what is feasible', it *cannot* be credibly claimed that 'economic selection forces drive individual firms and whole systems to *optimal* behavior'.[21] The fact that selection can select only the best of what has actually been tried – not what ought to have been tried – is one reason why they maintained that the diversity of firms is a key feature of evolutionary theory.[22]

> Firms facing the same market signals respond differently, and more so if the signals are relatively novel. Indeed, one would hope for such a diversity of response in order that a range of possible behaviors might be explored. One function of competition, in the structural sense of many firms, then would be to make possible that diversity.[23]

Presumably a perfectly competitive market would contain so many firms that the optimal variation would be bound to be included amongst these firms' very diverse range of responses to an external change. But as perfect competition is more the exception than the rule in real-world economies, the process of economic evolution is likely to produce imperfect, suboptimal responses. This may be why Schumpeter described economies as only *tending* to adapt themselves to changes in their environments.[24] It is more likely, though, that he was referring to economic rigidity's resistance to adaptation, which can delay or prevent even a merely useful variation being selected as the appropriate, adaptive response (see Chapters 2 and 3). In recognising that economic evolution can be so inefficient, Schumpeter may have been going outside the tradition but to a lesser extent than if he had included revolutionary, discontinuous changes within an evolutionary perspective.

Yet, somewhat paradoxically, to have viewed this sort of change as evolutionary might not have seemed so heretical to biologists. Some of them had claimed that biological evolution contains cases of discontinuous variation and indeed is based upon this form of variation. Darwin's emphasis upon the gradualness of evolution may well have been motivated by his opposition to these theories of evolution based on 'saltation' – from the Latin word *saltus* meaning 'a jump'.[25] In later times such theories used the notion of *macro*mutation (a genetic mutation that has a large effect on the organism) to argue that 'new species arise abruptly by *discontinuous variation*' that has been produced in a single generation rather than being produced through the accumulation of continuous changes by a series of generations.[26] The most well-known proponent of this approach, Goldschmidt, argued that a macromutation usually turns out to be disastrous, to be a 'monster', but occasionally might turn out to be a 'hopeful monster' and 'adapt an organism to a new mode of life'.[27] However, his major work was published long after (1940) Schumpeter's theory of development. Although the eminent economist Georgescu-Roegen has argued that Schumpeter anticipated Goldschmidt's idea by some thirty years, Schumpeter did not take the opportunity of using the notion of macromutation when he published *Capitalism, Socialism and Democracy* in 1942 but instead referred to the standard notion of genetic mutation, which had first appeared in the 1920s.[28]

In more recent times even such an orthodox Darwinist as Dawkins has acknowledged that a relatively simple type of macromutation might play a part in biological evolution, though as no more than a rare and minor supplement to the standard forms of mutation. Dawkins clarified and refined the concept of macromutation by pointing to the difference between (1) complex and (2) modifying types.[29] Both types are mutations that have a large effect and produce a discontinuous change, without any 'gradual series of intermediaries'.[30] But while one type produces a complex organ, such as an eye, the other type only modifies an existing design, such as by elongating segments. Although Dawkins declared that complex macromutations 'do not exist and have no connection with Darwinism', he acknowledged that modifying macromutations do occur and that it is 'not (quite) totally inconceivable' that even the dramatic elongation of the elephant's trunk could have been produced in a single-generation macromutation.[31]

It is true that the modifying macromutation lacks the revolutionary, complex nature of developmental changes, such as Schumpeter's example of the change from mail coaches to railways.[32] But this type of change is analogous in structure to Dawkins's hypothetical (for purposes of argument) *complex* type of macromutation. Its failure to occur in biological practice highlights the exceptional nature of the analogous revolutionary economic changes, and also highlights the difference between types of discontinuous economic change (revolutionary/complex versus reforming/modifying) that is noted in Chapter 2's discussion of entrepreneurship.

From an entrepreneurial perspective in fact the most important aspect of Schumpeter's theory of economic development is the distinctive way in which these discontinuous, developmental changes occur. 'By "development", therefore, we shall understand only such changes in economic life that are *not forced* upon it from without but arise from its *own initiative*, from within.'[33] Adaptive responses are forced upon the economy by such external changes as variations in natural conditions, the effects of war, and new public policies.[34] In contrast, developmental changes are initiated *from within* the economy as entrepreneurs (whom Schumpeter described as the bearers of the economy's mechanism for revolutionary change) use their initiative to instigate discontinuous economic change.[35]

However, Darwinian biological evolution has room for an equivalent of entrepreneurial initiative. 'Darwinism is not a mechanistic theory of environmental determinism'; organisms may alter their environment by 'behavioral innovation' and many adaptations 'must be preceded by a shift in behaviour'.[36] A famous case occurred in modern times when several species of English birds learned to use their bills to pry the tops off milk bottles and drink some of the contents. The birds had 'established new selective pressures by altering their own environment. Bills of a different shape will now be favored by natural selection'.[37] Although this altering of the environment has exploited an external change (the advent of bottled milk), the external change did not force an adaptive response but merely provided an opportunity for behaviourial innovation. It was the use of some initiative by the innovating birds that led to the environment being altered and to a redirection of selection (to favour bills with a different shape).

An evolutionary approach to economics could therefore have readily accommodated Schumpeter's distinction between change that occurs (1) in the usual forced, adapting way and (2) in the spontaneous, developmental way arising from entrepreneurs using their initiative. During his description of entrepreneurs, Schumpeter noted that what he called the 'adapting–spontaneous' contrast could be substituted for his contrast between (1) small variations at the margins and (2) entrepreneurs' large 'disturbances' of economic life.[38] He explained that he gave greater prominence to the small–large contrast rather than adapting– spontaneous contrast only 'because the latter method of expression is much easier to misunderstand than the former and really would demand still longer explanation'.[39]

The key point, however, is that Schumpeter's theory of economic development through discontinuous economic changes could have been accommodated within an evolutionary perspective – and been presented as part of an overall theory of economic evolution. He himself seems to have been thinking along these lines when the English translation was being prepared for publication, as in a 1934 letter describing his intellectual interests, he referred to the book as 'The Theory of Economic *Evolution*'.[40] By the time he wrote *Capitalism, Socialism and Democracy*, he was quite prepared to describe revolutionary as well as marginal changes as capitalist *evolution*.

Notes

1 Schumpeter's Leadership Model of Democracy

1. However, the leadership aspect of his theory seems to be gaining more recognition, as 2005 saw the publication of not only the first edition of this book but also an article that recognised Schumpeter to be a founder of the 'leader theory of democracy' (Körösényi, 2005).
2. Schumpeter, 1974 [1947]: 269, 271.
3. Downs, 1957. Downs acknowledged that 'Schumpeter's profound analysis of democracy forms the inspiration and foundation for our whole thesis, and our debt and gratitude to him are great indeed' (ibid.: 29 n. 11).
4. Schumpeter, 1974 [1947]: 272, 272 n. 6.
5. Ibid.: 283.
6. Ibid.: 285.
7. Ibid.: 286 n. 3.
8. Ibid.: 282.
9. Schapiro and Hacker-Cordon, 1999: 4. They assert that Schumpeter actually 'modeled' his theory of democracy 'on the neoclassical theory of price competition'.
10. Schumpeter, 1974 [1947]: 271.
11. Ibid.: 265.
12. Olson, 1971 [1965].
13. Schumpeter, 1974 [1947]: 250.
14. Ibid.: 269.
15. Ibid.: 267.
16. Ibid.: 245 n.14, 246.
17. Ibid.: 270.
18. Tucker, 1995 [1981]: 15.
19. Körösényi, 2005: 358–9. His leader theory of democracy takes a different view of Schumpeter, and even Downs, than the one presented in this chapter and the next. He describes Schumpeter's model of democracy as using the analogy with the entrepreneur, depicting the politician as an entrepreneur supplying new policies rather than a mere producer catering to the existing demand for policies (ibid.: 367). And he contrasts this notion of the political entrepreneur with the role of politicians in Downs's model, where 'they are simply *"producers"* who satisfy the existing demand' (ibid.: 367).
20. Beetham, 1974: 230. See Weber, 1968: 268 and 269 for examples of the term *Fuehrerdemokratie* being left in the original German rather than being translated into English. It has often been pointed out that Weber's ideas on democracy are similar to and presumably influenced Schumpeter's (Swedberg, 1991: 278 n. 141). The similarity with Weber's now famous 'Politics as a Vocation' includes not only the emphasis on leadership and the rise of the professional politician but also Weber's remarks about politicians striving for power through 'party campaigns in the market of election votes'

and about 'the competitive struggle to win the favor of the voters' (Weber [1918] 1991: 100, 110).
21. Beetham, 1974: 232–7.
22. Brooker, 1985.
23. Ibid.: 53–4.
24. See Medearis, 2001: 73–5 on Nazi sympathics. See Swedberg, 1991: 141, 145–50 for a slightly different and more mitigating assessment of Schumpeter's attitudes to the Nazi regime.
25. Schumpeter, 1974 [1947]: 257.
26. Ibid.: 293–4.
27. Ibid.: 273 n. 9.
28. Ibid.: 270.
29. Ibid.: 271, 273, 284, 285.
30. Ibid.: 269 n. 1.
31. Ibid.: 278.
32. Burnham, 1942: 83.
33. Ibid.: 105 on social revolution; 68–9, 71, 73, 99 on ruling class; 183, 191–2 on ideology. Burnham portrayed this 'revolution' as involving an extension of state control and of public-sector managers overshadowing private-sector counterparts – not vice versa – because this had recently been happening during the New Deal era in the US and, to a more extreme degree, in Nazi Germany and the communist Soviet Union (see chs 8, 14, 15, 16).
34. Brooker, 2009: 253.
35. See ibid.: 41.
36. Scott, 1970: 4–5.
37. Weber, 1947 [1922]: 359.
38. Freud, 1961 [1930]: 100.
39. Ibid.: 100.
40. Ibid.: 70.
41. Schumpeter, 1974 [1947]: 269.
42. Ibid.: 263.
43. Such a manufactured will of the people also shows that it may be possible in the short run 'to fool all the people all the time' and to fool the people 'step by step into something they do not really want' (ibid.: 264).
44. Ibid.: 295.
45. Ibid.: 272.
46. Ibid.: 295.
47. Ibid.: 264, 270.
48. Ibid.: 270.
49. Ibid.: 263–4.
50. Downs, 1957: 87.
51. Ibid.: 77.
52. Ibid.: 87. My emphases.
53. Brechtel and Kaiser, 1999: 20.
54. Downs, 1957: 87, 88.
55. Although Downs prefers the term 'government' to 'state', this government is a specialised organisation in society that 'can coerce all the other groups into obeying its decisions' (ibid.: 23).
56. Ibid.: 23, 25.

57. Ibid.: 38–9, 44–5.
58. For example, he implied that in elections the competing political leaders will be distinguishing themselves from one another by appealing to or attacking particular interests and ideals, for he declared that it should be 'possible for every would-be leader' to present his case to voters even if he is 'attacking their most vital interests or offending their most cherished ideals' (Schumpeter, 1974 [1947]: 295).
59. Downs, 1957: 98.
60. Ibid.: 98–9.
61. Ibid.: 100, 86.
62. Schattschneider, 1960: 139.
63. Ibid.: 141. Emphasis removed from the first sentence.
64. Ibid.: 141, 142.
65. Ibid.: 138.
66. Ibid.: 140.
67. Ibid.: 115–16.
68. Ibid.: 139.
69. His theory of 'the primacy of foreign policy' argued that the US as a state was involved in 'a titanic struggle for survival', namely its Cold War struggle against the communist countries, and was therefore having to place such heavy burdens on the American public that consent needed to be changed into public *support*: 'because consent is no longer enough'(ibid.: 112). He went on to argue that this public support could be achieved either by the dictatorial way of propaganda or by the democratic way of greatly increasing the scale of the public's participation in public life – greatly expanding the participating political community – by such means as reducing the amount of non-voting in national elections. It may be difficult to imagine how a political scientist of the 1950s–60s era could have viewed the Cold War as such a titanic struggle and burden but he was writing at the time when Kennedy was telling the world in his inaugural address that the US would 'pay any price, bear any burden, meet any hardship, support any friend, oppose any foe to assure the survival and the success of liberty', and several years later Johnson would conscript hundreds of thousands of young Americans to fight in support of 'any friend' in South Vietnam. If the US had continued to fight such burdensome wars, Schattschneider's theory might well have proved very applicable and, in any case, it highlighted an important aspect of the state-as-firm analogy and of the notion that the acceptance of leadership involves consent – sometimes leaders will be asking their political community for more than consent.
70. Ibid.: 72 on institutions and football rules; 48 on the rules of the game.
71. Elgie, 1995: 204.
72. Ibid.: 204, 205.
73. Schumpeter, 1974 [1947]: 243 on variations in time as well as place and situation.
74. Schattschneider, 1960: ch. 5 on electoral/party system and 110 on comparison with Britain.
75. Kriesi, 2005: 45.
76. Ibid.: 2.
77. Webb and Poguntke, 2005: 340, 354.

78. Ibid.: 355.
79. Ibid.: 355, 353.
80. Schumpeter, 1974 [1947]: 275.
81. Ibid.: 287.
82. Ibid.: 287.
83. Ibid.: 274 n. 10.
84. Ibid.
85. Lijphart, 1999: 105. Schumpeter suggested that the nearest functional equivalent in the US of a parliamentary government's Ministers were leaders in Congress. The 'President is not only prime minister but sole minister ... unless we find an analogy between the functions of an English Cabinet Minister and the functions of the managers of the administration's forces in Congress' (Schumpeter, 1974 [1947]: 274 n. 10). Here he was foreshadowing Neustadt's famous argument that the United States' functional equivalents of British Cabinet Ministers were not only Secretaries and White House staffers but also Senators and Representatives, notably the floor leaders and committee chairmen (Neustadt, 1969: 133).
86. Schumpeter, 1974 [1947]: 274 n. 10.
87. Ibid.: 278.
88. Ibid.: 273.
89. Lijphart, 1999.
90. Schumpeter, 1974 [1947]: 274.
91. Ibid.: 273 n. 9, 276.
92. Ibid.: 276.
93. Ibid.: 276 n. 16.
94. Ibid.: 276.
95. By the 1990s the argument about prime-ministerial versus cabinet government had staked out well-known positions and arguments, with the prime-ministerialists pointing to the Prime Minister's various public/party powers and political opportunities while the cabinetists pointed to the various constraints on the Prime Minister (Rhodes, 1995: 13). But Schumpeter's approach, as described in the next section of this chapter, is perhaps best compared to Smith's use of a power-dependence model to analyse the relationship between Prime Minister Thatcher and her Cabinet colleagues (Smith, 1994 and 1995).
96. Schumpeter, 1974 [1947]: 278. He viewed the parliamentary election of the government as being parliament accepting the Prime Minister's choice of who will be Ministers in 'his' government. However, parliament not only 'accepts but also influences his choice' of Cabinet and other government Ministers (ibid.). Any Prime Minister will select from among his party's parliamentarians a set of Ministers and a Cabinet that includes second-rank leaders as well as worthy veterans, some rising stars and a few experts in specialised areas of government (ibid.: 274–5). The Prime Minister is therefore politically required to offer Cabinet posts to 'leaders of the second rank', whom 'the leader has no choice but to put into appropriate offices' (ibid.: 273 n. 9). This is also true of the more modern examples of British and British-style Prime Minister (James, 1995: 77; Weller, 1985: 78).
97. Schumpeter, 1974 [1947]: 278, 281. My emphasis.

98. Few Cabinet Ministers will ever even consider an open challenge for party and government leadership, as most of them are only third-rank leaders, relative novices or politically neutered experts. History suggests that there are likely to be no more than 'two or three other members of the cabinet who are potential claimants' for the post, and in fact only very rarely has a modern (post-First World War) British Prime Minister been overthrown (James, 1995: 77, 79). But the other Ministers may rally behind the standard of a challenger to the Prime Minister, and they may deliberately or indirectly encourage a challenger by making it clear that their allegiance to the Prime Minister's standard is in decline – with resignation from the government being the most drastic means of displaying this declining allegiance.
99. Schumpeter, 1974 [1947]: 278.
100. Rhodes, 1995: 20; Andeweg, 1997: 77. The latter points out that this is the reason, not their being captured or housetrained by their departments, for Ministers' departmentalism: their reputation 'depends almost exclusively on their performance as head of department'. Rose and Davies argue that there is a 'personal career incentive to promote new programs or to repeal inherited programs' because 'such actions will enhance the minister's political visibility in the party, in Parliament, and with the public' (Rose and Davies, 1994: 124). In fact this can result in competition between specialised Ministers when their areas of policy interest overlap: 'their political fortunes rise and fall with the outcome of inter-department disputes' (Rose, 2001: 31).
101. Schumpeter, 1974 [1947]: 281. My emphases. The Prime Minister's cautious playing of the game is also noted by Weller. He argues that looking at the number of times Prime Ministers have been deposed by a party revolt is too crude an indicator of their vulnerability because this vulnerability will lead them to be cautious (Weller, 1985: 47). In fact the degree of security that Prime Ministers feel is likely to affect the way that they lead the government (ibid.: 45).
102. Cambray, 1932.
103. Quoted by James, 1995: 79. My emphasis.
104. Ibid.: 78–9, for example, contrasts Wilson's and Thatcher's ranges of policy interests, as Wilson had 'clear views on a minority of issues, mostly economic and diplomatic, but in other areas was content to let colleagues provide a lead'.
105. Riddell, 2001: 22, citing Cabinet Secretary Wilson; Kavanagh, 2001: 5.
106. Riddell, 2001: 22.
107. Ibid.: 22, 39.
108. Weller, 1985: 197–8.
109. Ibid.:104–5, and also 122 on intellectual weight.
110. Ibid.: 14 on adjusting the rules of the game, and 209 on how this illustrates what Weller sees as the flexibility built into the office.
111. Schumpeter, 1974 [1947]: 280.

2 Pioneering and Adaptive Leadership

1. Schumpeter, 1974 [1947]: 133–4.
2. Brooker, 2005: ch.4.

3. For example, Frohlich and Oppenheimer in their 1978 book on political economy defined a 'political entrepreneur' as an individual who is motivated 'to set up an organization purportedly to supply collective goods' (69), and Moe's 1980 book on the organisation of interests viewed the political entrepreneur as playing a key role in the formation and maintenance of an interest group (36–7 and ch.3). But in both cases there was no Schumpeterian emphasis on the innovative nature of the group – that it was a new type of group – and in the case of Frohlich and Oppenheimer there was no analysis of the variety of possible motives for this entrepreneurial activity. In contrast, Mintrom's more recent use of the term 'policy entrepreneur' at least included an explicit recognition of the 'extraordinary' nature of entrepreneurship and its distinction from business-as-usual incremental policy change (2000: 289–90). Other examples of the application of the concept of entrepreneurship to political or policy-making activities include: Apter, 1965; Wagner, 1966; Ilchman and Uphof, 1969; Salisbury, 1969; Breton and Breton, 1969; Frohlich, Oppenheimer and Young, 1971; Olson, 1971; Barry, 1978; Schlesinger, 1984; Dunleavy, 1991; and Hopkin and Paolucci, 1999.

4. Medearis, 2001: 180–1. My emphasis. The other passage that he cites as evidence of analogy seems to be Schumpeter's description of Gladstone using his rhetorical skills in 1879 to rouse the country against 'Turkish atrocities so successfully as to place him on the crest of a wave of popular enthusiasm for him personally' (Schumpeter, 1974 [1947]: 275). This would therefore seem to be readily interpreted as a careerist-motivated innovation that did indeed result in his becoming Prime Minister (ibid.: 276).

5. Przeworski, 2003: 214. He and other political economists are using a broad definition of state institutions that goes beyond the 'rules of the game' to include such rule-making and/or rule-enforcing organs and organisations as legislatures, courts and central banks (ibid.: 141, 214). In contrast, some institutional economists, such as North, prefer a narrower definition of institutions that views them as solely the rules of the game – 'the constraints that human beings impose on human interaction' – and as quite distinct from organisations: 'Institutions are the rules of the game, organizations are the players' (North, 2005: 59). Elsewhere North indicated that entrepreneurs, too, can be players in the game but he was using a definition of economic and political entrepreneurs that included incremental as well as innovative change and that viewed them as motivated solely and merely by a desire to improve their position (ibid.: 2–3).

6. Schumpeter, 1974 [1947]: 285. His emphasis on professional politicians as careerists is very similar to parts of Weber's much earlier 'Politics as a Vocation', and even the distinction between careerists and crusaders seems to be foreshadowed by Weber's description of a crusading leader coming to power (Weber, 1991 [1919]: 125). But Weber's crusading leaders are the charismatic prophets of revolutionary new political faiths; not merely someone pursuing an innovative issue for non-careerist reasons. Moreover, when Weber drew an analogy with entrepreneurship, it was in relation to an especially professional type of politician – the vote-supplying boss of a political machine – and not to any form of innovator, whether careerist or crusading (ibid.: 86, 102–3, 109).

7. Przeworski, 2003: 214–15.

8. Schumpeter, 1974 [1947]: 282, 281.
9. Downs, 1957: 28.
10. Schumpeter, 1961[1934]: 88–9. Olson, 1971: 174. 'When Joseph Schumpeter developed the notion of the entrepreneur, he focused upon the businessman who did pioneering things' (ibid.).
11. Schumpeter, 1961[1934]: 84, 87, 86.
12. Ibid.: 87.
13. Ibid.: 88.
14. Ibid.
15. Ibid.: 89.
16. Ibid.
17. Ibid.
18. Schlesinger, 1986: 430, 421.
19. Schumpeter, 1961[1934]: 81 n. 2, 80 n. 2.
20. Ibid.: 92. See 93 for his description of entrepreneurial motivations.
21. Cringely, 1996: 101, 183.
22. Downs, 1957: 28.
23. Ibid.: 30. Downs's definition of a party is not just a coalition of individuals cooperating to achieve certain ends in common but a 'team' coalition whose members agree on all their goals, not just part of them (ibid.: 24, 25).
24. Ibid.: 81. He actually titled part II of the book: 'The General Effects of Uncertainty'.
25. Schumpeter, 1961[1934]: 66.
26. Schumpeter, 1989 [1947]: 222.
27. The creative response was described as having three essential features: (1) the content of the response could not have been predicted beforehand, (2) the response has a significant and lasting effect and (3) the frequency of such creative responses has something to do with the quality of the available personnel and their individual patterns of behaviour (ibid.).
28. Schumpeter, 1961[1934]: 78, 75.
29. Schumpeter, 1989 [1947]: 223. And a few years later he noted that 'the entrepreneurial element may be present to a very small extent even in very humble cases' (Schumpeter, 1989 [1949]: 259).
30. Schumpeter, 1974 [1947]: 132.
31. Schumpeter, 1961[1934]: 78.
32. Ibid.: 81 n. 2, 82 n. 2.
33. Schumpeter, 1974 [1947]: 132.
34. Schumpeter, 1961[1934]: 89.
35. Ibid.: 88.
36. Ibid.
37. Ibid.: 79.
38. Mintrom, 2000: 290.
39. See Rioux, 1987: 308–9; Berstein, 1993: 6–15.
40. Criddle, 1992: 110–11.
41. Schumpeter, 1974 [1947]: 64–5. Swedberg argues that he had soon adopted a very critical attitude towards Roosevelt and the New Deal because Schumpeter believed the Depression should be allowed to run its course – that it was wrong to interfere with the workings of the business cycle (Swedberg, 1991: 148).

42. Schumpeter, 1974: 214 n. 10.
43. Medearis, 2001: 78–80, 90–5, 4.
44. Ibid.: 20 and see also 15, 100, 102. See also Swedberg, 1991: 148 on Schumpeter fearing that the Depression would accelerate the trend towards socialism.
45. Medearis, 2001: 181, 189.
46. Schumpeter, 1989 [1949]: 258.
47. Schumpeter, 1974 [1947]: 290 n. 5.
48. Schumpeter, 1989 [1947]: 222.
49. Kennedy, 1999: 777–8.
50. Drucker, 2007 [1985]: 125–6.
51. Ibid.: 31.
52. Ibid.: 25.
53. Ibid.: 25.
54. Ibid.: 127.
55. Ibid.: 127, xv.
56. Cringely, 1996: 329, and see 303–6 on prophecies of doom about the old IBM.
57. Schumpeter, 1974 [1947]: 105.
58. Quoted in T. P. Coogan, 1995: 33.
59. Polsby, 1984: 100.
60. Ibid.: 147 n. 1.
61. See Offner, 2002: 223, 235 on the President and Secretary Marshall publicly promoting the Plan in political and national-security terms, and most of Congress agreeing with this assessment.
62. Polsby, 1984: 75.
63. Offner, 2002: 202, 204, 210.
64. Ibid.: 198–205, 210.
65. Schumpeter, 1961[1934]: 76. But he included the important proviso that these must be first-time, new (discontinuous) combinations of factors. The same point was made rather differently in a 1949 essay where he distinguished between simply repeating or adapting inherited combinations and setting up new combinations – and argued that in the latter case Say's definition would be applying to a distinctive function (Schumpeter, 1989 [1949]: 258).
66. Schumpeter, 1974 [1947]: 132.
67. Schlesinger, 1986: 425.
68. Ibid.: 424, 426. My emphasis.
69. Kasza, 1987: 856, 869. His article was focused on the use of these organisational tools by radical military regimes but acknowledged that such tools – 'supraministerial planning agencies, low-ranking agencies and new specialized ministries' – have been used 'by all types of political regimes', including democracies, 'to further innovation' (ibid.: 867).
70. Ibid.: 869. He also cited Lewis's 1980 work on public entrepreneurs, which will be used in the chapter on administrative entrepreneurship.
71. Wilson, 1989: 227.
72. See Brooker, 2009: ch.8 on semidemocracies.
73. Przeworski, 1999: 23.
74. Brooker, 2009: 8, citing Schumpeter, 1974 [1947]: 290–6.

75. Schumpeter, 1974 [1947]: 290 n. 5.
76. Ibid.: 246 on environmental conditions; 243 on times, places and situations.
77. North, 2005: 16. See also 19, which gives the technical, statistical definitions of ergodicity as the probability of past-observed/calculated data recurring in the future, and also North's point that to an economic historian 'the ergodic hypothesis is a-historical'.
78. The Library of Congress cataloguing on the flyleaf is '1. Evolutionary economics. 2. Economics – Sociological aspects. 3. Institutional economics'. North acknowledges that he has 'drawn inspiration' from attempts to extend evolutionary biology to human evolution but declares that he has preferred a different approach because there are two differences between biological and economic evolution: (1) in how 'variation' occurs and (2) in the 'selection mechanisms' (ibid.: 66). However, economists who explicitly use an evolutionary perspective have been more interested in the presence of this two-stage, variation and selection process in the economy than in the differences between its economic and biological forms (see Appendix). And North so often uses evolutionary terminology in his accounts of economic change that it is hardly surprising that the book has been viewed as being at least implicitly or tacitly a work of evolutionary economics.
79. He refers to the 'evolving structure' of political as well as economic markets, to the 'evolution' of polities, and to the way in which political and economic organisations 'evolved' (ibid.: 2, 51, 140). He also makes a series of evolutionary comments about how political units in medieval Europe 'gradually evolved into nation states'; the competition between 'evolving nation states'; that a particular nation-state 'evolved into an absolutist monarchy'; and that another polity 'evolved the elements of political representation and democratic decision rules' – that is, evolved some democratic institutions (ibid.: 141, 144, 142).
80. Ibid.: 124.
81. Ibid.: 2–3.

3 From Economic to Political Evolution

1. Nelson, 1995: 68.
2. Schumpeter, 1974 [1947]: 82, 83.
3. Ibid.: 68.
4. Ibid.
5. Ibid.: 83.
6. Ibid.
7. Dawkins, 1997: 93.
8. Jones, 2000: 296, 293–4.
9. In those cases where change goes on between punctuations, it does not accumulate over the generations because fluctuations in the local environment prevent any long-term shift in the changing feature, which wobbles to and fro around the average in a form of long-term stasis (Sterelny, 2001: 76).
10. Ibid.: 75. By geological-time standards 'a speciation that took 50,000 years would seem instantaneous' (ibid).
11. Schumpeter, 1974 [1947]: 83 n. 2.

12. For a branching-bush/tree conception of evolution see 'Life's Little Joke' in Gould, 1991, and 'Full of Hot Air' and 'The Declining Empire of Apes' in Gould, 1993. For Schumpeter's cyclical conception see Schumpeter, 1974 [1947]: 83 n. 2. When Baumgartner and Jones applied the concept of punctuated equilibrium to agenda-setting, they explicitly distinguished their evolutionary, punctuated equilibrium approach from cyclical theories of American politics (Baumgartner and Jones, 1993: 245–6).

13. Schumpeter, 1974 [1947]: 79, 84–5.

14. Ibid.: 32.

15. Ibid.: 85. Fifty years later the threat of competition was still disciplining oligopolistic firms in technologically advanced industries, who were spending large amounts on basic research 'to ensure that the company remains a dominant player in its industry twenty years from now. It's cheap insurance, since failing to do basic research guarantees that the next major advance will be owned by someone else' (Cringely, 1996: 79).

16. Bagehot used the subtitle 'Thoughts on the Application of the Principles of "Natural Selection" and "Inheritance" to Political Society' for his book *Physics and Politics* (London, 1887). See also Krasner, 1984: 242–3 on the state; Baumgartner and Jones, 1993: 18–19 n. 1, on adopting the terminology of punctuated equilibrium 'because it evokes the images of stability interrupted by major alterations to a system'. As will be seen later in this chapter, Carmines and Stimson used the concept of punctuated equilibrium in their 1989 book on issue evolution.

17. Duverger, 1959: 312–23.

18. Jones, 2000: 147.

19. Ibid.: 177.

20. Darwin, 1996 [1859]: 104–5. My emphases. Earlier in the chapter he had declared: 'This preservation of favourable variations and the rejection of injurious variations, I call Natural Selection' (ibid.: 68).

21. Gould, 2002: 247.

22. Metcalfe, 1998: 6, 36.

23. Gould, 1989: 277, 283.

24. Riker, 1982: 210–11.

25. Ibid.: 209. Riker had in mind the overall population of issues in a democracy, not merely the population of issue-responses to a particular external change, and he linked the natural selection of issues to the fate of the entrepreneurial politicians who introduced them: 'the rise and fall of issues is a process of natural selection in which politicians, like genes, seek to survive and flourish' (ibid.: 210).

26. Carmines and Stimson, 1989: 8. In their revised, 1993 version of this opening chapter they made two modifications to the passage in which they argue for a biological-style, historical and unpredictable approach to the study of issue evolution. 'A sense of predestination or inevitability is not to be found in any of these paths to issue development. That is a central theme of the literature on natural selection and *it is equally true, we believe, of the evolution of political issues*. We see development paths as sensible and explainable after the fact. But given a world dependent upon context, variation, and chance, any possible outcome, including the one that did in fact occur, has a prior probability so low as to be all but unpredictable. That view of history

and evolution ... *is central to our treatment of issue evolution*' (Carmines and Stimson, 1993: 156. My emphases).

27. Carmines and Stimson, 1989: 7, quoting Riker, 1982: 210.
28. Carmines and Stimson, 1989: 11.
29. Ibid.: 157.
30. Ibid.: 5, 4.
31. Ibid.: 10–11, 12.
32. Ibid.: 8.
33. Ibid. Such a local variation is not always easily distinguished from an 'organic extension' type of issue, which is a new issue that continues an existing conflict (or becomes interpreted in that way) and may at most reinvigorate an old issue and conflict by redefining it 'in the direction of more current issue debates' (ibid. 9–10).
34. Ibid.: 190–1, 157.
35. Gould, 2002: 247.
36. Kingdon, 1995: 223, 224.
37. Jones, 2000: 400–1. My emphasis. Gould, 1999: 359, quoting Lankester.
38. Gould, 1999: 355.
39. The most prominent example of the crises/stages approach emerged from the series *Studies in Political Development*, published in the 1960s under the aegis of the Social Science Research Council's Committee on Comparative Politics. 'Explicit in the Committee's thought is the idea that political change has a direction – toward greater equality, capacity, and differentiation' (Grew, 1978: 9).
40. Price, 1971: 319; Polsby, 1984: 127–8, 153.
41. Butler *et al.*, 1994: chs 3, 4 and 5.
42. Carpenter, 2001: 6.
43. Harmel and Svåsand, 1993: 71.
44. Ibid.: 76.
45. Ibid.: 87 n. 16.
46. Downs, 1967: ch. 2 and 24–5.
47. Ibid.: 24–5.
48. Ibid.: 9–10.
49. Ibid.
50. Riker, 1982: 229, referring to the slavery issue displacing the other issues that the Federalist-Whig-Republican party had tried out in the 1830s–50s.
51. Downs, 1967: 22, 23.
52. Huntington, 1968: 15.
53. Rose, 2001: 187.
54. Ibid.: 67–8.
55. The term 'evolution' replaced 'descent with modification' because of the urgings of the social theorist Herbert Spencer (Gould, 2000: 258–9).
56. Gould, 1991: 61.
57. Nelson, 1995: 75. See 73–5 for his survey of evolutionary economic models that include path dependency.
58. Schumpeter, 1974 [1947]: 92.
59. Ibid.: 98–104. He also pointed to cases where perfect competition produced imperfect results in handling crisis situations, such as wheat farmers responding to bad weather, which showed that there are 'attempts at

adaptation that intensify disequilibrium' in the market and lead to sympathetic economists acknowledging 'that what looks like rigidity may be no more than regulated adaptation' (ibid.: 105, 95).
60. Ibid.: 105, and 104 on loss to the community.
61. Tucker, 1995: 45.
62. Schumpeter, 1974 [1947]: 281.
63. Ibid.: 281 n. 23.
64. Schumpeter, 1961 [1934]: 84–6.
65. Schumpeter, 1974 [1947]: 281.
66. Ibid.: 281–2.
67. Although their conception of inheritance is a socio-legal rather than biological one, there is obvious similarity between Darwin's notion of descent with modification and their notion of 'cumulative changes in the legacy' of policy programmes inherited by each new generation (Rose and Davies, 1994: ch. 5). They considered a particular programme to have become part of the continuing inheritance if it has been in place for *three* generations (ibid.: 66). But a period of several decades 'while not long comparable to successive generations of a family, is sufficient to allow choices of one decade to be repudiated by a successor generation or incorporated into a legacy that persists without choice' (ibid.: 68).
68. Ibid.: 81–2.
69. Ibid.: 111, and 88 on the pre-1945 programmes.
70. Ibid.: 181, 183. The planned-achievement category accounted for 9 per cent of programmes and the ad hoc category for 13 per cent of programmes.
71. Ibid.: 182, 205–6, 211, 218.
72. Ibid.: 183.
73. Ibid.: 180. Inherited programmes may experience 'fine-tuning' amendments but they are more likely to be favourable than unfavourable alterations (ibid.: 181).
74. Ibid.: 180.
75. Ibid.: 38, and 29 on political inertia. See also 30 on proposals to terminate a programme being resisted by self-interested officials, together with recipients and interest groups.
76. Selznick, 1957: 17, 18–19. My emphasis.
77. Ibid.: 19.
78. Ibid.: 16. Selznick's emphasis on the creation of vested interests by the *organisation* illustrates why he has been described not only as one of the most influential theorists of the institutional focus on organisations but also as emphasising the importance of history in the biological, 'natural history' sense of the evolution of the organisation as a living form that is adaptively changing over time (Scott, 1987: 493, 494).
79. Selznick, 1957: 7, 21. In fact Selznick declared that a key task of any leader of a new organisation is the choice of a social base, such as a clientele, to which the organisation's operations will be oriented (ibid.: 104).
80. March and Olsen, 1989: 55.
81. Ibid.
82. Ibid.: 7, 54. See 54–6 on criticism of that assumption.
83. Schattschneider, 1960: 68.
84. Mueller, 1989: 240, 241.

85. Ibid.: 240. My emphasis.
86. Hanson Leung's analysis of the role of leadership in economic adaptation in the Soviet Union and China described Deng Xiaoping's 1978 revival of household contracts for agricultural production as having to overcome 'torrents of ideological and bureaucratic resistance', even though it seems to have been an only minimal adaptive innovation (Hanson Leung, 1985: 243). It is true that Deng was not deterred from going on to implement a creative-response innovation that amounted to the dismantling of collective farming and creation of a tenant-farming system with the state as the landlord (ibid.: 244). But this case not only showed how such substantive reform 'requires an effective and creative leadership' – it also provided 'a convincing case for determined and tenacious leadership' (ibid.: 244, 245).
87. Kingdon, 1984: 192, 76.
88. Greenfield and Strickon, 1979: 349.
89. Ilchman and Uphoff, 1969: 204.
90. See Dolowitz and Marsh, 2000: 10, 16, on policy entrepreneurs and policy transfer; Dolowitz, 2000: 17 on importance of policy entrepreneurs in policy transfer; Dolowitz, 1998: 70, on role of US administrators promoting policy internationally, and 82–3 on the transferring role of Ministers Young, Fowler and Moore.
91. Polsby, 1984: 166.
92. Weber, 1991 [1919]: 128.

4   The Leadership-Evolutionary Model

1. Schumpeter, 1974 [1947]: 145.
2. Prisching, 1995: 315, 319 n. 27.
3. Simon, 1997: 291–8 provides a recent summary of not only his notion of bounded rationality but also his notion of 'satisficing'.
4. Schumpeter, 1961 [1934]: 80. Nelson and Winter, 1982: 40 present this argument as an example of Schumpeter's being a theorist of bounded rationality.
5. Simon, 1997: 296.
6. Kuran, 1991: 71.
7. Some rational choice theorists would agree with Schumpeter that voters are vulnerable to being manipulated by political advertising and are unlikely to develop informed and rational political opinions. Kuran pointed out that the 'group-centered economic theory of politics', unlike the voter-centred theory, acknowledges that groups of individuals are able to impose their preferences on society by influencing other voters' preferences (ibid.: 74). This is very similar to Schumpeter's warnings about the influence that economic interests, and anyone else with an axe to grind, can have over public opinion and elections. And one of the ways in which groups' political advertising might influence the electorate was indirectly tested and confirmed by psychological experiments on framing, which indicated that variations in the framing of an issue or decision can have a marked effect on preferences and the coherence of preferences (Tversky and Kahneman, 1981: 453, 458). Furthermore, many rational choice theorists would agree with Schumpeter's view that voters are not well informed about political

matters. For rational choice theorists contend that it would be irrational for a voter to spend time and money becoming well-informed about political matters when an individual voter has so little effect on the outcome of elections (Prisching, 1995: 305). In fact Downs and other rational choicers have had trouble showing why it is rational for voters to even make the effort of going to the polls, and 'there is a sense among some rational-choice scholars that voter turnout is a distinctively recalcitrant area of application' (Green and Schapiro, 1994: 51, 71).

8. Santoro, 1993: 141. See 130 on electoral preferences being always to some extent manufactured.

9. See Schumpeter, 1974 [1947]: 273 n. 9 on the pathological state of not providing a lead. According to Tucker's definition: 'A political leader is one who gives direction, or meaningfully participates in the giving of direction, to a political community' (Tucker, 1995: 15). He also describes a government as being the formal leadership structure of a political community (ibid.: 18). But Tucker's theory of politics as leadership takes a quite different approach from Schumpeter's in distinguishing democratic from non-democratic cases: 'From the leadership perspective, democratic government entails primarily the institutionalized possibility of active public participation in the defining of problem situations for the political community' (ibid.: 68).

10. Schumpeter, 1974 [1947]: 274 n. 10.

11. Prisching, 1995: 313; Mitchell, 1984: 83, 84.

12. Dunleavy, 1985: 322.

13. Ibid.: 301. The central departments of pre-privatisation Britain's civil service contained about 800 of them, spread over nearly 50 departments (ibid.: 301 n. 5). However, Page and Jenkins's, recent book *Policy Bureaucracy: Government with a Cast of Thousands* has emphasised the policy-drafting role of thousands of *middle*-ranking bureaucrats in the British civil service. However, they do not have such a significant role in 'key major policies', where Ministers 'claim with justification that they make decisions and choices' and so presumably only the senior ranks of the civil service is likely to have much of a policy role (Page and Jenkins, 2005: 184). Furthermore, in other areas of policy the middle-ranking officials 'work hard to fashion policies that that they think their ministers will like' and therefore it is difficult to apply any notion of leadership to their activities; in fact 'it may be hard to find *anyone* responsible for making choices, least of all conscious ones' (ibid.).

14. Wood and Waterman, 1993: 498. Responses can be delayed and uncertain because of ambiguity in political signals, dealing with multiple political principals, or simply 'shirking' any requirements that conflict with the bureaucracy's interests (ibid.: 503–4).

15. Mitchell, 1984: 83, 82.

16. Schumpeter, 1974 [1947]: 295.

17. Sabatier, 1988: 138–9.

18. Ibid.: 139, 142, 139.

19. Sabatier pointed out that in most cases a policy subsystem will be the home or arena of only one advocacy coalition or one dominant coalition and one or more minority coalitions (ibid.: 140, 148).

20. Marsh, 1998: 3, 14, 16 table 1.1. A policy community is not to be confused with an 'epistemic community', which is more like an advocacy coalition with a shared system of knowledge that defines policy problems and shapes the available policy responses (Dolowitz, 2000: 22). An epistemic community need not include administrators and legislators, and it may face one or more rival epistemic communities that are competing against it – in similar fashion to rival groupings of scientists seeking to have their group's 'interpretation of the data' vindicated by being adopted by the policy makers (ibid.).
21. Peters, 1998: 26.
22. Ibid.: 25. Marsh acknowledged that there is also a problem in integrating the 'meso-level' network analysis with 'macro-level' analysis of the broader political system and with 'micro-level' analysis of individual actions – which must be 'underpinned by a theory of human behaviour, such as rational choice theory' (Marsh, 1998: 13, 15). The LE model meets these requirements by locating the policy-based subsystems within the broader political system and including a careerist theory of individuals' political behaviour. This careerism's limited or bounded rational self-interest also meets Daugbjerg and Marsh's requirement that the micro-level theory used in an integrated analysis has to include realistic assumptions about individuals' behaviour: 'it is crucial to operate with a model of bounded rationality' (Daugbjerg and Marsh, 1998: 71).
23. Schumpeter, 1974 [1947]: 290.
24. The following argument about cartelisation is similar not only to Sabatier's earlier cited point about advocacy coalitions but also to Raymond Breton's argument that a policy field becomes institutionalised to the extent that 'competition ceases among entrepreneurs established in the field' and instead takes place between them and aspiring new entrants, who will discover that the established occupants of the field 'can construct quite effective resistance to innovation and change' (Breton, 1991: 109).
25. For example, see Sabatier, 1988 on defending the status quo against proposals that challenge it, on secondary aspects of a basic policy, and on intra-coalition arguments and learning about these secondary aspects – including experimenting with different variations and even learning from opposing coalitions.
26. Schumpeter, 1974 [1947]: 267.
27. Ibid: 67.
28. Stokes, 2001: 179–80.
29. Ware, 1996: 158.
30. Ibid: 157, 409 n. 8. See Lipsey and Chrystal 1995: 256 on market concentration and power.
31. Lipsey and Chrystal, 1995: 216.
32. Schumpeter, 1974 [1947]: 271.
33. Market power 'often arises naturally because in many industries the least costly way to produce is to have few producers' but 'some market power is maintained through artificial barriers to entry' (Lipsey and Chrystal, 1995: 418). See also 263, 270–1, on such natural factors as economies of scale and scope versus such firm-created factors as not only artificial barriers to entry but also the anti-competitive strategies of buying out rivals, merging with rivals or using predatory practices against them. Artificial barriers to entry

are not always firm-created factors; they may be such state-created factors as legal prohibitions or government interventions (ibid.: 273, 263, 218).
34. Ibid.: 270.
35. Parker, 1992: 17–18, 26–8.
36. Katz and Mair, 1995: 17, 16, 19.
37. Koole, 1996: 515–17.
38. See Hazan, 1996.
39. Schumpeter, 1974 [1947]: 85. See also 84 on competition through innovation, and 132 on entrepreneurs introducing such innovations.

5   Electoral Pioneering

1. Duverger, 1959: xxiii–xxv. In his classic work on political parties Epstein noted that 'the degree of organization is often taken as an important mark distinguishing a party from a faction', but he preferred to define a party as 'any group, however loosely organized, seeking to elect governmental office-holders under a given label' (Epstein, 1980 [1967]: 9).
2. Duverger, 1959: xxiii.
3. Epstein, 1980 [1967]: 20–1.
4. Charles, 1961: 85, 90.
5. Epstein, 1980 [1967]: 21.
6. Hopkin and Paolucci, 1999: 328.
7. Ibid.: 324–9.
8. Ibid.: 330–1.
9. Brechtel and Kaiser, 1999. See 21 on creative response, quoting from Schumpeter, 1989 [1947]: 222, 229.
10. Brechtel and Kaiser, 1999: 23.
11. Macfarlane, 1986: 3, 9.
12. Ibid.: 9.
13. Kingdon, 1995: 213, 217.
14. Macfarlane, 1986: 9.
15. Downs, 1972.
16. Ibid.: 47.
17. Downs, 1957: 47.
18. Dunleavy, 1991: 143. Yet he categorised such innovations as 'preference-*accommodating*' strategies, not as further examples of the 'preference-*shaping*' strategies that he had been describing earlier in the chapter, such as capitalising on social tensions or agenda-setting by bidding up the voters' expectations of what is economically or technically feasible (ibid.: 125–7).
19. Ibid.: 127.
20. Page, 1978: 269.
21. Ibid.: 269–70.
22. Loomis, 1996: 69, 182 figure 10.1.
23. Ashbee, 2001.
24. Hennessy, 2001: 508.
25. Young, 1989: ch. 7.
26. Kavanagh, 2001: 7. Riddell quoted by Hennessy, 2001: 512. Rose, too, points out that the major constitutional reforms 'were a legacy from the old Labour

Party' that preceded Blair's transformation of it into New Labour (Rose, 2001: 21).
27. Page, 1978: 271.
28. Ibid.
29. Nadel, 1971: 46–7.
30. Bean and Marks, 1993: 253. My emphasis.
31. Ibid.: 255, 256.
32. Ibid.: 256. My emphasis.
33. Warhurst, 2000: 2. Although Howard's Liberal-National coalition government was nervous about GST as an election issue, they wanted a pro-GST mandate before they went ahead with the policy, and Prime Minister Howard personally was 'politically becalmed and under criticism from business for a lack of vision' (Warhurst *et al.*, 2000: 169, 168).
34. Carmines and Stimson, 1989: 27–8.
35. Ibid.: 29. See 30–1 on politicians keeping race off the political agenda and 185 on parties not finding it advantageous to stake out a distinctive position on race.
36. Ibid.: 186.
37. Macfarlane, 1986: 3.
38. Carmines and Stimson, 1989: 114.
39. Ibid.
40. See Outshoorn, 1986, and van der Eijk and Kok, 1984, on similar complexity in the pre-policy life cycle of public issues.
41. Downs, 1972: 41.
42. Baumgartner and Jones, 1993: 87–8.
43. Ibid.: 57, 59, 100.
44. Riker, 1982: ch. 9.
45. Ibid.: 213.
46. Ibid.: 229.
47. Riker, 1986: ix–xi, and 147 on the three kinds of manipulation. The term 'heresthetic' was based on the ancient Greeks' word for choosing and electing, and was meant to be a counterpart of rhetoric, the art of persuasion.
48. Ibid.: 66, 151, 2–3.
49. Ibid.: 1, 51, 150.
50. Ibid.: ix. Paine's analysis of manipulation and persuasion pointed out that both he and Riker considered an audience's sincere acceptance of a new dimension's importance to be a case of persuasion (a changing of beliefs) rather than manipulation (Paine, 1989: 48). In fact he argued that manipulation of dimensions occurs only when its target pragmatically concludes that he should change his stance because an audience with the power to benefit/cost him, such as his constituents, have been persuaded by his manipulator that a new dimension is salient.
51. McLean, 2001: 232. See also ch. 2.
52. Ignazi refers to 'political entrepreneurs who exploited a favourable structure of opportunity' in establishing several new extreme-right parties in Europe in the 1980s, such as the National Front in France, but he does not explore their use of the anti-immigration issue – apart from suggesting that the rightist 'defence of the national community from foreigners' is linked to 'the identity crisis produced by atomisation' (Ignazi, 1996: 557, 560).

53. Tversky and Kahneman, 1981: 453, 457.
54. Goffman, 1974: 10–11.
55. Fisher and Strauss, 1979: 460; Coser, 1979: 315. The notion of 'defining the situation' was developed by Thomas, who pointed to definitions' organising of experience and to the fact 'that people do not only respond to objective features of a situation, but also, and often mainly, to the meaning that a situation has for them' (Coser, 1979: 315). However, it has been argued that Goffman had developed his own approach in his theory of frame analysis that was a kind of structuralism rather than the subjectivist and/or cultural approach of the 'situational', interactionist theorists (Gonos, 1977). Yet even if they are coming at the issue from different perspectives, Goffman and the interactionists seem very close in their practical implications. For example, Gonos acknowledges that (1) frame analysis 'retains a place for the notion of situation', which refers to temporary aspects of a frame that individuals may be able to adjust, and (2) Thomas recognised that such social situations as weddings are defined and carried out with a degree of uniformity – that there are 'predetermined' definitions of situation – which seems in practice very similar to Goffman's notion of a frame (ibid.: 864 n. 18, 858–9).
56. Tucker, 1995: 18, and 17–18 on Thomas's notion of defining the situation.
57. Goffman, 1974: 41, 345, 573. 'Keying' is where the transformation involves something meaningful in terms of a primary framework being transformed into something patterned on it but seen by the participants as quite different, as a process of 'transcription' (ibid.: 44). 'Fabrication' is where an intentional effort is made to induce someone to have 'a false belief about what it is that is going on' (ibid.: 83). Third, there is the self-imposed fabrication, the illusion, which has to be distinguished, too, from 'errors' in framing that may involve misperception and thus 'misframing' (ibid.: 116, 111, 308).
58. Fabrication can be either benign or exploitative, with the former claimed to be engineered for the victim's benefit (or at least not to be against his interests) and the latter clearly against the victim's interests (ibid.: 87, 103). He also makes the distinction between deceits meant to delude only a few and 'those designed to delude a wide public' (ibid.: 104).
59. Baumgartner and Jones, 1993: 31, 11, 239.
60. Ibid.: 38, 42, 4.
61. Ibid.: 16.
62. Ashbee, 2001: 159, 166.
63. Harmel and Svåsand, 1993: 77–8, 82–3.
64. Ibid.: 82, 78.

6   Governmental (Executive) Pioneering

1. In a presidential democracy, the governmental selling of leads is by the President to the legislature, as when he sends it a bill that he believes should be passed into law.
2. Downs, 1957: 107–8.
3. Budge and Hofferbert, 1990: 112, 129. See also Stokes, 2001: 8–9.
4. Stokes, 2001: 165.
5. Headey, 1974: 166. See also 207, 215. Headey described Ministers who imposed their own or their *party*'s policy objectives on their departments as

performing the role of 'policy initiator', as distinct from the 'policy legitimator' and 'policy selector' roles of merely accepting a departmental policy proposal by, respectively, rubberstamping or choosing among options (ibid.: 44–5). See also 191, and 157 on policy initiators and party policy pronouncements in the electoral manifesto.

6. Schumpeter, 1974 [1947]: 276, 278.
7. James, 1995: 64.
8. Edwards and Wayne, 2003: 412.
9. Schumpeter, 1974 [1947]: 280.
10. Moon, 1995: 5. His conception of innovative leadership has little in common with pioneering and sometimes seems similar to adaptive leadership, as when noting that innovative leadership 'identifies changing attitudes, moves with and legitimizes them, and provides new directions' (ibid.: 8).
11. Ibid.: 5; Theakston, 2003: 99.
12. See Thompson, 1995 and Smith, 1995.
13. Headey, 1974: 48. But it is true that the nature of the 'traditional' Cabinet changed several times in the 1940s–90s (James, 1995: 68–9). And the nature of the Cabinet as a forum also includes the extensive set of powerful Cabinet committees that is a distinctive characteristic of the British form of Cabinet government when compared to even the British-derived Canadian and Australian examples as well as to European examples of collective government (Andeweg, 1997: 77, 81).
14. Headey, 1974 [1947]: 49.
15. Ibid.: 66, 160, 164, 205.
16. Weller, 1985: 48. See also 190.
17. Edwards and Wayne, 2003: 124, 138; Neustadt, 1960: 100.
18. Baumgartner, 1989: 122.
19. Weller, 1985: 195–6.
20. Ibid.: 183.
21. See Johnston *et al.*, 1993.
22. Wilson, 1977: 69; James, 1995: 76.
23. See Thompson, 1995 and Smith, 1995 on the case of Thatcher's veto of membership of the EU Exchange Rate Mechanism eventually being overridden through pressure from her most senior Ministers.
24. Schumpeter, 1974 [1947]: 280.
25. Weller, 1985: 104, 123; Wilson, 1977: 75–6.
26. Weller, 1985: 126–7.
27. Ibid.: 129.
28. James, 1995: 78–9.
29. Ibid.: 79.
30. Burch, 1983: 407–8; Hennessy, 2001: 424.
31. Headey, 1974: 166.
32. Ibid.
33. For example, see ibid.: 166, 207, 215.
34. Theakston, 2003: 107, 109, 111.
35. Ibid.: 109.
36. Hennessy, 2001: 449.
37. Ibid.: 452, 451.
38. See Moon, 1995.
39. Quoted by Marsh, 1991: 460.

234 *Notes*

40. Smith, 1995: 115.
41. Young, 1989: 141, 149.
42. Burch, 1983: 411.
43. Young, 1989: 141–5.
44. Burch, 1983: 411.
45. Ibid.: 401–3.
46. Young, 1989: 218.
47. Ibid.: 218–20.
48. James, 1995: 85.
49. Young, 1989: 300, 280, 241.
50. Burch, 1983: 412.
51. Ibid.: 410.
52. Young, 1989: 367, 503.
53. Ibid.: 502.
54. Ibid.: 503.
55. Rose and Davies, 1994: 161–2.
56. Marsh, 1991: 465 table 1; 471 table 2.
57. Ibid.: 463.
58. See Allington *et al.*, 1999 on marketing efforts aimed at first-time sharebuyers; Marsh, 1991: 463 on increase in shareowners.
59. Dunleavy, 1991: 120. Research into voting behaviour has shown that the privatisation share sales did provide a significant electoral payoff, and were also markedly more electorally beneficial than the council-housing sales because there were many more first-time share buyers than the 1.2 million council-house buyers (Marsh, 1991: 463, 476).
60. Zahariadis, 1995: 61.
61. Quoted by Young, 1989: 498–9. See also Allington *et al.*, 1999 on it being portrayed as mass democracy, and Marsh, 1991: 474 quoting Moore on breaking down divisions between owners and earners.
62. Zahariadis, 1995: 64; Marsh, 1991: 463, 470–2; Allington *et al.*, 1999: 627, 632–3, and 640 on ideas vacuum; Young, 1989: 500, 537.
63. Zahariadis, 1995: 61; Campbell, 2000: 387.
64. Zahariadis, 1995: 75, 77.
65. Ibid.: 89.
66. Young, 1989: 330.
67. Allington *et al.*, 1999: 636.
68. As the title of the Butler *et al.*, 1994 study of the poll tax proclaims, it is viewed as a classic case of policy failure.
69. Ibid.: 56–9.
70. Ibid.: 68–9, 65.
71. Ibid.: 70. However, half of the Cabinet, including Chancellor Lawson, were not present at this crucial meeting. The Chancellor opposed the idea of a poll tax before and after the Chequers meeting but did not attend, nor attempt later to veto the proposal in Cabinet, because the poll tax was a local-government rather than Treasury matter and therefore was not in his feudal bailiwick or cabbage patch (ibid.: 75, 86, 87).
72. Young, 1989: 430.
73. Butler *et al.*, 1994: 76.
74. Ibid.: 82.

75. Ibid.: 107. See 104–6 on the Labour party deciding not to make an election issue of the poll tax's flaws – a decision which apparently baffled even the Conservatives.
76. Ibid.: 82.
77. Ibid.: 58.
78. Ibid.: 76; Young, 1989: 225, 544.
79. Weller, 1985: 124.
80. Thompson, 1995: 258. She made this claim in her mid-1980s vetoing of a proposal to join the ERM.
81. Young, 1989: 464.
82. Bunce's model of honeymoon decision making by US Presidents emphasises the structural or objective factors involved in the honeymoon tendency towards innovation rather than incrementalism, but also includes a personal, subjective element that is similar to the 'choose' element of the adage about the office of Prime Minister being what the holder chooses and is able to make of it. For example, she refers to a President's combination of *desire* and capability to act, to new leaders *wanting* to do more when they are novices, and to leaders being more *willing* to look for new agenda items during the honeymoon period (Bunce, 1981: 137, 138, 139). Moreover, she acknowledges that reelections produce less policy change than replacements, which suggests that a President experiences some form of burn-out in terms of energy and/or goals that a return to the campaign trail and a reelection honeymoon can only partly rectify (ibid.: 138, 137).
83. Gamble, 1988: 22, as quoted by Moon, 1995: 15.
84. Rose, 2001: 233.
85. Kavanagh, 2001: 10.
86. Hennessy, 2001: 517, 482–3, 518.
87. Ibid.: 520; Riddell, 2001: 33; Kavanagh, 2001: 11.
88. Hennessy, 2001: 536; Kavanagh, 2001: 14.
89. Riddell, 2001: 25 on factionalism between Blair and Brown; Hennessy, 2001: 508 on sharing of power.
90. Hennessy, 2001: 477, 522, 527.
91. Kavanagh, 2001: 14; Hennessy, 2001: 480.
92. Hennessy, 2001: 493, 513.
93. Riddell, 2001: 37.
94. Hennessy, 2001: 526.
95. Ibid.: 513; Kavanagh, 2001: 14.
96. Hennessy, 2001: 513, 528.
97. Lam, 1999: 365. But although Zhu had a personal following among the technocrats in the party, he was not seen as a potential successor to Jiang as party leader; only as a very able economic specialist best qualified to hold the post of Premier (ibid.: 23, 364–5).
98. Hennessy, 2001: 477.
99. Kavanagh, 2001: 11.
100. Quoted by Hennessy, 2001: 483.
101. Rose, 2001: 21; Kavanagh, 2001: 8; Riddell, 2001: 37.
102. Theakston, 2003: 120.
103. Hennessy, 2001: 487.
104. Ibid.: 485–6, citing a source from within the prime-ministerial staff.

105. Riddell, 2001: 30–1.
106. Mandelson speaking soon after his resignation in December 1998 and quoted by Hennessy, 2001: 507.
107. Kavanagh, 2001: 12; Riddell, 2001: 28.
108. Kavanagh, 2001: 15. Also cited by Riddell, 2001: 39.
109. Rose, 2001: 218, 227.
110. Ibid.: 220.
111. Riddell, 2001: 26.
112. Theakston, 2003: 119.
113. Seldon, 2007: 266.
114. Norton, 2007: 270 . He also confirms the key role of John Smith in preparing the way for the programme, which Blair committed himself to when he inherited the leadership from Smith in 1994.
115. Ibid.
116. Seldon, 2007: 266.
117. Thomson: 2007: 56.
118. Ibid.: 53–4.
119. Seldon, 2007: 266.
120. Thomson, 2007: 53 on expressing the targets in 'a way the public can understand'.
121. Ibid.: 56.
122. Hills, 2004: 19.

7   Presidential Pioneering and Foreign Policy

1. Brooker, 2009: ch.1.
2. Neustadt, 1990 [1960]: ix, 188.
3. Colomer and Negretto, 2005: 88 on not now ruling absolutely and 76–7 on proactive/agenda-setting relationship and formal powers, which were possessed by eight South American presidencies. It has been suggested that the US model is applicable to at least six Latin American countries, all in Central America, but some of these six cases must be more presidential than the US model if 'most' Latin American congressional legislatures have not developed 'full legislative initiative – in contrast to the typical US feature' (ibid.: 76, 88).
4. Neustadt, 1990 [1960]: 29.
5. Ibid.: 11, 28.
6. Ibid.: 7, 9.
7. Ibid.: 18. Each of the administrative departments and agencies 'has a different set of specialized careerists inside its own bailiwick' and while all agency administrators are responsible to the President, 'they are also responsible to Congress, to their clients, to their staffs and to themselves' (ibid.: 34).
8. Ibid.: 34.
9. Ibid.: 8, and 7–8 on giving a lead over a huge range of policy.
10. Schumpeter, 1974 [1947]: 274 n.10.
11. Neustadt, 1966: 68, 65–6, 64.
12. Neustadt, 1990: 38, 30.

13. Ibid.: 11, 32.
14. Ibid.: 38, 42, 11.
15. Ibid.: 30, 31.
16. Ibid.: 50, 52.
17. Ibid.: 73, 74, 76–7.
18. Ibid.: 81–4. Another example of Neustadt's almost pessimistic attitude towards presidential popular prestige is his point that public standing is not simply a matter of personality because there can be sharp changes in the popularity of a President who has 'projected the same human qualities' as before: 'the values men assign to what they see can alter rather quickly. "Decisiveness" may turn into irascibility; "cleverness" may come to seem deceitfulness; "openmindedness" to seem softheadedness; "courage" to seem rashness'(ibid.: 79, 80).
19. Campbell and Jamieson, 2008: 24.
20. Graebner, 1993: 31–2.
21. Ibid.: 47, 42.
22. Campbell and Jamieson, 2008: 8–9, 351.
23. Ibid.: 253.
24. Neustadt, 1966: 68. See also 65 on bipartisanship in practice.
25. Neustadt, 1990: 17–18.
26. Graebner, 1993: 44.
27. Ibid.: 33. My emphases.
28. Dallek, 1995: 545.
29. Quoted by Smith, 2008: 69.
30. DeConde, 1966: 126–7.
31. Smith, 2008: 66; DeConde, 1966: 3.
32. DeConde, 1966: 126.
33. Ibid.: 127.
34. Smith, 2008: 69.
35. DeConde, 1966: 127 confirms that he 'first availed himself of the phrase [Good Neighbour] in his inaugural address'.
36. Ibid.: 127; Smith, 2008: 69, 66. See Dallek, 1995: 38–9 on FDR as early as 12 April 1933 (Pan-American Day) publicly applying the concept to the Western hemisphere.
37. Kimball, 1993: 95 and on Roosevelt ensuring that military proposals conformed to his grand strategy.
38. Larrabee, 2004: 16, 638–9.
39. Ibid.: 36; Dallek, 1995: 255.
40. Casey, 2001: 22, 23.
41. Dallek, 1995: 267.
42. Larrabee, 2004: 53, 56–7
43. Ibid.: 61.
44. Ibid.: 46. It was during these years that Schumpeter noted that a President's loss of a vote in Congress on major issues 'will in general so weaken his prestige as to oust him from a position of leadership' (Schumpeter, 1974: 279 n.20).
45. Dallek, 1995: 292.
46. Ibid.: 310–11.
47. But he 'never forgot the depth of isolationist sentiment in the years before Pearl Harbor, especially the public's dogged and stubborn opposition to a

full and formal involvement in the war'; thus as late as 1944 he was still worried about whether the public would support a long-term commitment of US troops against Germany on the European continent (Casey, 2001: 214).

48. Leuchtenberg, 2009 [1963]: 327–8; Larrabee, 2004: 17.
49. Neustadt, 1990 [1960]: 132. My emphasis.
50. Larrabee, 2004: 65 quoting Arthur Schlesinger Jr.
51. Dallek, 1995: 532.
52. Allison, 1971: 159–60.
53. Ibid.: 179. Allison also uses the aphorism 'Where you stand depends on where you sit' in arguing that in budgetary, procurement and similar sorts of relatively routine issues the stance of individual subordinates can be predicted by where they 'sit' in organisational and career terms (ibid.:176).
54. Quoted by George, 1972: 754.
55. George, 1972: 753.
56. Ibid.: 755. Its staff 'reached deeper into departments and bureaus in order to identify and gain control over a wider range of issues at earlier stages' (ibid.: 754).
57. Ibid.: 760, 761.
58. Ibid.: 759.
59. Lambright, 1976: 203.
60. Ibid.
61. Spanier, 1981: 444.
62. Ibid.
63. Neustadt, 1990 [1960]: 270, 276–8. A more positive summary of Reagan by Neustadt was that 'his Presidency restored the public image of the office to a fair (if perhaps rickety) approximation of its Rooseveltian mold: a place of popularity, influence and initiative, a source of programmatic and symbolic leadership, both pacesetter and tonesetter, the nation's voice to both the world and us, and – like or hate the policies – a presence many of us loved to see as Chief of State' (ibid.: 269).
64. Ibid.: 278.
65. Pach, 2006: 76.
66. Ibid.: 77.
67. Ibid.: 82. The ban would be lifted in October 1986 but re-imposed soon afterwards when revelations emerged about the Iran-Contra affair.
68. Scott, 1996: 19.
69. Ibid.: 19–20, 21.
70. Neustadt, 1990 [1960]: 280–1. Casey was also first CIA Director to be made a member of the Cabinet.
71. Lettow, 2006: 14–17.
72. Ibid.: 28, quoting from a 1976 interview with Reagan and from a 1975 radio commentary written and broadcast by him.
73. Scott, 1996: 11.
74. Ibid.: 4–5. Apart from the Afghanistan case (which was also continuing an existing policy instituted by President Carter), there was no consistent commitment to implementing the doctrine (ibid.: 5). There was early but later erratic, 'on-again, off-again' military assistance for the Contra insurgents fighting against the revolutionary Sandinista regime in Nicaragua.

And there was a delayed application (again erratic) of the doctrine in favour of the UNITA insurgents fighting against the African Marxist-Leninist regime in Angola. But only 'non-lethal' supplies were given to the Cambodian insurgents fighting against communist Vietnam's occupying forces and their Cambodian puppet regime, while the insurgents fighting against the African Marxist-Leninist regime in Mozambique were given only indirect and non-military 'support', with the US resorting to diplomacy and inducements to encourage Mozambique's regime to adopt a less pro-Soviet stance.

75. Ibid.: 227, 228. Mann describes 'breezily avoiding the disputes within his administration' as the President's 'operating style' (Mann, 2009: 314).
76. Scott, 1996: 12 on bureaucracy and 239 on Congress. The presidential dis-interest and inaction that prompted congressional action occurred in the 'Afghanistan, Angola, Cambodia, and Mozambique cases'. See also ibid.: 11, 237 on policy being formulated in Congress and on congressional leader-ship of foreign policy.
77. Neustadt, 1990: 273.
78. Ibid.
79. Scott, 1996: 237, 241. This description applies not only to the foreign-policy bureaucracy but also to what Scott described as rival inter-branch alliances that might include the President and groups in Congress as well as in the bureaucracy.
80. Speech of 23 March 1983 in support of his defence budget. Quoted by Lettow, 2006: 111. My emphases.
81. Lettow, 2006: 21–3.
82. Ibid.: xi. See ibid.: 110 on Reagan being undeterred by opposition to SDI.
83. Mann, 2009: 336. See also Nixon's and other conservatives' later opposition to the INF Treaty eliminating intermediate-range nuclear weapons (ibid.: 286–8).
84. Ibid.: 345–6.
85. Bunch, 2009: 74–5.

8 Legislative Pioneering

1. Kingdon, 1984: 81. The independence of Congress from the executive is exemplified by the fact that the staff of congressional committees 'do detailed policy work of the kind done by the executive civil servants in the UK' (Page and Jenkins, 2005: 174).
2. Neustadt, 1960: 43.
3. Mayhew, 1974: 26.
4. Loomis, 1996: 94–8. By the mid-1990s the personal office allowance allowed a member of Congress to employ up to eighteen full-time staff and four part-time (ibid.: 97).
5. Dodd, 1977: 397.
6. Mayhew, 1974: 47–8.
7. Ibid.: 49, 67–8, 68.
8. Ibid.: 69, 69 n. 118.
9. Dodd, 1977: 398.
10. Bradshaw and Pring, 1981: 276.

11. Quirk, 1995: 228; Loomis, 1988: 110.
12. Wawro described legislative entrepreneurs as engaging in 'legislative inno-
    vation' when they introduce an issue that has never before been addressed
    by Congress or introduce a new way of combining issues that have been
    previously addressed (Wawro, 2000: 10–11). But he discussed legislation
    innovation only as part of the wider topic of bill drafting, and referred only
    obliquely to innovation when describing his indicator for measuring entre-
    preneurial ability in bill-drafting: the number of titles and index items in a
    bill (ibid.: 33–4). Many years earlier, Walker had mentioned both legislative
    initiative and innovation but did not explain how they differed, if at all,
    from merely introducing a new bill on the discretionary part of the legisla-
    tive agenda (Walker, 1977: 428, 426).
13. Schiller, 1995: 186 n. 1.
14. Ibid.: 188, 199.
15. Ibid.: 191.
16. Hall's definition of entrepreneurship in Congress was a legislator and
    his staff 'exceeding some high threshold of issue-specific participation',
    which might include *obstruction* of a bill (Hall, 1996: 233). See also 30, 30
    n. 4.
17. Ibid.: 41.
18. Ibid.: 193. See 206–7 on what this political entrepreneurship entailed.
19. Ibid.: 67 n. 19.
20. Wawro, 2000: 28.
21. Ibid.: 27.
22. Ibid.: 34, 33, 30–2.
23. Ibid.: 36–43, 101. But the results failed to support the hypothesis in the case
    of minority-party members and their prestigious positions in the House.
24. Ibid.: 103, 107.
25. Bullock and Loomis, 1985: 65.
26. Ibid.: 66, 77. Seniority remained the dominant criterion for promotion on
    committees even after its formal relaxation in the early 1970s but appar-
    ently had comparatively little effect upon the 'vagaries of attaining top
    party leadership positions' (Deering, 1996: 6, 19).
27. Ibid.: 77, 69, 78.
28. Wawro, 2000: 101, 20.
29. Ibid.: 111, citing Mayhew, 1974: 141.
30. Mayhew, 1974: 5, 145–7.
31. Wawro, 2000: 20–1. See Fenno, 1973: 1 on House, 139 on Senate.
32. Mayhew referred only to the Speaker and Majority Leader party leader-
    ship positions and to what he termed the three 'control' committees in the
    House: Rules, Appropriations, and Ways and Means (Mayhew, 1974: 147).
33. Wawro, 2000: 104–6.
34. Ibid.: 110–11.
35. Bullock and Loomis, 1985: 66.
36. Ibid.: 77–8.
37. Loomis, 1988: 19.
38. Loomis, 1996: 178.
39. Mayhew, 1974: 15, 16.
40. Ibid.: 68, and 68 n. 116 citing Price, 1972: 29, 78 on the Magnuson case.
    Less dramatic but more general evidence of an electoral careerist motivation

for bill-selling is that Schiller's statistical and interview research indicated that serving constituents' economic interests was a major factor in Senators' decisions to introduce bills (Schiller, 1995: 192, 194).
41. Price, 1972: 297.
42. Price, 1971: 320–1.
43. Ibid.: 322.
44. Fenno, 1973: 13, 142; Mayhew, 1974: 76; Loomis, 1988: 107.
45. Polsby, 1984: 162.
46. Ibid.: 162, 163.
47. Wawro, 2000: 109.
48. Hall, 1996: 204.
49. Parker, 1992: 15, 97, 5.
50. Ibid.: 11, 108, 33.
51. Walker, 1977: 425–6.
52. Ibid.: 426, 432.
53. Schuck, 1995: 57.
54. Ibid.: 58.
55. Ibid.: 55.

9 Administrative Pioneering

1. Aberbach *et al.*, 1981: 231.
2. Ibid.: 231, 234–5.
3. Doig and Hargrove, 1987: 18. My emphasis.
4. Ibid.: 19, 20.
5. Lewis, 1980: 9.
6. Ibid.: 206.
7. Ibid.: 8–9.
8. Polsby, 1984: 164.
9. Ibid.: 144.
10. Ibid.: 171–2.
11. Lewis, 1980: 240–1, 243–4.
12. Carpenter, 2001: 4. He pointed out that agencies and their leaders also need reputational 'uniqueness', as in the case of Comstock's reputational uniqueness as a moral protector enabling him not only to achieve the 1873 anti-pornography law but also to become a 'legislative force unto himself, pressing numerous extensions of his authority through Congress' (ibid.: 5, 2).
13. Ibid.: 6, 288.
14. Nadel, 1971: 9. See also Carpenter, 2001: 257–74.
15. Lewis, 1980: 237.
16. Ibid.: 25.
17. Ibid.: 10, 17, 235, 247.
18. Ibid.: 109–10.
19. Ibid.: 115–21. The Bureau was also designated the *Federal* Bureau of Investigation in 1935, which symbolised its increasingly autonomous and national status as something more than just a Bureau of the Justice Department.
20. Ibid.: 23, 143–4, 153.
21. Ibid.: 55. See also 43–55 on the selling skill and effort – and luck – required to accomplish this triumph.

22. Ibid.: 55, 20, 59.
23. Ibid.: 81–2, 252.
24. Ibid.: 23.
25. See Peter Drucker's letter to James Doig, quoted in Doig, 1987: 173 n. 62.
26. Lewis, 1980: 21, 206–11.
27. Ibid.: 9.
28. Ibid.: 219–20.
29. Ibid.: 122–3, 74–5. Rickover himself emphasised that one of the key characteristics of a successful manager in a large bureaucracy was 'ownership' of the job (Stoecker, 1998: 139).
30. Lewis, 1980: 20.
31. Ibid.: 18. Unlike ordinary politicians and bureaucrats, they were able to project a politically and popularly appealing image of professional, even scientific, neutrality (ibid.: 233).
32. Ibid.: 240.
33. His conception of bureaucratic autonomy included the requirement that politicians 'must believe that it will be costly to resist the agency's innovations', and these costs not only may be electoral but also can be substantial enough to influence even Presidents (Carpenter, 2001: 33).
34. Lewis, 1980: 154.
35. Cooper, 1987: 85.
36. Lewis saw a 'struggle for autonomy' as a promotional activity that strengthens and consolidates the position of the entrepreneur's new organisation or policy, with the public entrepreneur having to 'bargain, threaten and seduce others into allowing him autonomy over his mission' (Lewis, 1980: 18).
37. Doig and Hargrove, 1987: 15.
38. See Cornell and Leffler, 1987: 397–9 on Forrestal; Shapley, 1987: 425–6 on McNamara; Cooper, 1987: 87–8 on Pinchot; Wyszomirski, 1987: 233, 234 on Hanks; Lambright, 1987: 183, 186 on Webb; Hargrove, 1987: 53 on Lilienthal and the TVA; and Doig, 1987: 166 on Tobin.
39. Lewis, 1980: 88, 224–6.
40. Ibid.: 10. However, the list also included three cases that have not been mentioned here because they clearly were not good examples of a prominent, let alone pioneering, public administrator: Staats, the legislative administrator; Eccles, the leader of the Federal Reserve; and O'Keefe, the private-sector political entrepreneur.
41. Doig and Hargrove, 1987: 7–8, 8.
42. Ibid.: 5. My emphasis.
43. Shapley, 1987: 432. My emphasis.
44. Ibid.: 416, 419.
45. Cooper, 1987: 78–9.
46. Hargrove, 1987: 51–2.
47. Ibid.: 52.
48. Wyszomirski, 1987: 231, 232.
49. Ibid.: 229–30.
50. Ibid.: 237.
51. Doig, 1987: 172 n. 39, 169.
52. Ibid.: 166.

53. Marmor, 1987: 262.
54. Ibid.: 263, 270. He described how it was in their retirement, when fighting to defend social security from cutbacks in the mid-1970s–mid-1980s, that Ball and Cohen had their greatest effect upon policy and did indeed make a large difference (ibid.: 264–8, 269–70).
55. Ibid.: 267, 246, 251, 268, 260.
56. Lambright, 1987: 177–8, 180–1.
57. See ibid.: 176, 191–4.
58. See Lewis, 1980: 59 on Rickover's attitude.
59. Lambright, 1987: 182–5.
60. Ibid.: 184.
61. Ibid.: 185.
62. Ibid.
63. Ibid.: 200, 197.
64. Lambright, 1995: 201–2.
65. Cornell and Leffler, 1987: 388. See 387 on Forrestal's patriotic rather than careerist motivation for proposing the NSC.
66. Ibid.: 400, 390, 391–9.
67. Carpenter, 2001: 365, 366.
68. Lewis, 1980: 250.
69. Ibid.: 11.
70. Ibid.: 11–12.
71. Ibid.: 239, 240. In fact Rickover's technical knowledge may well have saved him from the usual fate of iconoclasts in the Navy (Stoecker, 1998: 139).
72. Lewis, 1988: 112.
73. Ibid.: 115–16.
74. Ibid.: 117–18. He suggests that the modern era has seen a shift from the traditionally religious to the politically religious to the technological secular religion (ibid.: 117).
75. Ibid.: 121, 124.
76. Ibid.: 124.
77. Ibid.: 123.
78. Mintrom, 2000: 289–90.
79. Landy, 1995: 225, 226.
80. Page and Jenkins, 2005: 175.
81. Landy, 1995: 226.
82. See Breton and Wintrobe, 1986: 924, 912–15 on encouraging of competitiveness, notably Hitler's role in encouraging competition and choosing among competing policy proposals as the key buyer of policy proposals and the key market selection process.
83. Ibid.: 915. See 916 for an example of his 1938 speeding up of forced emigration.
84. Ibid.: 916.
85. Ibid.: 918, 923, 925. They also described the 'competition between bureaucrats for jobs' as possibly taking the form of coming up with innovations and initiatives that leads to 'what is now often called Schumpeterian competition or entrepreneurship' (ibid.: 909). But here they are only following the view of Schumpeterian entrepreneurial competition presented in their book on the logic of bureaucratic conduct, which did not mention Schumpeter's emphasis on pioneering motivation even when referring to his *Development* account of entrepreneurship (Breton and Wintrobe, 1982: 109).

86. Browning, 1993: 75.
87. Quoted by Browning (ibid.).

10 Policy Advocates' Pioneering

1. Wilson, 1973: 331, 335.
2. Baumgartner and Jones, 1993: 177; Loomis, 1996: 35.
3. Loomis, 1996: 35.
4. Kingdon, 1984: 188–9, 214.
5. Ibid.: 129. It could also be advocacy for the prominence of a policy idea.
6. Ibid.
7. Ibid.: 113.
8. Ibid.: 128–9.
9. Ibid.: 128, 124, 126.
10. Ibid.: 135–7.
11. Ibid.: 193, 191. It can also involve coupling political events to policy problems.
12. Kingdon described his theory as a revised 'garbage can' model adapted to understand agenda setting in the federal government (ibid.: 92). As well as adding the role of entrepreneurs, he had replaced two of the four streams – participants and choice opportunities – with a politics stream. But he retained much of Cohen, March and Olsen's approach to this 'organised anarchy' of problems and solutions being dumped by participants into the choice-opportunities stream as if it were a garbage can, with any particular choice outcome being a product of the particular mix of garbage in the can at the time and of how the mix was processed: the particular coupling, or lack of coupling, of participants, problems and solutions (Cohen *et al.*, 1972).
13. Kingdon, 1984: 181.
14. Ibid.: 192.
15. Ibid. My emphases.
16. Ibid.: 190. The other qualities contributing to success were an entrepreneur's political connections, negotiating skill and claim to a hearing, as an expert or as the spokesperson for an interest group (ibid.: 189–90).
17. Ibid.: 179.
18. Nadel, 1971: 42; McCarry, 1972: 110; Ashbee, 2001: 159.
19. Wilson, 1980: 370. His other example of policy entrepreneurship in the regulation of business was Dr Wiley, the pioneering administrator described in Chapter 9, and he pointed out that policy entrepreneurship is found in other areas of politics, such as when Howard Jarvies helped to pass Proposition 13 in California and when Senator Joseph McCarthy galvanised sections of the public into an anti-communist crusade (ibid.).
20. Nadel, 1971: 43. He argued that although Nader had a major role in developing and publicising the consumer protection issue, 'he came along at a time when other conditions also pushed the issue forth' (ibid.: 42).
21. McCarry, 1972: 18.
22. Nadel, 1971: 141, 111; McCarry, 1972: 86.
23. Walker, 1977: 435.
24. McCarry, 1972: 121.

25. Nadel, 1971: 209, 210, 207.
26. McCarry, 1972: 166–7, and see 141–51 on the meat safety bill and 234–5 on failing in 1970 to prevent weakening of the bill to establish a consumer protection agency.
27. Ibid.: 115, 155.
28. Ibid.: 164, 154, 158.
29. Ibid.: 155. See 154–5, 158, 167 on Nader's frustration with the bills' weakness, notably the lack of criminal penalties and non-implementation.
30. McCraw, 1984: xi. The following account of Brandeis's career is based upon McCraw's ch. 3, 'Brandeis and the Origins of the FTC'.
31. Ibid.: 82, 83, and 106–7 on his lack of interest in consumer advocacy and actual contempt for the consumer.
32. Ibid.: 122.
33. See Nellis, 2000, on the judge's invention and its fate.
34. Lewis, 1980: 137–9.
35. Ibid.: 88.
36. Cooper, 1987. See also Carpenter, 2001: 275–85.
37. Cooper, 1987: 83.
38. Ibid.: 89.
39. See Mintrom, 2000: 180 n. 9.
40. Ibid.
41. The continuing expansion in the movement's corps of policy advocates is illustrated by a sample of 7 environmental groups whose staff numbers increased from 668 to 1731 in the 1970s and then increased further to 2916 in the 1980s (Baumgartner and Jones, 1993: 184 table 9.4).
42. Ibid.: 236. My emphases. They acknowledged that the term 'punctuated equilibrium' was first proposed by Eldredge and Gould to describe a pattern of biological evolution (ibid.: 19 n. 1). In the revised, 1995 edition of his book Kingdon agreed with Baumgartner and Jones that 'agenda-setting looks like punctuated equilibrium' but suggested that a gradualistic, more Darwinian form of evolution operates in an earlier part of the process; he pointed out that in ch. 6 he had portrayed the development of policy proposals as being similar to the Darwinian, gradualistic evolution of biological natural selection (Kingdon, 1995: 226–7).
43. Baumgartner and Jones point to the 1960s–70s as such a period, when the mobilisation of new participants and destruction of policy monopolies brought about a transformation in the US interest-group system (Baumgartner and Jones, 1993: ch. 9).
44. Ibid.: 17.
45. Ibid.: 35, 89. See 86–9, 239 on contrast with the Downsian type of mobilisation.
46. Ibid.: 6–8, 100–1, 238–9 and ch. 4 case study of the rise and fall of the nuclear power policy monopoly. Baumgartner's earlier paper on leadership strategies had mentioned other examples of policy monopoly destroyed by conflict expansion: social security, child abuse and aviation policy (Baumgartner, 1989: 116–17).
47. Baumgartner and Jones, 1993: 248.
48. Ibid.: 32, 35. My emphasis.
49. Nadel, 1971: 140–1.

50. Baumgartner and Jones, 1993: 36.
51. See Haggard and McCubbins, 2001: 2 n. 5 on Tsebelis's work, which is oriented towards bicameral legislatures, and also ibid.: 5 on Haggard and McCubbins measuring the degree of separation of powers by measuring the potential number of veto players but also emphasising that the separation or unity of *purpose* determines the effective number of vetoes, which may be near only one if each separate institution is working with a unified purpose towards a common goal. A somewhat similar effect occurs when positive feedback leads to an increasingly rapid opening of veto gates to let through the increasingly laden bandwagon.
52. Baumgartner and Jones, 1993: 16.
53. Ibid.: 239, 240.
54. Kingdon, 1984: 190.
55. Ibid.: 153. My emphasis.
56. Baumgartner and Jones, 1993: 249.
57. Ibid.: 191–2.

Conclusion

1. Finley, 1983: 117.
2. Saward, 1997: 34; Rosenau, 1989: 37, quoted by Saward, 1997: 33.
3. Schumpeter, 1974 [1947]: 290.
4. Ibid.: 132.
5. Drucker, 2007 [1985]: 160. This seems comparable to a distinction that Bernier and Hafsi made in a recent article on the changing nature of public entrepreneurship. They drew the distinction between (1) the past's heroic individual public entrepreneurs creating new things or organisations and (2) today's systemic teams of public entrepreneurs seeking to do things better or more efficiently through less dramatic innovations (Bernier and Hafsi, 2007).
6. Drucker, 2007 [1985]: 31.
7. Schumpeter, 1974 [1947]: 132–3.
8. Greenstein, 2000:3.
9. Leuchtenburg, 2009 [1963]: 327.
10. Ibid.: 328–9. See also Badger, 2002: 6 on innovators descending on Washington and 193 on the new administrators 'receptivity to new ideas from unlikely sources'.
11. Leuchtenburg, 2009 [1963]: 327 n. 3.
12. Ibid.: 133; Badger, 2002: 234 and Kennedy, 1999: 267 on contributory insurance for pensions and payroll taxes for unemployment benefits; Badger, 2002: 232, Kennedy 1999: 263 on political concerns or obstacles preventing the envisaged extension of Social Security to health care.
13. Badger, 2002: 311.
14. Leuchtenburg, 2009: 264–5 n. 35.
15. See ibid.: 152–4 and Kennedy, 1999: 278, 283–4, 351–2 on the business community's attitudes and on Roosevelt's measures and rhetoric being partly motivated by threat from populism on the left.
16. McElvaine, 1993: 320.
17. Badger, 2002: 311.

Appendix

1. Schumpeter, 1961 [1934].
2. By the time of his 1939 work on business cycles he was specifying that the 'changes in the economic process brought about by innovation' that he had earlier described as development were now instead described as economic 'evolution' (Schumpeter, 1939: 1, 86. Cited by Hodgson, 1993: 145).
3. Hodgson, 1993: 146 and ch. 7, 'The Mecca of Alfred Marshall'. Hodgson argued that in fact 'Schumpeter's conception of evolution was closer to that of Hegel and Marx, rather than to Darwin and Lamarck' (ibid.: 147). He pointed out that the notion of inheritance, for example, does not play any significant part in Schumpeter's work, and he concluded that Schumpeter's conception of economic evolution was 'not sufficiently wide to incorporate an analogy with natural selection' (ibid.: 146). Thus he described Schumpeter's analogy with mutation as 'a cautious and passing reference to a single concept from biology' and as part of a 'developmentalist' rather than 'selectionist' theory (ibid.: 147).
4. Buchholz, 1999: 157, 154–5. On the other hand, Darwin could be viewed as the Malthus or Adam Smith of biology, as he had publicly acknowledged the debt he owed to Malthus, and it has been argued by Gould that Darwin's theory of natural selection was also consciously or unconsciously influenced by Adam Smith's economics (Gould, 1983: 57).
5. Buchholz, 1999: 155. My emphases. However, Marshall himself did not depict his approach in such explicitly evolutionary terms. Buchholz quotes such key phrases from the Principles as the 'The Mecca of the economist lies in economic biology' and 'The main concern of economics is thus with human beings who are impelled, for good and evil, to change and progress' (Marshall, 1961 [1920]: xiv, xv). But there seem to be few occasions in the Principles when such explicitly evolutionary terms as 'adaptation' are used, as on page 127. Marshall refers to Darwin's *The Origin of Species* not when applying a marginalist analysis but rather when discussing biological analogies of the fact that 'those properties of an economic institution which play the most important part in fitting it for the work which it has to do now, are for that very reason likely to be in a great measure of recent growth' (ibid.: 50).
6. Schumpeter, 1961 [1934]: 63.
7. Ibid.: 62. My emphasis. In making the distinction between discontinuous and continuous changes he argued that the former were changes 'which do not appear continuously and which change the framework, the traditional course itself' (ibid.: 61). More formally, these were 'that kind of change arising from within the system which so displaces its equilibrium point that the new one cannot be reached from the old one by infinitesimal steps. Add successively as many mail coaches as you please, you will never get a railway thereby' (ibid.: 64 n. 1).
8. Ibid.: 66. He specified that whenever he referred thereafter to new combinations of productive means, it would mean only discontinuous new combinations (ibid.).
9. Ibid.: 81. My emphases. He acknowledged that small changes may 'in time add up to great amounts', but he argued that the 'decisive point is that the businessman, if he makes them, never alters his routine' (ibid.: 81 n. 1). See

also 62 on how continuous changes 'may in time, by continual adaptation through innumerable small steps, make a great department store out of a small retail business'.

10. Ibid.: 59. My emphasis.
11. Metcalfe, 1998: 37.
12. Gould, 1983: 67. Gould also pointed out that Darwinists' tendency to describe genetic variation as 'random' was unfortunate 'because we do not mean random in the mathematical sense of equally likely in all directions. We simply mean that variation occurs with no preferred orientation in adaptive directions' (ibid.).
13. Metcalfe pointed out that there are no grounds in economic theory or research for believing that business firms will respond identically – they interpret the evidence in different ways and they may differ in their perception of market pressures (Metcalfe, 1998: 35).
14. Nelson and Winter, 1982: 11.
15. Ibid.: 399–400.
16. Ibid.: 4, 9, 17.
17. Ibid.: 142–3, 140.
18. Schumpeter, 1961 [1934]: 63. My emphasis.
19. Ibid.: 66, 67.
20. Nelson and Winter, 1982: 266.
21. Ibid.: 142, 140. My emphasis. See also 25–6 for criticism of models which specified that 'firms adapt to the changed conditions by changing their policies in an appropriate direction' but included the presumption that 'the direction of adaptive response' is towards 'profit maximization'.
22. Ibid.: 140, 402.
23. Ibid.: 276. My emphases.
24. Schumpeter, 1961 [1934]: 63.
25. Dawkins, 2000 [1986]: 302, 283.
26. Gould, 1983: 156. Gould of course is not one of these theorists of macromutation but in this article he was quite sympathetic to the macromutation view. He defended 'its postulate that macroevolution is not simply microevolution extrapolated, and that major structural transitions can occur rapidly without a smooth series of intermediate stages' (ibid.: 157). He pointed to and described 'two recently supported cases of discontinuous change' (ibid.: 157, 158), and went on to argue that to accept 'many cases of discontinuous transition in macroevolution' would be quite compatible with Darwinism – whose essence 'lies in a single phrase: natural selection is the major creative force of evolutionary change' (ibid.: 158). He also suggested that any need to reconcile macromutation with Darwinism might be met through an approach favoured by Goldschmidt, namely that perhaps relatively minor genetic mutations making small changes in the development of an embryo could produce large differences in the fully grown organism (ibid.: 159–60).
27. Ibid.: 156.
28. Georgescu-Roegen, 1992: 153. The Oxford Dictionary gives 1925 as the first use of the term 'gene mutation' (*Oxford Dictionary*, 2nd edn (Oxford, 1989) x, 146).

29. Dawkins, 2000 [1986]: 283, 288–300; Dawkins, 1997: 87, 90–3. In both books he refers to the complex type as the 'Boeing 747' macromutation and to the modifying type as the 'Stretched DC8' macromutation.
30. Dawkins, 1997: 91.
31. Ibid.: 90, 93. In an earlier book he had argued that Stretched DC8 macromutations are not truly macromutations at all because these large effects in the adult have been produced by micromutations in the genetic instructions for development of the embryo (2000 [1986]: 291).
32. Schumpeter, 1961 [1934]: 64 n. 1.
33. Ibid.: 63.
34. Ibid.: 63, 64, 62. Schumpeter did not include changes in consumer tastes as one of these external factors because it is 'the producer who as a rule initiates economic change, and consumers are educated by him if necessary; they are, as it were, taught to want new things' (ibid.: 65). In fact in *Capitalism, Socialism and Democracy* he referred to the railroads and the electricity industry having to 'create the demand for their services' (1974: 99).
35. See Schumpeter, 1961 [1934]: 61 n. 1 on entrepreneur as the bearer of the mechanism of change.
36. Gould, 1983: 68–9.
37. Ibid. But 'a subsequent evolution of bill shape to make the pilferage easier ... will probably be nipped in the bud by paper cartons and a cessation of home delivery' (ibid.: 69).
38. Schumpeter, 1961 [1934]: 81 n. 1.
39. Ibid.
40. Letter to S. S. Morgan quoted by Swedberg, 1989: ix.

References

Aberbach, J. D. *et al.* (1981) *Bureaucrats and Politicians in Western Democracies* (Cambridge, MA).

Allington, N. *et al.* (1999) 'How Marketing Changed the World – The Political Marketing of an Idea: A Case Study of Privatization', in B. I. Newman (ed.), *Handbook of Political Marketing* (London).

Allison, G. T. (1971) *Essence of Decision: Explaining the Cuban Missile Crisis* (Boston, MA).

Andeweg, R. (1997) 'Collegiality and Collectivity: Cabinets, Cabinet Committees, and Cabinet Ministers', in P. Weller *et al.* (eds), *The Hollow Crown: Countervailing Trends in Core Executives* (Basingstoke).

Apter, D. (1965) *The Politics of Modernization* (Chicago, IL).

Ashbee, E. (2001) 'The Also-Rans: Nader, Buchanan and the 2000 US Presidential Election', *Political Quarterly*, 72/2, 159–69.

Badger, A. J. (2002) *The New Deal: The Depression Years, 1933–1940.* (Chicago, IL).

Bagehot, W. (1887) *Physics and Politics* (London).

Barry, B. (1978 [1970]) *Sociologists, Economists and Democracy* (Chicago, IL).

Baumgartner, F. R. (1989) 'Strategies of Political Leadership in Diverse Settings', in B. D. Jones (ed.), *Leadership and Politics* (Kansas City, KS).

Baumgartner, F. R. and Jones, B. D. (1993) *Agendas and Instability in American Politics* (Chicago, IL).

Bean, C. and Marks, G. (1993) 'The Australian Federal Election of 1993', *Electoral Studies*, 12/3, 253–6.

Beetham, D. (1974) *Max Weber and the Theory of Modern Politics* (London).

Bernier, L. and Hafsi, T. (2007) 'The Changing Nature of Public Entrepreneurship', *Public Administration Review*, 67/3, 488–504.

Berstein, S. (1993) *The Republic of de Gaulle, 1958–1969* (Cambridge).

Bradshaw, K. and Pring, D. (1981) *Parliament and Congress* (London).

Brechtel, T. and Kaiser, A. (1999) 'Party System and Coalition Formation in Post-Reform New Zealand', *Political Science*, 51/1, 1–25.

Breton, A. and Breton, R. (1969) 'An Economic Theory of Social Movements', *The American Economic Review*, 59/2, 198–205.

Breton, A. and Wintrobe, R. (1982) *The Logic of Bureaucratic Conduct* (Cambridge).

Breton, A. and Wintrobe, R. (1986) 'The Bureaucracy of Murder Revisited', *Journal of Political Economy*, 94/5, 905–26.

Breton, R. (1991) 'Policy Decisions and the Competition for Symbolic Resources', in A. Breton *et al.* (eds), *The Competitive State* (Dordrecht, Netherlands).

Breton, R. (1998) 'Ethnicity and Race in Social Organization: Recent Developments in Canadian Society', in R. Helmes-Hay and J. Curtis (eds), *The Vertical Mosaic Revisited* (Toronto).

Brooker, P. (1985) 'The Nazi Fuehrerprinzip: A Weberian Analysis', *Political Science*, 37/1, 50–8.

Brooker, P. (2000) *Non-Democratic Regimes* (Basingstoke).

Brooker, P. (2009) *Non-Democratic Regimes*, 2nd edn (Basingstoke).

Browning, C. R. (1993) *Ordinary Men: Reserve Police Battalion 101 and the Final Solution in Poland* (New York).

Buchholz, T. (1999) *New Ideas from Dead Economists*, rev. edn (Harmondsworth).

Budge, I. and Hofferbert, R. I. (1990) 'Mandates and Policy Outputs: U.S. Party Platforms and Federal Expenditures', *American Political Science Review*, 84/1, 111–31.

Bullock, C. S. and Loomis, B. A. (1985) 'The Changing Congressional Career', in L. C. Dodd and B. I. Oppenheimer (eds), *Congress Reconsidered*, 3rd edn (Washington, DC).

Bunce, V. (1981) *Do New Leaders Make a Difference?* (Princeton, NJ).

Bunch, W. (2009) *Tear Down This Myth: How the Reagan Legacy has Distorted Our Politics and Haunts Our Future* (New York).

Burch, M. (1983) 'Mrs Thatcher's Approach to Leadership in Government: 1979– June 1983', *Parliamentary Affairs*, 36/4, 399–416.

Burnham, J. (1942) *The Managerial Revolution* (London).

Butler, D. *et al.* (1994) *Failure in British Government: The Politics of the Poll Tax* (Oxford).

Cambray, P. G. (1932) *The Game of Politics: A Study of the Principles of British Political Strategy* (London).

Campbell, J. (2000) *Margaret Thatcher: The Grocer's Daughter* (London).

Campbell, K. K. and Jamieson, K. H. (2008) *Presidents Creating the Presidency: Deeds Done in Words* (Chicago, IL).

Carmines, E. G. and Stimson, J. A. (1989) *Issue Evolution: Race and the Transformation of American Politics* (Princeton, NJ).

Carmines, E. G. and Stimson, J. A. (1993) 'On the Evolution of Political Issues', in W. H. Riker (ed.), *Agenda Formation* (Ann Arbor, MI).

Carpenter, D. P. (2001) *The Forging of Bureaucratic Autonomy* (Princeton, NJ).

Casey, S. (2001) *Cautious Crusade: Franklin D. Roosevelt, American Public Opinion, and War Against Nazi Germany* (Oxford).

Charles, J. (1961) *The Origins of the American Party System* (New York).

Cohen, M., March, J. and Olsen, J. (1972) 'A Garbage Can Model of Organizational Choice', *Administrative Science Quarterly*, 17, 1–25.

Colomer, J. M. and Negretto, G. L. (2005) 'Can Presidentialism Work Like Parliamentarism?', *Government and Opposition*, 40/1, 60–89.

Coogan, T. P. (1995) *The Troubles: Ireland's Ordeal 1966–1995 and the Search for Peace* (London).

Cooper, J. M., Jr (1987) 'Gifford Pinchot Creates a Forest Service', in J. W. Doig and E. C. Hargrove (eds), *Leadership and Innovation: A Biographical Perspective on Entrepreneurs in Government* (Baltimore, MD).

Cornell, C. S. and Leffler, M. P. (1987) 'James Forrestal: The Tragic End of a Successful Entrepreneur', in J. W. Doig and E. C. Hargrove (eds), *Leadership and Innovation: A Biographical Perspective on Entrepreneurs in Government* (Baltimore, MD).

Coser, L. A. (1979) 'American Trends', in T. Bottomore and R. Nisbet (eds), *A History of Sociological Analysis* (London).

Criddle, B. (1992) 'Electoral Systems in France', *Parliamentary Affairs*, 45/1, 108–16.

Cringely, R. X. (1996) *Accidental Empires: How the Boys of Silicon Valley Make Their Millions, Battle Foreign Competition, and Still Can't Get a Date*, rev. edn (New York).

Dallek, R. (1995) *Franklin D. Roosevelt and American Foreign Policy, 1932–1945* (New York).

Darwin, C. (1996 [1859]) *The Origin of Species*, 2nd edn (Oxford).

Daugbjerg, C. and Marsh, D. (1998) 'Explaining Policy Outcomes: Integrating the Policy Network Approach with Macro-Level and Micro-Level Analysis', in D. Marsh (ed.), *Comparing Policy Networks* (Buckingham).

Dawkins, R. (1997) *Climbing Mount Improbable* (Harmondsworth).

Dawkins, R. (2000 [1986]) *The Blind Watchmaker* (Harmondsworth).

DeConde, A. (1966) *Herbert Hoover's Latin-American Policy* (Stanford).

Deering, C. J. (1996) 'Career Advancement and Subcommittee Chairs in the U.S. House of Representatives', *American Politics Quarterly*, 24/1, 3–23.

Dodd, L. C. (1977) 'Congress, the Constitution, and the Crisis of Legitimation', in L. C. Dodd and B. I. Oppenheimer (eds), *Congress Reconsidered*, 2nd edn (Washington, DC).

Doig, J. W. (1987) 'To Claim the Seas and the Skies: Austin Tobin and the Port of New York Authority', in J. W. Doig and E. C. Hargrove (eds), *Leadership and Innovation: A Biographical Perspective on Entrepreneurs in Government* (Baltimore, MD).

Doig, J. W. and Hargrove, E. C. (1987) ' "Leadership" and Political Analysis', in J. W. Doig and E. C. Hargrove (eds), *Leadership and Innovation: A Biographical Perspective on Entrepreneurs in Government* (Baltimore, MD).

Dolowitz, D. P. (1998) *Learning from America: Policy Transfer and the Development of the British Workfare State* (Brighton).

Dolowitz, D. P. (2000) 'Policy Transfer: A New Framework of Policy Analysis', in D. P. Dolowitz *et al.* (eds), *Policy Transfer and British Social Policy: Learning from the USA?* (Buckingham).

Dolowitz, D. P. and Marsh, D. (2000) 'Learning from Abroad: The Role of Policy Transfer in Contemporary Policy-Making', *Governance*, 13/1, 5–24.

Downs, A. (1957) *An Economic Theory of Democracy* (New York).

Downs, A. (1967) *Inside Bureaucracy* (Boston, MA).

Downs, A. (1972) 'Up and Down with Ecology – the "Issue-Attention Cycle"', *The Public Interest*, 28, 38–50.

Drucker, P. F. (2007 [1985]) *Innovation and Entrepreneurship: Practice and Principles* (Oxford).

Dunleavy, P. (1985) 'Bureaucrats, Budgets and the Growth of the State: Reconstructing an Instrumental Model', *British Journal of Political Science*, 15, 299–328.

Dunleavy, P. (1991) *Democracy, Bureaucracy and Public Choice: Economic Explanations in Political Science* (Hemel Hempstead).

Dunleavy, P. (1995) 'Reinterpreting the Westland Affair: Theories of the State and Core Executive Decision Making', in R. A. W. Rhodes and P. Dunleavy (eds), *Prime Minister, Cabinet and Core Executive* (Basingstoke).

Duverger, M. (1959) *Political Parties: Their Organization and Activity in the Modern State*, 2nd edn (New York).

Edwards, G. C. and Wayne, S. J. (2003) *Presidential Leadership: Politics and Policy Making* (Belmont, CA).

Eijk, C. K. van der and Kok, W. J. P. (1984) 'Non-Decisions Reconsidered', *Acta Politica*, 10/3, 277–301.

Elgie, R. (1995) *Political Leadership in Liberal Democracies* (Basingstoke).

Epstein, L. D. (1980 [1967]) *Political Parties in Western Democracies* (New Brunswick, NJ).

Fenno, R. F. (1973) *Congressmen in Committees* (Boston, MA).

Finley, M. I. (1983) *Politics in the Ancient World* (Cambridge).

Fisher, B. M. and Strauss, A. L. (1979) 'Interactionism', in T. Bottomore and R. Nisbet (eds), *A History of Sociological Analysis* (London).

Freud, S. (1961 [1930]) *Civilization and its Discontents* (New York).

Frohlich, N. and Oppenheimer, J. A. (1978) *Modern Political Economy* (Englewood Cliffs, NJ).

Frohlich, N., Oppenheimer, J. A. and Young, O. R. (1971) *Political Leadership and Collective Goods* (Princeton, NJ).

Gamble, A. (1988) *The Free Economy and the Strong State: The Politics of Thatcherism* (London).

George, A. L. (1972) 'The Case for Multiple Advocacy in Making Foreign Policy', *American Political Science Review*, 66/3, 751–85.

Georgescu-Roegen, N. (1992) 'Nicholas Georgescu-Roegen about Himself', in M. Szenberg (ed.), *Eminent Economists: Their Life Philosophies* (Cambridge).

Goffman, E. (1974) *Frame Analysis: An Essay on the Organization of Experience* (New York).

Gonos, G. (1977) 'Situation versus Frame: The Interactionist and the Structuralist Analyses of Everyday Life', *American Sociological Review*, 42, 854–67.

Gould, S. J. (1983) *The Panda's Thumb* (Harmondsworth).

Gould, S. J. (1989) *Wonderful Life: The Burgess Shale and the Nature of History* (London).

Gould, S. J. (1991) *Bully for Brontosaurus* (New York).

Gould, S. J. (1993) *Eight Little Piggies* (New York).

Gould, S. J. (1999) *Leonardo's Mountain of Clams and the Diet of Worms* (London).

Gould, S. J. (2000) *The Lying Stones of Marrakech: Penultimate Reflections in Natural History* (London).

Gould, S. J. (2002) *I Have Landed: The End of a Beginning in Natural History* (New York).

Graebner, N. A. (1993) 'The President as Commander in Chief: A Study in Power', in J. G. Dawson (ed.), *Commanders in Chief: Presidential Leadership in Modern Wars* (Lawrence, KS).

Green, D. and Schapiro, I. (1994) *Pathologies of Rational Choice Theory* (New Haven, CT).

Greenfield, S. M. and Strickon, A. (1979) 'Entrepreneurship and Social Change: Toward a Populational, Decision-Making Approach', in S. M. Greenfield *et al.* (eds), *Entrepreneurs in Cultural Context* (Albuquerque).

Greenstein, F. I. (2000) *The Presidential Difference: Leadership Style from FDR to Clinton* (New York).

Grew, R. (1978) 'The Crises and Their Sequences', in R. Grew (ed.), *Crises of Political Development in Europe and United States* (Princeton, NJ).

Haggard, S. and McCubbins, M. D. (2001) 'Introduction: Political Institutions and the Determinants of Public Policy', in S. Haggard and M. D. McCubbins (eds), *Presidents, Parliaments, and Policy* (Cambridge).

Hall, R. L. (1996) *Participation in Congress* (New Haven, CT).

Hanson Leung, C. K. (1985) 'The Role of Leadership in Adaptation to Change: Lessons of Economic Reforms in the USSR and China', *Studies in Comparative Communism*, 18/4, 227–46.

Hargrove, E. C. (1987) 'David Lilienthal and the Tennessee Valley Authority', in J. W. Doig and E. C. Hargrove (eds), *Leadership and Innovation: A Biographical Perspective on Entrepreneurs in Government* (Baltimore, MD).

Harmel, R. and Svåsand, L. (1993) 'Party Leadership and Party Institutionalisation: Three Phases of Development', *West European Politics*, 16/2, 67–87.

Hazan, R. (1996) 'Presidential Parliamentarism: Direct Popular Election of the Prime Minister, Israel's New Electoral and Political System', *Electoral Studies*, 15/1, 24–41.

Headey, B. (1974) *British Cabinet Ministers: The Roles of Politicians in Executive Office* (London).

Hennessy, P. (2001) *The Prime Minister: The Office and its Holders Since 1945* (London).

Hills, A. (2004) *Future War in Cities* (London).

Hodgson, G. M. (1993) *Economics and Evolution* (Cambridge).

Hopkin, J. and Paolucci, C. (1999) 'The Business Firm Model of Party Organisation: Cases from Spain and Italy', *European Journal of Political Research*, 35, 307–39.

Huntington, S. P. (1968) *Political Order in Changing Societies* (New Haven, CT).

Huntington, S. P. (1991) *The Third Wave: Democratization in the Late Twentieth Century* (Norman).

Ignazi, P. (1996) 'The Crisis of Parties and the Rise of New Political Parties', *Party Politics*, 2/4, 549–66.

Ilchman, W. and Uphoff, N. (1969) *The Political Economy of Change* (Berkeley, CA).

James, S. (1995) 'Relations between Prime Minister and Cabinet: From Wilson to Thatcher', in R. A. W. Rhodes and P. Dunleavy (eds), *Prime Minister, Cabinet and Core Executive* (Basingstoke).

Johnston, R. *et al.* (1993) 'Free Trade in Canadian Elections: Issue Evolution in the Long and the Short Run', in W. H. Riker (ed.), *Agenda Formation* (Ann Arbor, MI).

Jones, S. (2000) *Almost Like a Whale: The 'Origin of Species' Updated* (London).

Kasza, G. J. (1987) 'Bureaucratic Politics in Radical Military Regimes', *American Political Science Review*, 81/3, 851–71.

Katz, R. and Mair, P. (1995) 'Changing Models of Party Organization and Party Democracy: The Emergence of the Cartel Party', *Party Politics*, 1/1, 5–28.

Kavanagh, D. (2001) 'New Labour, New Millennium, New Premiership', in A. Seldon (ed.), *The Blair Effect* (London).

Kennedy, D. M. (1999) *Freedom From Fear: The American People in Depression and War, 1929–1945* (Oxford).

Kimball, W. F. (1993) 'Franklin Roosevelt: "Dr Win-the-War" ', in J. G. Dawson (ed.) *Commanders in Chief: Presidential Leadership in Modern Wars* (Lawrence, KS).

Kingdon, J. W. (1984) *Agendas, Alternatives, and Public Policies* (Boston, MA).

Kingdon, J. W. (1995) *Agendas, Alternatives, and Public Policies*, 2nd edn (New York).

Koole, R. (1996) 'Cadre, Catch-all or Cartel: A Comment on the Notion of the Cartel Party', *Party Politics*, 2/4, 507–23.

Körösényi, A. (2005) 'Political Representation in Leader Democracy', *Government and Opposition* 40/3, 358–78.

Krasner, S. D. (1984) 'Approaches to the State: Alternative Conceptions and Historical Dynamics', *Comparative Politics*, 16/2, 223–45.

Kriesi, H. (2005) *Direct Democratic Choice: The Swiss Experience* (Lanham, MD).

Kuran, T. (1991) 'The Role of Deception in Political Competition', in A. Breton *et al.* (eds), *The Competitive State* (Dordrecht, Netherlands).

Lam, W. W-L. (1999) *The Era of Jiang Zemin* (Singapore).

Lambright, W. H. (1976) *Governing Science and Technology* (New York).

Lambright, W. H. (1987) 'James Webb and the Uses of Administrative Power', in J. W. Doig and E. C. Hargrove (eds), *Leadership and Innovation: A Biographical Perspective on Entrepreneurs in Government* (Baltimore, MD).

Lambright, W. H. (1995) *Powering Apollo: James E. Webb of NASA* (Baltimore, MD).

Landy, M. K. (1995) 'The New Politics of Environmental Policy', in M. K. Landy and M. A. Levin (eds), *The New Politics of Public Policy* (Baltimore, MD).

Larrabee, E. (2004) *Commander in Chief: Franklin Delano Roosevelt, His Lieutenants, and Their War* (Annapolis, MD).

Laver, M. (1980) 'Political Solutions to the Collective Action Problem', *Political Studies*, 28/2, 195–209.

Lettow, P. (2006) *Ronald Reagan and His Quest to Abolish Nuclear Weapons* (New York).

Leuchtenburg, W. E. (2009 [1963]) *Franklin D. Roosevelt and the New Deal* (New York).

Lewis, E. (1980) *Public Entrepreneurship* (Bloomington, IN).

Lewis, E. (1988) 'Public Entrepreneurship and the Teleology of Technology', *Administration & Society*, 20/1, 109–25.

Lijphart, A. (1999) *Patterns of Democracy: Government Forms and Performance in Thirty-Six Countries* (New Haven, CT).

Lipsey, R. and Chrystal, K. A. (1995) *An Introduction to Positive Economics* (Oxford).

Loomis, B. (1988) *The New American Politician: Ambition, Entrepreneurship, and the Changing Face of Political Life* (New York).

Loomis, B. (1996) *The Contemporary Congress* (New York).

Luttwak, E. and Koehl, S. L. (2000) *The Dictionary of Modern War* (New York).

Macfarlane, L. J. (1986) *Issues in British Politics Since 1945* (London).

Mann, J. (2009) *The Rebellion of Ronald Reagan: A History of the End of the Cold War* (New York).

March, J. G. and Olsen, J. P. (1989) *Rediscovering Institutions: The Organizational Basis of Politics* (New York).

Marmor, T. R. (1987) 'Entrepreneurship in Public Management: Wilbur Cohen and Robert Ball', in J. W. Doig and E. C. Hargrove (eds), *Leadership and Innovation: A Biographical Perspective on Entrepreneurs in Government* (Baltimore, MD).

Marsh, D. (1991) 'Privatization Under Mrs Thatcher: A Review of the Literature', *Public Administration*, 69, 459–80.

Marsh, D. (1998) 'The Development of the Policy Network Approach', in D. Marsh (ed.), *Comparing Policy Networks* (Buckingham).

Marshall, A. (1961 [1920]) *The Principles of Economics*, 9th edn (Guillebaud ed.) (London).

Mayhew, D. R. (1974) *Congress: The Electoral Connection* (New Haven, CT).

McCarry, C. (1972) *Citizen Nader* (New York).

McCraw, T. K. (1984) *Prophets of Regulation* (Cambridge, MA).

McElvaine, R. S. (1993) *The Great Depression: America, 1929–1941* (New York).

McLean, I. (2001) *Rational Choice and British Politics* (Oxford).

Medearis, J. (2001) *Joseph Schumpeter's Two Theories of Democracy* (Cambridge, MA).

Metcalfe, J. S. (1998) *Evolutionary Economics and Creative Destruction* (London).

Mintrom, M. (2000) *Policy Entrepreneurs and School Choice* (Washington, DC).

Mitchell, W. C. (1984) 'Schumpeter and Public Choice, Part I: Precursor to Public Choice?', *Public Choice*, 42, 73–88.

Moe, T. M. (1980) *The Organization of Interests* (Chicago).

Moon, J. (1995) 'Innovative Leadership and Policy Change: Lessons from Thatcher', *Governance*, 8/1, 1–25.

Mueller, J. (1989) *Retreat from Doomsday: The Obsolescence of Major War* (New York).

Murphy, R. D. (1971) *Political Entrepreneurs and Urban Poverty* (Lexington, KY).

Nadel, M. V. (1971) *The Politics of Consumer Protection* (Indianapolis, IN).

Nellis, M. (2000) 'Law and Order: The Electronic Monitoring of Offenders', in D. P. Dolowitz *et al.* (eds), *Policy Transfer and British Social Policy: Learning from the USA?* (Buckingham).

Nelson, R. R. (1995) 'Recent Evolutionary Theorizing about Economic Change', *Journal of Economic Literature*, 33, 48–90.

Nelson, R. R. and Winter, S. G. (1982) *An Evolutionary Theory of Economic Change* (Cambridge, MA).

Neustadt, R. E. (1960) *Presidential Power: The Politics of Leadership* (New York).

Neustadt, R. E. (1966) 'Shadow and Substance in Politics: White House and Whitehall', *Public Interest*, 2, 55–69.

Neustadt, R. E. (1969) 'White House and Whitehall', in A. King (ed.), *The British Prime Minister* (London).

Neustadt, R. E. (1990 [1960]) *Presidential Power and the Modern Presidents: The Politics of Leadership from Roosevelt to Reagan* (New York).

North, D. C. (2005) *Understanding the Process of Economic Change* (Princeton).

Norton, P. (2007) 'Tony Blair and the Constitution', *British Politics*, 2/2, 269–82.

Nutt, P. C. (2002) *Why Decisions Fail* (San Francisco, CA).

Offner, A. A. (2002) *Another Such Victory: President Truman and the Cold War, 1945–1953* (Stanford, CA).

Oliver, T. R. and Paul-Shaheen, P. (1997) 'Translating Ideas into Actions: Entrepreneurial Leadership in State Health Care Reforms', *Journal of Health Politics, Policy and Law*, 22/3, 721–88.

Olson, M. (1971 [1965]) *The Logic of Collective Action* (Cambridge, MA).

Outshoorn, J. (1986) 'The Feminist Movement and Abortion Policy in the Netherlands', in D. Dahlerup (ed.), *The New Women's Movement: Feminism and Political Power in Europe and the USA* (London).

Pach, C. (2006) 'The Reagan Doctrine: Principle, Pragmatism, and Policy', *Presidential Studies Quarterly*, 36/1, 75–89.

Page, B. I. (1978) *Choices and Echoes in Presidential Elections: Rational Man and Electoral Democracy* (Chicago, IL).

Page, E. C. and Jenkins, B. (2005) *Policy Bureaucracy: Government with a Cast of Thousands* (Oxford).

Paine, S. C. (1989) 'Persuasion, Manipulation, and Dimension', *Journal of Politics*, 51/1, 36–49.

Panebianco, A. (1988) *Political Parties: Organisation and Power* (Cambridge).

Parker, G. R. (1992) *Institutional Change, Discretion, and the Making of the Modern Congress* (Ann Arbor, MI).

Peters, G. (1998) 'Policy Networks: Myth, Metaphor and Reality', in D. Marsh (ed.), *Comparing Policy Networks* (Buckingham).

Polsby, N. (1984) *Political Innovation in America: The Politics of Policy Initiation* (New Haven, CT).

Price, D. E. (1971) 'Professionals and "Entrepreneurs": Staff Orientations and Policy Making on Three Senate Committees', *Journal of Politics*, 33, 317–36.

Price, D. E. (1972) *Who Makes the Laws? Creativity and Power in Senate Committees* (Cambridge, MA).

Prisching, M. (1995) 'The Limited Rationality of Democracy: Schumpeter as the Founder of Irrational Choice Theory', *Critical Review*, 9/3, 301–24.

Przeworski, A. (1999) 'Minimalist Conception of Democracy: A Defense', in I. Schapiro and C. Hacker-Cordon (eds), *Democracy's Value* (Cambridge).

Przeworski, A. (2003) *States and Markets* (Cambridge).

Quirk, P. J. (1995) 'Policy Making in the Contemporary Congress: Three Dimensions of Performance', in M. K. Landy and M. A. Levin (eds), *The New Politics of Public Policy* (Baltimore, MD and London).

Rhodes, R. A. W. (1995) 'From Prime Ministerial Power to Core Executive', in R. A. W. Rhodes and P. Dunleavy (eds), *Prime Minister, Cabinet and Core Executive* (Basingstoke).

Riddell, P. (2001) 'Blair as Prime Minister', in A. Seldon (ed.), *The Blair Effect* (London).

Riker, W. H. (1982) *Liberalism Against Populism* (San Francisco, CA).

Riker, W. H. (1986) *The Art of Political Manipulation* (New Haven, CT).

Rioux, J-P. (1987) *The Fourth Republic, 1944–1958* (Cambridge).

Rose, R. (2001) *The Prime Minister in a Shrinking World* (Cambridge).

Rose, R. and Davies, P. L. (1994) *Inheritance in Public Policy: Change without Choice in Britain* (New Haven, CT).

Rosenau J. N. (1989) 'The State in an Era of Cascading Politics: Wavering Concept, Widening Competence, Withering Colossus, or Weathering Change?' in I. A. Caporaso (ed.), *The Elusive State* (London).

Sabatier, P. A. (1988) 'An Advocacy Coalition Framework of Policy Change and the Role of Policy-Oriented Learning Therein', *Policy Sciences*, 21, 129–68.

Salisbury, R. H. (1969) 'An Exchange Theory of Interest Groups', *Midwest Journal of Political Science*, 13/1, 1–32.

Santoro, E. (1993) 'Democratic Theory and Individual Autonomy: An Interpretation of Schumpeter's Doctrine of Democracy', *European Journal of Political Research*, 23, 121–43.

Saward, M. (1997) 'In Search of the Hollow Crown', in P. Weller *et al.* (eds), *The Hollow Crown: Countervailing Trends in Core Executives* (Basingstoke).

Schapiro, I. and Hacker-Cordon, C. (1999) 'Promises and Disappointments: Reconsidering Democracy's Value', in I. Schapiro and C. Hacker-Cordon (eds), *Democracy's Value* (Cambridge).

Schattschneider, E. E. (1960) *The Semisovereign People* (New York).

Schiller, W. J. (1995) 'Senators as Political Entrepreneurs: Using Bill Sponsorship to Shape Legislative Agendas', *American Journal of Political Science*, 39/1, 186–203.

258 *References*

Schlesinger, A. M., Jr (1986) *The Cycles of American History* (Boston, MA).

Schlesinger, J. A. (1984) 'On the Theory of Party Organization', *Journal of Politics*, 46, 369–400.

Schneider, M. and Teske, P. with Mintrom, M. (1995) *Public Entrepreneurs: Agents for Change in American Government* (Princeton, NJ).

Schuck, P. H. (1995) 'The Politics of Rapid Legal Change: Immigration Policy in the 1980s', in M. K. Landy and M. A. Levin (eds), *The New Politics of Public Policy* (Baltimore, MD).

Schumpeter, J. A. (1939) *Business Cycles* (New York).

Schumpeter, J. A. (1961 [1st English edn 1934]) *The Theory of Economic Development* (New York).

Schumpeter, J. A. (1974 [1947]) *Capitalism, Socialism and Democracy*, rev. 2nd edn (London).

Schumpeter, J. A. (1989 [1947]) 'The Creative Response in Economic History', in J. A. Schumpeter, *Essays on Entrepreneurs, Innovations, Business Cycles, and the Evolution of Capitalism*, ed. R. I. Clemence (New Brunswick, NJ and Oxford).

Schumpeter, J. A. (1989 [1949]) 'Economic Theory and Entrepreneurial History', in J. A. Schumpeter, *Essays on Entrepreneurs, Innovations, Business Cycles, and the Evolution of Capitalism*, ed. R. I. Clemence (New Brunswick, NJ and Oxford).

Scott, A. M. (1970) *Competition in American Politics: An Economic Model* (New York).

Scott, J. M. (1996) *Deciding to Intervene: The Reagan Doctrine and American Foreign Policy* (Durham).

Scott, W. R. (1987) 'The Adolescence of Institutional Theory', *Administrative Science Quarterly* 32/4, 493–511.

Seldon, A. (2007) 'Blair in History', *British Politics*, 2/2, 264–8.

Selznick, P. (1957) *Leadership in Administration: A Sociological Interpretation* (New York).

Shapley, D. (1987) 'Robert McNamara: Success and Failure', in J. W. Doig and E. C. Hargrove (eds), *Leadership and Innovation: A Biographical Perspective on Entrepreneurs in Government* (Baltimore, MD).

Simon, H. E. (1997) *Models of Bounded Rationality, Volume 3: Empirically Grounded Economic Reason* (Cambridge, MA).

Smith, M. J. (1994) 'The Core Executive and the Resignation of Mrs Thatcher', *Public Administration*, 72, 341–63.

Smith, M. J. (1995) 'Interpreting the Rise and Fall of Margaret Thatcher: Power Dependence and the Core Executive', in R. A. W. Rhodes and P. Dunleavy (eds), *Prime Minister, Cabinet and Core Executive* (Basingstoke).

Smith, P. H. (2008) *Talons of the Eagle: Latin America, the United States and the World* (New York).

Spanier, J. (1981) *Games Nations Play: Analyzing International Politics*, 4th edn (New York).

Sterelny, K. (2001) *Dawkins vs. Gould: Survival of the Fittest* (Duxford).

Stoecker, S. W. (1998) *Forging Stalin's Army: Marshal Tukhachevsky and the Politics of Military Innovation* (Boulder, CO).

Stokes, S. C. (2001) *Mandates and Democracy: Neoliberalism by Surprise in Latin America* (Cambridge).

Swedberg, R. (1989) 'Introduction to the Transaction Edition', in J. A. Schumpeter, *Essays on Entrepreneurs, Innovations, Business Cycles, and the Evolution of Capitalism*, ed. R. I. Clemence (New Brunswick, NJ and Oxford).

Swedberg, R. (1991) *Joseph A. Schumpeter: His Life and Work* (Cambridge).

Theakston, K. (2003) 'Political Skills and Context in Prime Ministerial Leadership in Britain', in E. C. Hargrove and J. E. Owens (eds), *Leadership in Context* (Lanham, MD).

Thompson, H. (1995) 'Joining the ERM: Analysing a Core Executive Policy Disaster', in R. A. W. Rhodes and P. Dunleavy (eds), *Prime Minister, Cabinet and Core Executive* (Basingstoke).

Thomson, W. (2007) 'Tony Blair's Social Legacy: Transformational Leadership', *Policy Options*, June 2007, 51–6.

Tucker, R. C. (1995 [1981]) *Politics as Leadership*, rev. edn (Columbia, SC and London).

Tversky, A. and Kahneman, D. (1981) 'The Framing of Decisions and the Psychology of Choice', *Science*, 211, 453–8.

Wagner, R. E. (1966) 'Pressure Groups and Political Entrepreneurs: A Review Article', in G. Tullock (ed.), *Papers on Non-Market Decision Making*, No. 1 (Charlottesville, VA).

Walker, J. L. (1977) 'Setting the Agenda in the U.S. Senate: A Theory of Problem Selection', *British Journal of Political Science*, 7/4, 423–45.

Ware, A. (1996) *Political Parties and Party Systems* (Oxford).

Warhurst, J. (2000) 'Tax Attacks: The 1998 Australian Election Campaign', in M. Simms and J. Warhurst (eds), *Howard's Agenda: The 1998 Australian Election* (St Lucia, Queensland).

Warhurst, J. *et al.* (2000) 'Tax Groupings: The Group Politics of Tax Reform', in M. Simms and J. Warhurst (eds), *Howard's Agenda: The 1998 Australian Election* (St Lucia, Queensland).

Wawro, G. (2000) *Legislative Entrepreneurship in the U.S. House of Representatives* (Ann Arbor, MI).

Webb, P. and Poguntke, T. (2005) 'The Presidentialization of Contemporary Democratic Politics: Evidence, Causes, and Consequences', in T. Poguntke and P. Webb (eds) *The Presidentialization of Politics* (Oxford).

Weber, M. (1947 [1922]) *The Theory of Social Economic Organization*, edited by T. Parsons (New York).

Weber, M. (1968) *Economy and Society*, edited by G. Roth and C. Wittich (New York).

Weber, M. (1991 [1919]) 'Politics as a Vocation', in H. H. Gerth and C. Wright Mills (eds), *From Max Weber: Essays in Sociology* (London).

Weller, P. (1985) *First Among Equals: Prime Ministers in Westminster Systems* (Sydney).

Wilson, H. (1977) *The Governance of Britain* (London).

Wilson, J. Q. (1973) *Political Organizations* (New York).

Wilson, J. Q. (1980) 'The Politics of Regulation', in J. Q. Wilson (ed.), *The Politics of Regulation* (New York).

Wilson, J. Q. (1989) *Bureaucracy* (New York).

Wood, B. D. and Waterman, R. W. (1993) 'The Dynamics of Political-Bureaucratic Adaptation', *American Journal of Political Science*, 37/2, 497–528.

Wyszomirski, M. J. (1987) 'The Politics of Art: Nancy Hanks and the National Endowment for the Arts', in J. W. Doig and E. C. Hargrove (eds), *Leadership and Innovation: A Biographical Perspective on Entrepreneurs in Government* (Baltimore, MD).

Young, H. (1989) *One of Us: A Biography of Margaret Thatcher* (London).

Zahariadis, N. (1995) *Markets, States, and Public Policy: Privatization in Britain and France* (Ann Arbor, MI).